Investigations into Economic Class in America

Philip E. DeVol
Karla M. Krodel

Investigations into Economic Class in America
Philip E. DeVol and Karla M. Krodel
286 pp.
Bibliography pp. 265–271

ISBN 13: 978-1-934583-46-3
ISBN 10: 1-934583-46-4

Copy editing by Dan Shenk and Jesse Conrad
Workbook design by Paula Nicolella
Cover design by Naylor Design
Illustrations by Jill E. Garbe

Printed in the United States of America by Automated Graphic Systems, Inc.

Table of Contents

Acknowledgments   v

Module 1   1
Getting Started

Module 2   13
Mental Model of Poverty

Module 3   37
A Process for Change

Module 4   55
The Rich/Poor Gap and How It Works

Module 5   91
Hidden Rules of Economic Class

Module 6   109
Language Rules and Resources

Module 7   135
Eleven Resources

Module 8   161
Stages of Change

Module 9   167
Self-Assessment of Resources

Module 10   197
Community Assessment

Module 11   219
Building Resources

Module 12   229
Personal Plan for Building Resources

Appendix   251

Bibliography   265

Index   273

Acknowledgments

This work would not exist without the insights and experience of Ruby Payne. Her ground-breaking book *A Framework for Understanding Poverty* has sparked many applications in the practice of improving education for students of all ages. All the staff persons of aha! Process, Inc. provide tremendous support, but special thanks go to Peg Conrad, vice president of Publications, and Bethanie Tucker. Our gratitude also goes to Dan Shenk and Jesse Conrad for their editing expertise, as well as to Paula Nicolella for her outstanding work designing the book.

This book benefited greatly from the wisdom and insights from people who completed *Getting Ahead in a Just-Gettin'-By World* (the original version of this work) and those who reviewed content and activities contained in this book. They include co-facilitators Janae Books, Carlos Guajardo, Sonia Holycross, Yolanda Reed, and Terrell Wesley, along with Rebecca Banks, Brandy Bates, Alberta Bevly, Lisa Carlock, Remona Gordon, Jacqueline Hall, Tanavia Hodges, Malcom Horton, Karen Jones, Cathy Lenoir, Gracie Rollins, Maryann Rought, Lawarnda Smith, and Suzie Wright (who also helped in the design of the book).

In addition, several talented facilitators contributed their ideas and support, including Karen Kessler, Patricia Matthews, Kathy McPherson, Lenore Moore, and Gale Vaughn. Thank you for "keeping it real."

There are many "communities of practice" across North America using the concepts in Phil DeVol's books through Bridges Steering Committees and Move the Mountain's Circles™ Campaign. Thanks to Scott Miller, Vikki Boatman, Marian Brannon, Marlo Fox, Catherine Iannello, Clay Randall, Laura Solano, Lisa Stoddard, Judith Valade, Karin Van Zant, Tay Waltenbaugh, Dee Washington, and Lisa Yaeger. Thank you for sharing your insights and confirming the need for this work.

There are many people from colleges, universities, and trade schools who helped us with this work. Some became early adopters of Getting Ahead with postsecondary students and shared results, needs, and ideas; some reviewed and advised us about these books; and some contributed content in their areas of practice. Your expertise is much appreciated, and we hope you find it has been well used here. Thank you to Vicki Thompson and Linda Reader of Trumbull Career and Technical Center in Champion, Ohio, the first school we know of that incorporated the *Getting Ahead* workbook into an accredited educational program (licensed practical nursing); Bonnie Bazata, executive director of St. Joseph County Bridges Out of Poverty Initiative, South Bend Indiana; Gale Vaughn, facilitator and assistant director of Admissions at Ivy Tech, South Bend, Indiana, the first college-based Getting Ahead program we are aware of; and Diane Kloss, Sondra O'Donnell, and Pauline Tressler at Kent State University, Columbiana, Ohio, campuses, for pioneering Getting Ahead in career pathway and workforce initiatives.

The following scholars and practitioners consulted with us on aspects of the book as it was developed, and we are indebted to you: Bill Border, Sherri Harper-Woods, Henry Ingle, Cryshanna Jackson, Susan Jakes, Sherry Linkon, Guy Shebat, and Rebecca Wheeler.

A special thanks to our thoughtful reviewers whose insights and suggestions greatly improved this work and validated it: Karen Becker, reading and study skills coordinator and adjunct instructor at Youngstown (Ohio) State University; Virginia Calvin, chancellor, Ivy Tech Community College North Central (Indiana); Edward Carmien, associate professor of English, Mercer County (New Jersey) Community College; Lisa Horan, director, Center for Community Building to End Poverty, Lewiston, Idaho; Alicia Liss, former vice president, Warren County (New Jersey) Community College, director, College Circles Program, and Getting Ahead instructor, Sussex County (New Jersey) Community College; Karon J. Rosa, program director, Arkansas Department of Higher Education; Victoria Van Steenhouse, associate professor emeritus, Applied Behavioral Studies, Delta College, University Center, Michigan; and Monieca West, director, Carl D. Perkins CTE Post Secondary Program, Arkansas Department of Higher Education.

And finally, heartfelt thanks to Susan DeVol and Craig Paulenich, our respective spouses, whose unfailing love and support over the last two years have made this work possible.

MODULE 1
Getting Started

I. Introduction

Investigations into Economic Class in America is about the world that students currently live in and the future they will build for themselves and their communities. You will investigate what it takes to succeed at college and how to build a high-quality life during hard economic times.

Investigations is based on *Getting Ahead in a Just-Gettin'-By World,* which was first published in 2004 and has been used in many communities in the United States, Canada, Australia, and Slovakia. Thousands of people have already used this resource in workshop settings to change their lives, to build economic stability.

Investigations will be unlike any high school or college course you have ever taken. In terms of education, this course is as much about a learning *process* as it is about the content. Students are encouraged to use the learning process to identify and address problems. The discussions, activities, and assignments are invitations to learning—ways of modeling a process.

This course is as much about mastering yourself as it is about mastering a subject. The assignments will ask you to share what you know, rethink things you already know, make models, analyze cause and effect, compare, contrast, argue, describe—all of which education, careers, and life itself demand that you be able to do. If you do them well, you control your world rather than letting the world control you. The focus of the course is economic class—specifically poverty and its effects on individuals, communities, and society. Some of the group members might not be in poverty, but poverty affects us all, and most people don't understand it very well.

We study economic class to better understand how life works. For example:

- How does the economic environment in which a person lives affect that person?

- From a societal standpoint, what is the experience of people in poverty, middle class, and wealth?

1

- How different are the three environments of economic class?

- What does it mean to live in an unstable world where one is forced to attend to immediate, "concrete" problems all day long?

- What does it mean to live in a stable world where there is little fear for today, where solid resources support one's movement toward long-term goals?

We also study economic class to better understand ourselves in terms of our economic experience and to better understand people from other classes. We bring our own experience in society to college with us. Those who were raised in economic stability (middle or upper class) will find that college feels comfortable because for many decades in the U.S. the college experience has been an upper- and middle-class norm. But with the new economy many working-class people, as well as people from poverty, are enrolling in college. They will find that many colleges are still operating from largely middle-class norms and so will not feel as "at home" as most middle-class students feel.

Investigations into Economic Class in America addresses class issues that you encounter every day. It applies words and descriptions to the real world of economic class. The goal is twofold: to understand the impact that economic environments have on others, but more importantly to understand our *own* societal experience. Taking ownership of our own experience allows us to be much more open to the experiences of others. It can free us from judging people who come from different economic experiences. It allows us to question and seek understanding. And it gives us

a way to develop relationships of mutual respect, to resolve differences, and to solve problems.

This work is about helping you complete college and move toward economic stability or even prosperity. There is a critical difference between making informed choices and achieving economic stability, as opposed to "becoming middle class" and doing what others think you "should" or "ought" to do. This is not about "assimilation," "training," or "soft skills." Moving to economic stability or prosperity doesn't require conformity to the system or for you to embrace any particular ideology or political philosophy or to strive or want to become middle class. You can choose to use knowledge about the rules of economic classes and how to build resources without losing touch with community, family, or personal identity. Having more stability, choice, and power allows for different approaches to a reality of your *own choosing*.

This educational process also puts individuals in a position to become visible. Generally speaking, people from poverty are not present when decisions that affect their lives are made. They are invisible. Equipped with the information from this course, people who have lived in poverty can come to the table as problem solvers, advisers, and informed decision makers. Indeed, the visibility and civic engagement of those from poverty can have a positive effect on many of the conditions that contribute to poverty.

- The real **subjects** of the assignments are you, the campus, and the community in which we live.

- The **purpose** is to involve you with the process of thinking and using language to take apart and rebuild your world as you see fit.

- The **goal** is to put you in a position to create your own path for making a stable, secure life for you and your family.

In moving through this course, you aren't going to be handed a plan and told to follow certain steps. We know that each of us has our own story, and everyone is different, so one person's plan won't necessarily work for another. For that reason, it's important that each person create his or her own plan. We're all living out the stories of our lives. Part of that story comes from our past, from where we live, from the people in our lives, from community history, and from world or national events. And a part of our story is determined by the decisions we make. Who we are today was decided by what we did yesterday; who we'll be tomorrow is decided by what we do today. Whether we know it or not, we're all creating our future stories right now. This course offers a process for you to become more aware and therefore more in control of the possible paths to take as you intentionally create a new future story of your own.

It's important to be clear about our work together before we actually begin. We need to be clear about you and your education, how we relate to the information presented about economic class and to each other, and what to expect from each other. This is our agreement or contract.

II. Using *Investigations into Economic Class in America*

Expectations

In this class, students are invited to think of themselves as "investigators." Investigators dig out information, look into things, examine them, and find solutions. Investigators will be doing this form of learning for themselves and for the group.

A lot of what we do in this course will be connected to what the other people in the class are doing. Taking part in challenging and thoughtful discussions is important because the ideas and knowledge put forth by others is a wonderful way for everyone to learn. At times the group will divide up the tasks, and it's expected that each investigator will do his or her part. Some activities will take place in class, while others might be assigned as homework. This means that investigators must be *accountable to the group* for attending, investigating, and participating in the learning process.

The assignments will put you in a position to learn something about yourself from what you do as a student. You will learn *how* you learn and be able to take control of your own learning. The assignments set up conversations within the group that build throughout the modules of the workbook. To make it valuable, we cannot avoid the tough questions. There will be good times in class, but other times will be hard. The best thing this course can do is put you in a position to improve yourself *for yourself* and recognize your efforts and the result. This means that investigators must be *accountable to themselves,* as well as to the group.

The person heading your workgroup is both facilitator and co-investigator. When acting as a facilitator instead of an instructor, he or she will be making sure things run smoothly and the conversations stay on track. As a co-investigator, he or she will be working with you (and the other investigators) to uncover and explore new information that comes out of *your experience* and other sources. Collectively, you as a group bring a variety of backgrounds and experiences from many communities. Most of you have had jobs, and many may be working; all of you undoubtedly have your own ideas about the way the world works and why. The facilitator will keep introducing more information to investigate and help challenge the group to explore it fully.

What the facilitator will *not* do is impose his or her answers on the investigators or tell them what to do with their lives. This is an adult learning experience. Investigators will make up their own minds about what they will do with the information.

Depending on how and where this course is being offered, your facilitator might have other roles as well. For example, if the course is being offered for college credit, then the facilitator might also have to be an "instructor"; in that role, he or she makes, collects, and grades assignments. Take some time to talk about these expectations, including your expectations and the facilitator's expectations.

Support and Persistence

One thing we know from past experience with this information and process is that investigators tend to support each other during—and after—the course. They help each other with very practical problems: working in study groups, doing childcare in an emergency, and problem solving together so that everyone stays in college. Sometimes the persistence comes from other investigators and the facilitator: "Stick with it; I know you can do this, even when you think you can't."

What You Will Be Learning and Why

It's important that you know *what* will be covered, *why* it's important, and *how* the information fits together. At the beginning of each module or section you'll see a table that explains exactly that. Here's the table for this section.

Learning Objectives

WHAT'S COVERED	WHY IT'S IMPORTANT	HOW IT'S CONNECTED TO YOU
You will: Meet everyone in the group Learn about co-investigating Examine and understand the syllabus, the Process Triangle Find out what's expected of you Make and agree on the rules for the group	This module lets you know what to expect from *Investigations* and the group. If the sessions have a pattern or structure to them, it makes it easier to learn and manage the new information.	Each module will begin with a table like this to help you see where you've been and where you're going. The information and ideas build as we go. It's important to attend every session.

Learning Process

- You will read through this module during class as the facilitator reviews it with you.

- You'll review a syllabus that describes the course and shows you session by session what you'll be doing.

- You might make some notes in this workbook or in a notebook to help you remember important parts. You also may wish to note in a planner when assignments are due.

How the Workook Is Set Up

Numbering System

The book uses a simple numbering system to make it easier to find your place.

I. Information   The first number (like this Roman numeral "I") indicates where information is provided for you to use. This example would be the first piece of information in Module 1.

I. A. Activity   A capital letter designates an activity or discussion. Therefore, this example would be telling you that there is an activity or discussion after this first piece of information.

The Process Triangle

The Triangle you see on the next page is a symbol or **mental model** that includes, in capsule form, everything we'll be doing. It describes a process that can change lives—how we can use the *Investigations* process and the plans we create to build economic security for ourselves and our community. The Triangle will appear at the beginning of each module to show which part of the process we're working on. This Triangle is a quick and easy way to tell where we've been, where we're going, and how it all fits together. To understand what we'll be doing, we'll start at the bottom of the Triangle and work our way to the top.

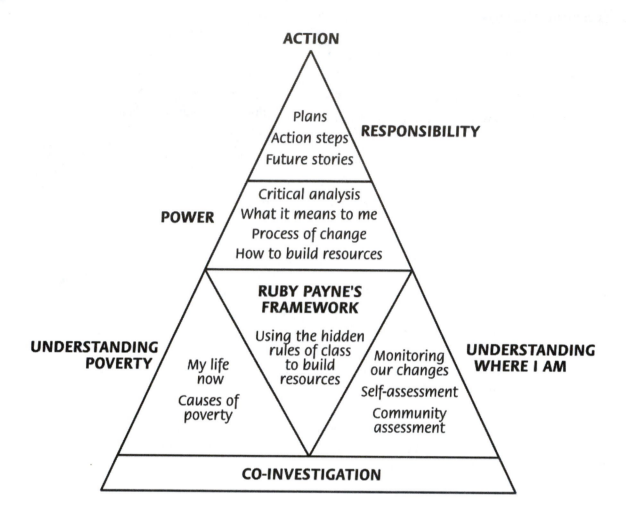

A. Bottom of Triangle: Co-Investigation

Module 1 sets the tone and expectations for the course.

Module 1   Co-investigation means that everyone in the group is a co-investigator (including the facilitator). It is the foundation of the work done by the group, so it is the foundation of the Triangle. Together, the group will investigate every part of the Triangle. Sometimes the group will study big issues that affect all people, and at other times the investigation will focus on your own unique experience. The point is: Everyone has something to offer, and everyone is a problem solver.

B. Bottom Left of Triangle: Understanding Poverty

In Modules 2 and 4, we'll investigate what it means to live in different economic classes.

Module 2	We'll investigate poverty, how it works in the lives of people toward the bottom of the economic ladder, and how it works for us individually. You'll make a mental model (or drawing) of "My Life Now."
Module 4	To better understand poverty, we have to understand it from different perspectives. This section introduces areas of research that tell part of the story. You'll learn that poverty is about much more than just the choices individuals make. Plans need to take into account *all* the causes of poverty.

C. Center of Triangle: Ruby Payne's 'Framework'

The centerpiece of the workbook is based on a framework for understanding economic class that was first described by Ruby K. Payne in the mid-1990s. Her work has been helping teachers do a better job, so that children from poverty do better in school. This is the first time these ideas have been put in writing especially for older students who are looking to postsecondary education to help them get ahead. When you understand better how the different economic classes work, you'll be in a better position to decide what you need and how to get it. Payne's hidden rules of economic class can be used to help build resources.

Module 5	The wealthy, the middle class, and the poor: Each group has its own hidden rules. If a person decides to take steps to build economic stability, he or she has to know and be able to use the hidden rules of middle class; if a person wants to get out of the middle class, he or she has to know and be able to use the hidden rules of wealth. In short, if we want to understand people from different classes, we need to be competent in our understanding and use of their hidden rules.
Module 6	Language is an especially important hidden rule. We can tell a lot about people by listening to how they speak. To get through college and get a good job, it's important to know how to speak—and even how to *hear* what other people are saying. "Formal register" and the language of negotiation are powerful tools.
Module 7	In order to build economic security, we have to know *which* resources to strengthen. This isn't just about money; it's about all aspects of life. Module 7 defines and describes the necessary resources for getting ahead.

D. Bottom Right Side of Triangle: Understanding Where I Am

Having investigated poverty, it's time to apply the information.

Module 8   Building economic stability means making some changes. Whatever plans you make, they should be yours and not someone else's. This module shows you how you can take charge of your changes, and it gives you a way to monitor how you're doing.

Module 9   Most agencies evaluate or assess people in some way. A self-assessment of resources is even more important because you can include everything, not just one part of your life, and you do it for yourself, rather than having it done to you or for you. This self-assessment is the foundation for your personal plans.

Module 10   In this module, we complete the work we began in Module 4 by doing an assessment of community resources. This is the foundation for our plan for community prosperity.

E. Center Section: Power

In this section we reflect back on everything we have learned. When we see the bigger picture, we can do a critical analysis and figure out what it means to us and what we want to do about our particular personal situations. With the information we have, we can gain power—both in our own lives and in our communities.

Module 3   If individuals or families go to agencies and the government for help, they find that they're expected to change and to make plans. The question is: Whose plan for change is it? Is it the individual's? Will the plan help the individual or family get out of poverty and build economic stability? The process of change—the idea behind this workbook—is that individuals can take charge of their own lives.

Module 11   Building resources is virtually the only way to establish economic stability, but it's hard to do. If it were easy, we wouldn't be getting together like this. The thinking we do here will be used when you make your individual plans.

F. Top Right Side of Triangle: Responsibility

People who have power are people who look for solutions. Now it's time to take responsibility for finding solutions. In this module you make your personal plans for moving toward prosperity.

Module 12   Here is where we work together to build individual plans for gaining economic stability. You'll be creating a vision of your future story. You also can be a problem solver on the college campus or in your community—and contribute to building prosperity. You might choose new roles as a planner and problem solver in the community.

G. Top of Triangle: Action

Investigations is designed to bring you right up to the point of action. This is when you take your knowledge, insights, and plans and put them to work.

Making It Challenging—and Safe

Know this up front: *Investigations* is going to be challenging. Sometimes it's hard to talk in a group, so we have to make it safe for everyone here. Below are some ground rules that should help. Your group can add to these or change the wording—whatever works for you and the group.

A. One person at a time talks

B. No putdowns, violence, or threats of violence

C. Show respect for each other by listening carefully

D. Respect people's privacy; don't share other people's stories without their permission (use common courtesy)

E. No volunteering advice

F. Honor differences

Once the ground rules or guidelines are established, you might discuss who it is you're accountable to. In college each student is expected to be responsible for his or her own behavior—being on time, for example. In *Investigations,* because the learning is done in a group process, it's important that the members agree to be accountable to each other. This applies to being on time and completing class and homework assignments.

How the Course Is Set Up

1. **Rooms, Space, and Learning Styles**
    College is different from high school, and this course is different from most other college courses. Sitting around a table or in a circle gives everyone equal access, and it encourages conversation. People learn in different ways, so discussions, stories, drawings, and activities will be the main ways to learn. Sometimes all we need is a little information to get the picture. *Activities* are designed to discover how the information relates to you specifically and your community. There aren't right or wrong answers. Discussions help you learn to listen and to express yourself. A good answer, communicated the wrong way, is not helpful.

2. **Keeping a Journal**
    Keeping a journal or diary lets you look back on where you started, as well as your journey up to the present. In your journal you get

to write about what *you* think or feel regarding the information being covered—or about some specific part of the module. The act of writing helps focus your thinking, sharpen your language, and craft your future story. Some modules have specific journal assignments, but most of the time you can take your journal response in whatever direction you wish.

3. Creating the 'Lexicon'—a Working Vocabulary for the Group

The language we use has a major impact not only on our relationships and work, but also on our own thinking and understanding. Information can be covered and understood more quickly if everyone in the room has the same understanding of what the words mean. Also, by creating short and "to the point" labels for bigger concepts, we can cover information more quickly and be more specific about what we say. So one of the "products" produced in this workbook is a list of words, terms, and labels—a lexicon. Each module

includes suggestions for the lexicon, and you can add more. Try using some of those words in your discussions and your journal. The lexicon for this introduction is brief (see below left). From this point forward, the lexicon will appear at the beginning of each module.

4. Assessments and Planning

At the end of *Investigations* you will be developing personal plans for building resources. We will be introducing and practicing assessment and planning skills so that you are ready to finish that final project.

5. Making a List of Things You Want to Do

The work you do here might cause you to think of all sorts of things you think need to happen in your life and the community. We'll be developing plans for the things that need to change, so we suggest that you write down your ideas in your journal as they come to you.

6. Personal and Private Problems

If something personal comes up that might interfere with your ability to participate in the group, ask to meet with the facilitator privately. The group process of analyzing personal stories and what is happening in the community might stir up feelings. And the plans you make for change might stir things up with people you care about. This is a normal part of the process, but sometimes you might want some extra help. Let your facilitator know if you need help or feel that things are getting out of control.

Lexicon for Module 1

Accountability
Assimilation
Concrete problems
Economic class
Environments
Facilitator
Investigations
Investigators, co-investigators
Lexicon
Mental model
Process Triangle
Soft skills

7. Group Projects and a Place in the Community

The way you work together in this class, along with the vocabulary you develop in the lexicon and the new knowledge you gain about economic class, helps prepare you for working with others on campus and/or in the community on issues that are important to you. Many investigators in previous groups have become community problem solvers by joining planning groups, committees, and boards.

You now have an overview of what the course is about, what it is designed to accomplish, and what is expected of you. You might come back to this overview in the middle and/or the end of the course to see if you understand it differently after learning new things. But for now, it's time to get started with the first investigation: what poverty is like.

MODULE 2
Mental Model of Poverty

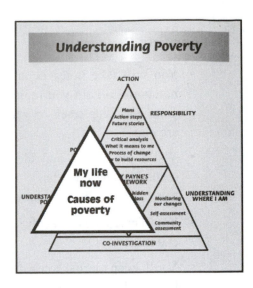

Understanding Poverty

ACTION

Plans
Action steps
Future stories

RESPONSIBILITY

Critical analysis
What it means to me
Process of change
to build resources

My life now
Causes of poverty

PAYNE'S FRAMEWORK

hidden class

Monitoring our changes

Self-assessment

Community assessment

UNDERSTANDING WHERE I AM

CO-INVESTIGATION

Learning Objectives

WHAT'S COVERED

You will:

Learn what mental models are

Investigate what it's like to live in poverty

Make a Mental Model of Poverty

Investigate income and wage information

Figure several personal financial indicators

Make a "My Life Now" mental model of your life

Figure estimated vs. actual use of time

WHY IT'S IMPORTANT

It's important to start with what is real. To do that we have to listen to each other and ask tough questions. Everything you do in *Investigations into Economic Class in America* is based on having a true (realistic and objective) picture of what your life is like.

It's also important that we begin to investigate community issues that foster poverty, such as housing and wages, because poverty isn't just about the choices individuals make.

When we go to college or otherwise work on improving our lives, it comes down to a vision, a dream, and a plan. Going through this workbook may well be the first step in creating a new vision and your *own* plan.

HOW IT'S CONNECTED TO YOU

These are the first mental models you will create. We will use mental models throughout the workbook.

The "My Life Now" mental model will show you where you are. In order to be able to make changes, you need to know where you are now.

The first investigations you do will be about your community and your personal situation. You will be learning some of the standard measures for determining financial stability.

Learning Process

- You will take notes in this book or in a notebook to help you remember important parts and keep track of when assignments are due.

- You'll put words and ideas into pictures (called mental models), which you will keep and look back at throughout the term.

- You'll calculate and analyze personal financial indicators.

- You'll keep journal notes about what you've learned, how you see it applying to you, and what you'd like to do with the information. Part of journaling is keeping track of your feelings and emotions. Your facilitator may need to read your journal to learn from it, but you can be sure that the facilitator will keep what you write confidential.

Lexicon for Module 2

Affordable housing payment
  threshold
Debt-to-income ratio
Inferences
Living wage
Mental Model of Poverty
Minimum wage
"My Life Now" mental model
Pro-innovative, anti-innovative
Savings cushion
Self-sufficient wage
Time Monitor

I. Mental Models—Background

We've used the term "mental model" several times already. Now we need to define what we mean because we'll be using mental models from this point forward. Mental models are stories, cartoons, analogies, metaphors, diagrams, charts, and drawings. Mental models are valuable because they help us remember, learn faster, see the whole picture and all of its parts, understand complex issues, and not rely on language (written or spoken).

Think, for example, of weather reports on TV. It would take a long time to talk about everything that we can see in seconds just by looking at symbols on a map.

Business, education, and the social service/workforce development sectors use mental models for planning and dealing with complex ideas. Peter Senge (1990) describes the mental models used by managers as theories-in-use. Some are simple generalizations, some are complicated, but they help determine how we act.

Michael Fairbanks (2000) identifies four principles for mental models:

1. A mental model consists of beliefs, inferences, and goals that are first-person, concrete, and specific. It is a mental map of how the world works.

2. Mental models are sets of beliefs that are pro-innovative or anti-innovative.

3. Mental models shape performance and can be tested against objectives.

4. Mental models can be changed.

Mental models can change our view of reality. They show us the bigger picture.

Mental Model of Poverty

As a group, you are going to investigate and describe what life is like for someone living in poverty in your community. If we're going to do something about poverty, we had better know what we're talking about. In other words, we need to have an accurate, specific, and complete picture of poverty in our community before we make plans to do something about it.

Questions to get started:
- What problems does a person in poverty have to solve?
- What do people worry about?
- Where does most of their time and energy go?

I. A. Activity: Group Mental Model of Poverty
(make a pie chart showing all aspects of life in poverty)

Time: 30 minutes

Materials: Chart paper, markers

Procedure:

1. At the top of the page write: Mental Model of Poverty.

2. Draw a big circle on the page; it should just about fill the page.

3. As the group discusses life in poverty, have someone draw in and label the pieces of the pie. You can make a copy for yourself in your journal or in the space below.

NOTE: This is the first of many mental models the group will create. Keep all of them so that later the group can refer to them and add, subtract, or modify information.

I. B. Discussion

1. How have the investigators (including you) described life in poverty? What are the biggest problems for people in poverty? What problems take the most time and energy? Does that make them the most important problems—or merely the most urgent?

2. How is poverty the same for everyone? How is it different?

3. What kinds of things do you think middle-class and wealthy people know about living in poverty? What kinds of things don't they know?

4. What is it about poverty that makes it hard to get out? Why? What happens to someone who lives in poverty for a long time?

5. How do people solve problems when living in poverty? What strengths and skills are needed?

6. Have the leaders in the community seen mental models like this? What would be the value of having people like the mayor, police chief, or school superintendent have this information? List other leaders, organizations, and associations that could use this information.

"Survival = Anger x Imagination.
Imagination is the only weapon
on the reservation."

—Sherman Alexie, *The Lone Ranger
and Tonto Fistfight in Heaven*

Journal Reflections

What did you learn from this? What conclusions have you come to about poverty in the United States?

II. Housing

The "Mental Model of Poverty" that we made is a general picture representing people in the community. The next step is creating a clear picture of your specific life circumstances. In order to make changes in your life, you'll need to examine it as carefully as possible and create a mental model of "My Life Now."

For example, when we did the Mental Model of Poverty, we talked about housing and jobs in a general way. The lack of affordable housing is one of the engines that drive chaos and insecurity. Some people are in subsidized housing, while others are on their own to find a solution. This means that people are returning to live with relatives or are crowding into apartments, houses, and trailers with friends. People are living in campgrounds, long-term motels, cars, shelters, and on the street.

Now we need to really investigate housing and wage issues in detail and understand how they connect with your life. One way to gain perspective on your personal housing situation is to calculate how much of your income can safely be spent for housing. When a person goes to a bank for a loan, the banker calculates the Affordable Housing Payment Threshold. Let's investigate this threshold.

II. A. Activity: Affordable Housing Payment Threshold Calculator

Time: 10 minutes

Materials: Calculator

Procedure: Review the example, then enter your information into the blank worksheet.

Example: Affordable Housing Payment Threshold

Calculation A Monthly Income (before taxes)	x 30%	$ 4,000 $ 1,200 A.	Payment threshold is 30% of monthly income
Calculation B Monthly Income (before taxes) Monthly Loan Payments (car loans, school loans, other loans) Monthly Utility Payments (phone, electric, water, etc.) Balance	 - - = x 35%	 $ 4,000 $ 500 $ 300 $ 3,200 $ 1,120 B.	 Payment threshold is 35% of monthly income minus loan and utility payments
Affordable Housing Payment Threshold (enter the amount in A. or B., whichever is less): $ ___1,120___			

ACTUAL			
Calculation A Monthly Income (before taxes)	x 30%	$ $ _____ A.	Payment threshold is 30% of monthly income
Calculation B Monthly Income (before taxes) Monthly Loan Payments (car loans, school loans, other loans) Monthly Utility Payments (phone, electric, water, etc.) Balance	 - - = x 35%	$ $ _____ $ _____ $ _____ $ _____ B.	Payment threshold is 35% of monthly income minus loan and utility payments
Affordable Housing Payment Threshold (enter the amount in A. or B., whichever is less): $ _____			

Note. Worksheet provided courtesy of Paul J. Pfeiffer, MBA, CFP.®

 ## II. B. Discussion

1. How does the housing payment recommended by the Affordable Housing Payment Threshold calculator compare to what members of the group are paying in rent?

2. How does this information relate to the recent housing crisis in the U.S.?

If the cost of housing for you is more than 35% of your income, Activity III. A. will help you figure how much you need to earn.

Journal Reflections

What did you learn from this? How does it apply to you and your family?

II. C. Activity: Mental Model of the Floor Plan of My Apartment/House

Time: 15 minutes

Materials: Pencil, pen, paper

Procedure: Draw the floor plan of the house or apartment where you are living now. Put the initials of everyone who sleeps at your house in the room in which they sleep. See the example below.

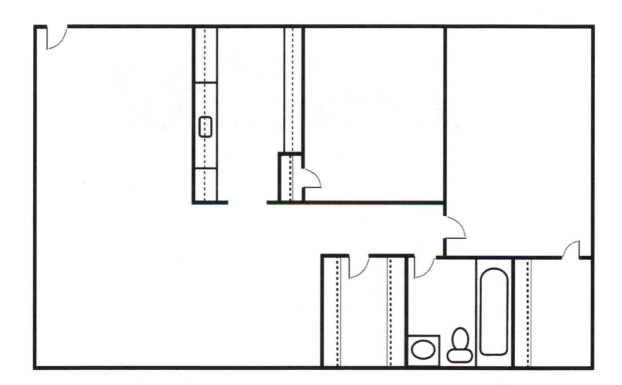

 ## II. D. Discussion

1. What are the conditions of the house or apartment in terms of lighting, bathrooms, kitchen fixtures, furniture, and entertainment centers?

2. How many people are staying where you live?

3. Are people doubling up or "couch surfing"?

4. What are the liabilities or drawbacks of crowded living?

5. What is the impact on children?

III. Wages

The Affordable Housing Payment Threshold is an exercise that immediately brings up the idea of wages. How much does your current job (or last one, if you aren't working now) pay, and how many hours a week could you work? What kind of job can you do that would earn enough to make the rent affordable?

What is the relationship between housing costs and wages? The questions we need to answer are: "How much do we have to make an hour to afford the rent? And how much is left over for the rest of your expenses?"

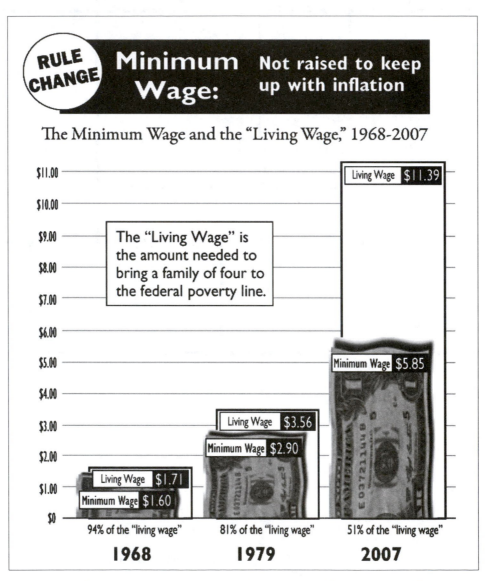

RULE CHANGE

Minimum Wage: Not raised to keep up with inflation

The Minimum Wage and the "Living Wage," 1968-2007

The "Living Wage" is the amount needed to bring a family of four to the federal poverty line.

Living Wage $11.39

Minimum Wage $5.85

Living Wage $3.56
Minimum Wage $2.90

Living Wage $1.71
Minimum Wage $1.60

94% of the "living wage"
1968

81% of the "living wage"
1979

51% of the "living wage"
2007

Note. Adapted from *The Growing Divide: Inequality and the Roots of Economic Insecurity,* 2009, Boston, MA: United for a Fair Economy. Copyright 2009 by United for a Fair Economy.

The graph on the previous page looks at the federal minimum wage in 1968, 1979, and 2007 and compares it to a "living wage" in each of those three years. A *living wage* is the hourly pay a full-time worker needs to lift his or her family of four to *only* the Federal Poverty Line. It could more accurately be called a "poverty wage." People pushing for living-wage laws in cities or counties require that the city, as well as businesses contracting with the city, pay at least a poverty-line wage to their employees.

The minimum wage is worth much less now than it was in 1968. The chart shows that in 1968 a minimum-wage worker was making only 11 cents an hour below a living wage. In 2007 the gap had widened to $5.54 an hour.

NOTE: The recommended federal minimum wage was increased to $7.25 on July 24, 2009. A living wage in 2009 would be $10.19. So the gap had narrowed to $2.94, which is still far worse than 1968. For your information:

Federal Poverty Guidelines:
Family Size and Monthly Income, 2009

Family Size	1	2	3	4	5	6	7	8
Poverty Line	$798	$1,069	$1,341	$1,613	$1,884	$2,156	$2,428	$2,699

Note. Adapted from The Growing Divide: Inequality and the Roots of Economic Insecurity, *2009, Boston, MA: United for a Fair Economy. Copyright 2009 by United for a Fair Economy.*

III. A. Activity: Getting Ahead or Just Getting By?
Calculate the hourly wage needed to pay the rent and have enough money left over to meet your other expenses.

Time: 15 minutes

Materials: None

Procedure:

1. How much do you earn? In the chart on the next page find the full-time hourly wage (in Column 1) or the monthly income (in Column 3) that is closest to what you are earning now—or at your last job—or in a job you might be qualified for *today* (check the newspaper). *Circle that dollar amount.*

2. How much do you pay for housing? Next, in Column 5 find the dollar amount closest to what your rent or mortgage is now *in the 35% rows only.*

3. Now you can see what hourly or monthly wage you would need to be making to afford the rent.

Income Related to Cost of Housing

1 Hourly wage	2 Hours worked per month full time	3 Monthly income	4 Percentage of income for rent	5 Cost of rent	6 Money available for other expenses	7 How much *more* money is left over for other expenses when you pay 35% instead of 50% of your income for rent
$6.00	173	1,038	35%	363	675	156
			50%	519	519	
$7.00	173	1,211	35%	424	787	181
			50%	606	606	
$8.00	173	1,384	35%	484	900	208
			50%	692	692	
$9.00	173	1,557	35%	545	1,012	233
			50%	779	779	
$10.00	173	1,730	35%	606	1,125	260
			50%	865	865	
$11.00	173	1,903	35%	666	1,237	285
			50%	952	952	
$12.00	173	2,076	35%	727	1,349	311
			50%	1,038	1,038	

Note. Adapted from work of Glenn Corliss, Columbiana County (Ohio) One Stop.

Example of how to read the table: If John worked eight hours a day, five days a week, he would be working an average of 173 hours a month. If he earned $7 an hour and his rent was 35% of his income, he would be paying $424 for rent and would have $787 left over for other expenses. If John paid 50% of his income on rent, he would be paying $606 for rent and have only $606 left over for other expenses. When paying rent at 35%, John would have an extra $181 to use for other expenses.

III. B. Discussion

1. What are the "other" expenses mentioned in Columns 6 and 7 that people have?

2. Discuss some ways that people can balance the wage/rent issue in the short term. How do people solve this problem?

3. Discuss some ways that people can solve the wage/rent problem in the long term.

4. What's the minimum wage in your state? How does it compare with the Federal Poverty Guidelines shown earlier?

5. How many people in your group are working more than one job? Or ever did?

6. How many of the employers provide health insurance? Has that changed in recent years? If so, how?

Investigate This!

- What is a living wage? What is the self-sufficiency standard?

- How much income does a single mom with an infant and a toddler need to cover housing, transportation, taxes, utilities, food, childcare, clothing, and healthcare costs without using any governmental support at all?

- How many cities and counties in the United States have passed a living-wage ordinance? How many states have worked out the self-sufficiency standard for every county?

Where might you go to learn more about this?

Now that we've examined housing conditions, the cost of housing, and wages, it's time to calculate our savings cushion and debt-to-income ratio.

IV. Savings

Economic security is hard to achieve. What would happen if the main wage earner in your family lost his or her job? One way to become economically secure is to create a savings cushion. Money stored up in a savings account can tide a family over through a layoff, illness, or other emergency. Financial planners say that a family's first financial goal should be to accumulate an emergency fund of ready cash that equals six months of wages or salary.

IV. A. Activity: What Is Your Savings Cushion?

Time: 20 minutes

Materials: None

Procedure: Review the example, then fill out the Savings Cushion worksheet with your information below.

Example: Savings Cushion Calculation

If you or your family's main breadwinner lost a job today, how long could the family survive at the poverty line before running out of money? Estimate your cash savings and enter the figure in Line a.	a. $600
To determine your monthly level minimum, look at the Family Size/Poverty Line table from the Federal Poverty Guidelines presented earlier in this module. Enter that amount on Line b.	b. $1,341
Divide Line a. by Line b. The result is the number of months your family could live at the poverty level before your savings run out.	$600/$1,341 = .45 month

Example: In this case the individual has $600 ready cash in a savings account, and there are three people in the family. The family could live at the poverty line for almost half a month.

Worksheet: Savings Cushion Calculation

If you or your family's main breadwinner lost a job today, how long could the family survive at the poverty line before running out of money? Estimate your cash savings and enter the figure in Line a.	a. _____
To determine your monthly level minimum, look at the Family Size/Poverty Line table from the Federal Poverty Guidelines presented earlier in this module. Enter that amount on Line b.	b. _____
Divide Line a. by Line b. The result is the number of months your family could live at the poverty level before your savings run out.	

Note. Adapted from *The Growing Divide: Inequality and the Roots of Economic Insecurity,* 2009, Boston, MA: United for a Fair Economy. Copyright 2009 by United for a Fair Economy.

V. More Rules of Money

Very few people in the U.S. learn the rules of money management in high school, so they have to learn them from their families or on their own by reading books or (the hard way) by making mistakes.

The rules of money management change with our age and stage of life. However, there are some basic measures of financial health that everyone should know. We have already covered two—the percentage of income that goes to housing and the savings cushion. Another basic metric is the *debt-to-income (DTI) ratio.* There are two types of DTIs: The first ratio is the percentage of income that goes to housing, which we've already addressed. The second ratio covers all income and all debts. A debt load of more than 37% is generally regarded as a sign of trouble.

In the housing bust that started in 2007, many people broke this rule to their regret. Even Edmund L. Andrews, an economics reporter for the *New York Times,* got into trouble. On the strength of his credit rating he bought a home he couldn't afford and—despite the help of (or perhaps because of) a loan officer from a mortgage corporation—Andrews plunged into a series of go-go mortgages, liar loans, piggyback loans, and a no-ratio mortgage that led to foreclosure (Andrews, 2009).

Although not designed to be a course in financial literacy, this final investigation into your own DTI ratio provides a window into your financial realities.

V. A. Activity: Calculating Your Debt-to-Income Ratio

Time: 20 minutes

Materials: Calculator

Procedure: Review the example, then fill in the worksheet with your information and do the calculations.

Debt-to-Income Ratio: Example

1. How much is your monthly rent or house payment?	$400
2. How much do you owe in car payments per month?	$100
3. How much do you pay on credit cards per month?	$50
4. How much do you pay for loans, payday lenders, lease/purchase per month?	$50
5. How much do you pay for renters/home insurance per month?	-0-
TOTAL DEBT: ITEMS 1–5	$600
6. How much gross income (before taxes and deductions) do you have per month?	$800
7. How much do you get in food stamps per month?	$50
8. How much child support do you get each month?	$200
TOTAL INCOME: ITEMS 6–8	$1,050
Divide your DEBT by your INCOME. This is your DEBT-TO-INCOME RATIO.	57.14 57%

Debt-to-Income Ratio: Personal Worksheet

1. How much is your monthly rent or house payment?	
2. How much do you owe in car payments per month?	
3. How much do you pay on credit cards per month?	
4. How much do you pay for loans, payday lenders, lease/purchase per month?	
5. How much do you pay for renters/home insurance per month?	
TOTAL DEBT: ITEMS 1–5	
6. How much gross income (before taxes and deductions) do you have per month?	
7. How much do you get in food stamps per month?	
8. How much child support do you get each month?	
TOTAL INCOME: ITEMS 6–8	
Divide your DEBT by your INCOME. This is your DEBT-TO-INCOME RATIO.	

V. B. Discussion

1. What DTI did members of the group have?

2. What are the largest debts that people are carrying?

VI. 'My Life Now'

We began by investigating the impact that poverty has on our community, after which we investigated housing, wages, and three personal financial metrics. The activities focused on your individual situations. The intent of this activity is to clarify your perspective of your life as it is now. No doubt your group talked about other aspects of life like school, health, relationships, neighborhood conditions, children, transportation, safety, entertainment, college, and spirituality. All of those are things you might consider when creating this mental model.

VI. A. Activity: Personal Mental Model—'My Life Now'

Time: 20 minutes
Materials: Notebook paper
Procedure:

1. Draw a large circle on a separate piece of paper in your notebook.

2. Using a pencil (so that you can change things as you learn more), draw in the pieces of the pie for every part of your life and label them. Make each piece of

the pie large or small according to how important it is. For example, if health issues are a huge concern, then make that piece of the pie larger.

 ## VI. B. Discussion

1. What is the largest piece of your pie? How might it be argued that the biggest piece is also the most significant piece of your life? How might you argue that this is not true?

2. What makes it hard to make changes? Come up with a list of the reasons why change is difficult and complicated. How is change about more than simply "putting your mind to it"?

3. What did you learn about poverty by doing this mental model?

4. What did you learn about your community or "the system" by doing this mental model?

5. What were your feelings after doing this mental model?

6. This model represents what you are already doing—what you are living with each day—but you might not have ever considered it this way. What thoughts or comments do you have now that you have finished your mental model?

7. What words and phrases do you say to yourself to encourage yourself to keep going?

Journal Reflections

To what extent have you thought about your life like this before? Is your thinking about poverty starting to change? If so, how?

VII. Time Management and Planning

Being in school is only one aspect of your life. Most students have other things to be responsible for as well, such as family and work. Adding school—classes, studying, new friends, and responsibilities—requires some planning. But you can't plan your time if you don't know where it goes … how you spend the hours in a day. For the next seven days, you will investigate exactly what you do with your time in one week's time (even if it isn't a completely typical week). This information is personal; share with others only what feels comfortable.

VII. A. Activity: Time Management (Where Does the Time Go?)

Time: 5 minutes, 3 times a day—morning, noon, and night for 7 days

Materials: One Estimated Time vs. Actual Time (below) and one Weekly Time Monitor

Procedure:

1. First, estimate how many hours a week you spend in the following activities and record that in the second column.

Estimated Time vs. Actual Time

Activity	Estimated time spent in a week	Actual time spent in a week
Grooming		
Eating		
Classroom		
Studying		
Working		
On the Internet		
Traveling/commuting		
Watching TV		
With friends		
Childcare		
With family		
Church		
Clubs		
Sleeping		
Other		

2. Beginning today, fill in the Time Monitor sheets (see next two pages) with all your activities since you got out of bed in the morning.

   Next to the time you got out of bed, write what you did first (for example, showering, shaving, and dressing could be shortened to "grooming").

   Round off to the nearest 15-minute block. If you got up at 6:55 a.m., record that as 7 a.m.

   Continue to record how you spend your time in 15-minute increments—for example, breakfast, travel to school, English class, math class, lunch, study, communications class, work, and so on.

3. Keep the Time Monitor with you and fill it in every few hours, or at least three times a day so that you don't forget anything significant.

After seven days, add up the categories of time to see how much time you actually were in class, studying, with friends, and so on, then record that in the third column of the **Estimated Time vs. Actual Time** table on the previous page.

 ## VII. B. Discussion/Journal

After the week is over, you can come back to answer these questions:

1. What did you learn from monitoring your time during this time-management assignment?

2. Where do you spend more time than you thought you would?

3. Where did you spend less time than you thought you would?

4. Where would you *like* to spend more time? How *should* you spend more time?

5. How much of the time was spent doing the things you planned on doing?

6. Did the fact that you knew you were doing this exercise change (in any way) how you spent your time during the week? If so, in what way(s)?

Time Monitor Sheets

Monday ___ / ___ / ___		Tuesday ___ / ___ / ___		Wednesday ___ / ___ / ___	
7:00 7:15 7:30 7:45	7:00	7:00 7:15 7:30 7:45	7:00	7:00 7:15 7:30 7:45	7:00
8:00 8:15 8:30 8:45	8:00	8:00 8:15 8:30 8:45	8:00	8:00 8:15 8:30 8:45	8:00
9:00 9:15 9:30 9:45	9:00	9:00 9:15 9:30 9:45	9:00	9:00 9:15 9:30 9:45	9:00
10:00 10:15 10:30 10:45	10:00	10:00 10:15 10:30 10:45	10:00	10:00 10:15 10:30 10:45	10:00
11:00 11:15 11:30 11:45	11:00	11:00 11:15 11:30 11:45	11:00	11:00 11:15 11:30 11:45	11:00
12:00 12:15 12:30 12:45	12:00	12:00 12:15 12:30 12:45	12:00	12:00 12:15 12:30 12:45	12:00
1:00 1:15 1:30 1:45	1:00	1:00 1:15 1:30 1:45	1:00	1:00 1:15 1:30 1:45	1:00
2:00 2:15 2:30 2:45	2:00	2:00 2:15 2:30 2:45	2:00	2:00 2:15 2:30 2:45	2:00
3:00 3:15 3:30 3:45	3:00	3:00 3:15 3:30 3:45	3:00	3:00 3:15 3:30 3:45	3:00
4:00 4:15 4:30 4:45	4:00	4:00 4:15 4:30 4:45	4:00	4:00 4:15 4:30 4:45	4:00
5:00 5:15 5:30 5:45	5:00	5:00 5:15 5:30 5:45	5:00	5:00 5:15 5:30 5:45	5:00
6:00 6:15 6:30 6:45	6:00	6:00 6:15 6:30 6:45	6:00	6:00 6:15 6:30 6:45	6:00
7:00 7:15 7:30 7:45	7:00	7:00 7:15 7:30 7:45	7:00	7:00 7:15 7:30 7:45	7:00
8:00 8:15 8:30 8:45	8:00	8:00 8:15 8:30 8:45	8:00	8:00 8:15 8:30 8:45	8:00
9:00 9:15 9:30 9:45	9:00	9:00 9:15 9:30 9:45	9:00	9:00 9:15 9:30 9:45	9:00

Time Monitor Sheets

Thursday __ / __ / __		Friday __ / __ / __		Saturday __ / __ / __	
7:00 7:15 7:30 7:45	7:00	7:00 7:15 7:30 7:45	7:00		
8:00 8:15 8:30 8:45	8:00	8:00 8:15 8:30 8:45	8:00		
9:00 9:15 9:30 9:45	9:00	9:00 9:15 9:30 9:45	9:00		
10:00 10:15 10:30 10:45	10:00	10:00 10:15 10:30 10:45	10:00		
11:00 11:15 11:30 11:45	11:00	11:00 11:15 11:30 11:45	11:00		
12:00 12:15 12:30 12:45	12:00	12:00 12:15 12:30 12:45	12:00		
1:00 1:15 1:30 1:45	1:00	1:00 1:15 1:30 1:45	1:00		
2:00 2:15 2:30 2:45	2:00	2:00 2:15 2:30 2:45	2:00	Sunday __ / __ / __	
3:00 3:15 3:30 3:45	3:00	3:00 3:15 3:30 3:45	3:00		
4:00 4:15 4:30 4:45	4:00	4:00 4:15 4:30 4:45	4:00		
5:00 5:15 5:30 5:45	5:00	5:00 5:15 5:30 5:45	5:00		
6:00 6:15 6:30 6:45	6:00	6:00 6:15 6:30 6:45	6:00		
7:00 7:15 7:30 7:45	7:00	7:00 7:15 7:30 7:45	7:00		
8:00 8:15 8:30 8:45	8:00	8:00 8:15 8:30 8:45	8:00		
9:00 9:15 9:30 9:45	9:00	9:00 9:15 9:30 9:45	9:00		

Readings

An Atlas of Poverty in America: One Nation, Pulling Apart, 1960–2003 by Amy Glasmeier. Comprehensive data on poverty in the U.S.

The Fifth Discipline: The Art and Practice of the Learning Organization by Peter Senge. The value of mental models.

Rich Dad, Poor Dad by Robert Kiyosaki and Sharon Lechter. Describes how people in different classes think of money.

The Shock Doctrine: The Rise of Disaster Capitalism by Naomi Klein. Describes how the tyranny of the moment works in war and natural disasters.

The Spirit Level: Why More Equal Societies Almost Always Do Better by Richard Wilkinson and Kate Pickett. From the book jacket: "Almost every modern social and environmental problem— ill health, lack of community life, violence, drugs, obesity, mental illness, long working hours, big prison populations—is more likely to occur in a less equal society." See also Chapter 3 on how inequality gets under the skin, pages 31–48.

MODULE 3
A Process for Change

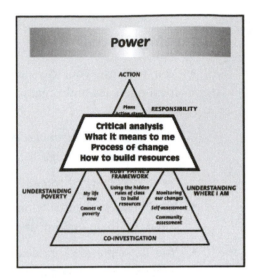

Power

ACTION

Plans
Action steps

RESPONSIBILITY

Critical analysis
What it means to me
Process of change
How to build resources

RUBY PAYNE'S FRAMEWORK

UNDERSTANDING POVERTY

My life now

Using the hidden rules of class to build resources

Monitoring our changes

UNDERSTANDING WHERE I AM

Causes of poverty

Self-assessment

Community assessment

CO-INVESTIGATION

Learning Objectives

WHAT'S COVERED

You will:

Examine which agencies require clients to change

Investigate how plans are made in agency settings

Explore ways people change

Explore changes you might need to make to succeed in college and to build a prosperous life

Learn the process of change for *Investigations*

Learn time-management techniques

WHY IT'S IMPORTANT

Learning about change is important because, to succeed in college or to build resources for yourself and your family, you might need to think and act differently.

Agencies have some of the resources that you may need, so you'll probably have to work with them, at least for a while. Most agencies are based on middle-class values, and so middle-class organizations are all about change.

To be in charge of the changes you make, you'll want to know the process of change that *Investigations* is based on.

HOW IT'S CONNECTED TO YOU

Changes are harder to make when a person lives in an unstable environment.

The process of change can help you stay focused on your future story, even when you are living in an unstable setting.

If you want to establish economic stability, *you* will need to be in charge of the investigation, the plans, the action, and the monitoring.

Once free of the tyranny of the moment, you'll need to know how to manage time effectively.

Learning Process

- You will use your own experiences with local agencies and organizations to understand:

  - *How those agencies expect their clients to change*

  - *Processes of change*

- You'll review the mental models in Module 2 and use them to think about change.

- You'll "step aside" or detach yourself emotionally from the mental models so that you can think about them and your life objectively.

- You'll examine the processes of change used by organizations in your community, including the college or university.

- You'll watch the facilitator develop a mental model of the Process of Change that is the foundation of this course.

Lexicon for Module 3

Abstract
Metacognition
Proactive planning strategies
Procedural steps
Process of change
Psychological reactance
Quadrant
Reactive problem solving
Righting reflex
Stability
Time-management matrix
Tyranny of the moment

I. Who Wants You to Change?

You will be supplying most of the information in this module, and you'll use it to revise the Mental Model of Poverty from Module 2. We'll begin by investigating how change and plans are handled by the agencies we use. This investigation can best be done by the group.

"The conflict lies in the fact that theory, in a field like medicine, education, or [the] sciences, may dictate one course of behavior, and the bureaucratic structure, set up supposedly to carry out these ends, may dictate another. There are certain structural needs or pressures which may conflict with theory, yet they may come to dominate practice."

—Chandler Washburne, "Conflicts Between Educational Theory and Structure"

I. A. Activity: Examining Agency Approaches to Change

Time: 30 minutes

Materials: Chart paper, markers, group Mental Model of Poverty from Module 2

Procedure:

1. Make a list on the chart paper of the agencies and programs used by the members of your family or members of the group. Examples might include schools, substance abuse treatment programs, mental health clinics, homeless shelters, probation/parole offices, welfare-to-work agencies, and employment agencies.

2. List the departments and offices on campus with which you have had contact; these might include admissions, financial aid, a health clinic, tutoring, and/or other student services.

3. Match the agencies and departments to the mental model. On the Mental Model of Poverty that you created as a group, draw a line pointing to a piece of the pie and write on that line the name of the agency that is meant to help in that area. For example, Metropolitan Housing would be written on a line pointing to the piece of the pie marked "housing."

4. Now mark an "X" beside the name of any agency that *requires* you to make changes in the way you think or behave.

5. Mark a second "X" by those agencies that *suggest* plans for how you "should" change. Sometimes these plans are called by different names, such as "reunification plans," "treatment plans," "contracts," or "commitments."

The Mental Model of Poverty now looks different because the pie is surrounded by names of agencies, programs, organizations, and other helping entities.

I. B. Discussion

1. Are there any parts of the pie where there is no agency or organization trying to assist people?

2. About what percentage of the agencies require you to make a plan for change?

3. Pick a piece of the pie that has an agency working on it. How does that agency deal with the rest of the pieces of the pie? What might they do differently?

4. How do you feel when you look at the agencies surrounding the Mental Model of Poverty?

5. What have your "change" experiences been like with agencies? How much has your life changed as a result of going to an agency?

6. What difference does it make if you make your *own* plans, taking into account the entire picture?

7. Why do you think change by the client is so important to people who work at agencies?

II. Change Meets the 'Righting Reflex'

Almost all agencies and organizations that serve people in poverty are about change—the changes that they believe clients need to make. Agencies, like people, have what is called a *"righting reflex,"* so when they see something that isn't right, they usually have an idea about how to make it better or "fix" it (Miller & Rollnick, 2002, pp. 20–22).

For most people, the righting reflex works like this: You want to watch TV and you can't locate the remote. You eventually find it in the other room, and your righting reflex is, "Hey, you kids! I've told you a thousand times to leave the remote on the coffee table!" It's a simple "fix." Sometimes the righting reflex is applied to adults by friends, family, people in authority, and society in general. These messages are basically "you should" and "you ought," and people get tired of hearing them.

- "You should get busy."
- "You should get a job, any job."
- "You ought to leave that man/woman."
- "You should quit smoking."

The righting reflex (even when the intentions are good) is often met with what is called **psychological reactance,** which goes like this: "I'm sick and tired of everyone telling me to quit smoking! If I want to kill myself by smoking, I will" (Miller & Rollnick, 2002, p. 18). But the righting reflex also works in deeper ways, because inside all of us is that place where we know the difference between right and wrong. It's an internal guide or compass.

The righting reflex is basically a good thing, something we all have and need. And yet there can be problems with the righting reflex. The first is when we don't take charge of our own life and make our own plans for righting things that have gone wrong. The second is when the agencies and institutions impose their plans without taking the person's complete situation into account. One agency may even require actions and behaviors that contradict what another agency is ordering.

Some people hate change. They almost never want to change, they don't want things to change, and they don't want others to change. We've already discussed some things about living in poverty that make it difficult to change. Richard Farson, author of *Management of the Absurd* (1997), noticed that the more resources a person has, the easier it is for him or her to change. The reverse is also true: The fewer resources a person has, the more difficult it is to change.

If you want to determine which process of change an agency has, look carefully at what the agency workers have you do while you're with them. Keep track of what happens step by step as you work through the program.

- What do you learn about?

- Do you work on personal issues?

- Do you make a plan to change your behavior?

- Do you meet in groups or individually with a counselor?

- What kinds of support do you get?

- How do the agency workers measure the changes you make?

- What happens when you do make changes?

- What does the agency do if you don't make changes?

Following are just a few of the approaches—or models—that many agencies use to try to help clients change. Some change models are very sophisticated and are based on research, while others are based on best practices and/or good intentions. To one degree or another, all of these models have value, but they also have some self-evident limitations.

1. *Education model:* If we give you accurate information—in other words, educate you—then you will change.

2. *Support model:* If we provide support (transportation, childcare, etc.) and remove other barriers that keep you from participating, then you will change.

3. *Access model:* If we design the program so that you can participate, then you should be able to change.

4. *Incentive model:* If we raise your awareness about the benefits of a change, then you'll become motivated to try new behaviors.

5. *Sanctions model:* If it's painful or you feel personally threatened by the problem, then you'll be willing to change.

6. *Skilled self-interest model:* If the benefits outweigh the costs and if you believe that you have the skills or abilities to change, then you'll change.

7. *Accountability model:* If you are held accountable for your choices and behaviors, then you will change.

8. *Redemption model:* If you believe in ____ and pray, ____ will provide.

III. College and the Process of Change

At college, there is certainly the expectation that you will change, even that the college experience will change you.

Use the same pattern of questions we asked about agencies to examine the school's process of change. There are two major parts of any college that you'll be dealing with—the academic side and the student services side. What do **in-**

structors have you do when you are with them in class or during one-on-one conferences? In what ways are your classes the same? In what ways are they different?

- What do you learn about?
- Do you work on personal issues?
- Do you make a plan to change your behavior?
- Do you meet in groups or work individually?
- What kinds of support do you get?

- How do the instructors measure the changes you make?
- What happens when you do make changes?
- What does the instructor do if you don't make changes?

Ask the same questions about the **student services departments.** What do the student services people have you do? Keep track of what happens step by step as you work through their programs.

"Now suddenly I was expected to sit in a room and communicate with a bunch of strangers in an entirely new way. Compared with South Street, school was artificial and pointless. I had received no preparation to help me adjust to it or do what was expected of me."

—Carl Upchurch, *Convicted in the Womb*

Journal Reflections

Describe what it was like the first time you came to campus. Why did you decide to go to college? Were you hoping to change something? If so, how will college help you make that change? If you aren't clear about this, where on campus can you find help? (If there are no changes you hope to make, how do you account for that?)

The feeling of

III. A. Activity: Deciding to Change

Time: 15 minutes

Materials: Chart paper, markers

Procedure: As a group, add more processes of change to the above list.

- Discuss which strategies have been used on you and which strategies you've used on others. Which strategies "worked" for you—and which ones didn't? Why?

- Expand on the reasons why living in poverty makes it harder to change.

- Think of a time when you made a change. This should be a time when it was a conscious choice, not something that someone else controlled, but something you did out of your own motivation. For example, it could be that you broke up with someone, took a class, or quit smoking.

1. What was different about the way you thought about the experience of change that made it work?

2. What might it mean to follow the example of someone else who has been successful in making a change?

3. What might it mean to learn by observing the mistakes made by someone else?

4. What might it mean to have the support of family or friends to make the change? How did they help (or hinder) you?

5. Did you repeat a pattern or strategy that you had used before?

6. What new ideas or information did you have that made it easier to change?

IV. *Investigations'* Process of Change

It's important that you understand the process of change that is a foundational piece of this workbook because (1) it provides a context for the information provided in the book and developed by your classroom discussions and (2) you will be asked to take steps and prepare a plan of action for yourself. At this point, we aren't asking for a commitment—just an open mind.

Watch as the facilitator draws a mental model for the Process of Change that is "at work" throughout the process in this workbook. You might want to reproduce it in your notes. The mental model will use the following elements and terms:

- The **"My Life Now"** mental model that you drew in Module 2.

- The term **"Concrete"** is used to describe a situation in which a person must spend a lot of time and energy solving immediate problems—for example, fixing broken-down cars, putting food on the table, finding a place to stay, finding money to keep the heat and lights on.

- The term **"Abstract"** means to think and to analyze, to detach from concrete problems and think about them objectively. It means new information, learning, and education.

- The phrase **"Tyranny of the Moment"** means being in the grip, control, or dominance of the *immediate concrete situation*. This happens to civilian populations in war, in natural disasters, and in persistent poverty. When individuals are in the tyranny of the moment they have trouble focusing on the future. They say things like "That's all I know" … "I can't see past next week" … "I'm too busy to worry about that."

- The phrase **"Reactive Problem Solving"** refers to the skills a person has to solve problems on the fly, pulling together the resources to solve concrete problems. If a person cannot focus on the future but is stuck in the moment, he or she ends up having to solve the same immediate problems again and again. These individuals are resourceful, creative, and resilient, but they aren't getting ahead.

- The phrase **"Proactive Planning Strategies"** refers to the skills a person has to think past the present moment, to develop plans that provide new solutions.

- The phrase **"Procedural Steps"** involves a detailed list of actions that can be taken to achieve a plan.

- This mental model is about freeing one's mind from the tyranny of the moment. When a person can think about the way he or she thinks, that is **"Metacognition."** Once an individual has that ability, he or she can live in unstable and chaotic situations and still be free to think of the future.

The process of change just described is an abstract concept: "This is how change might occur" … "This is a way to think about how you solve problems" (metacognition). In more specific terms, the process of change behind *Investigations* follows this thought process:

- Living in poverty makes it hard for people to change. Poverty is a trap that forces many people to live in the tyranny of the moment, even in chaos.

- Because of this, it's especially important that people explore macro-economic issues, to learn that poverty is about more than the choices that individuals make.

- It's also important to understand and describe how poverty impacts individuals. That means learning about the hidden rules of economic class, resources, family structure, and language issues is crucial to doing an objective analysis of the situation.

- When people in poverty analyze the bigger picture, as well as their own issues, they will know what to do—that is to say, they will be in a position to make informed decisions.

- Doing an assessment of both personal resources and community resources will allow individuals to make their own plans for economic stability.

- Understanding and using the hidden rules of economic class (poverty, middle class, wealth) to build resources will ease the transition to stability.

- Partnerships with the middle class and those in wealth will build vital social support for people in poverty.

- Working on individual plans is not enough because poverty is a systemic problem too. People in poverty must be at the planning tables to help reduce poverty, resolve community problems, and bring about systemic change.

Employees from Clarian Health Partners in Indianapolis met again several months after completing a course like this and developed the "post" mental model (below) of what meant the most to them from the Getting Ahead course. One item referred to the process of change: "No longer thinking Concrete—Abstract." This is taken to mean: *We are no longer stuck in concrete problem solving but can choose to think about the future, even if our lives are still not completely stable.*

IV. A. Discussion

1. Have you ever lived in the tyranny of the moment, even for a short time? What does the tyranny of the moment feel like?

2. How fast can the situation change from stability to instability, from a future orientation to a focus on "right now"?

3. In what ways does the tyranny of the moment interfere with your ability to think clearly? With your ability to learn? In what ways does it sharpen your ability?

4. How might this process of change help you focus on the future even when you may be faced with immediate problems?

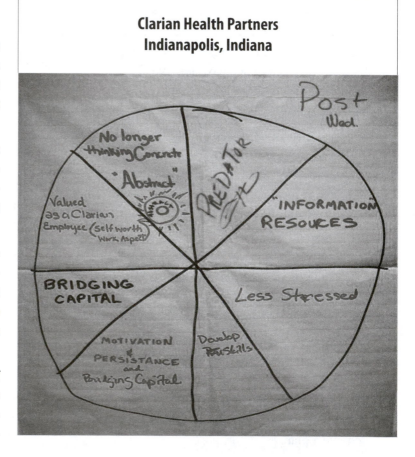

Journal Reflections

In your journal, write a letter to yourself describing why you are here in school and how this process of change might help you.

V. Time Management

Once free of the tyranny of the moment, you can learn to really manage your time. Everyone will agree that to be successful in college you need to spend time in class, study outside of class, and do other things associated with coursework. The challenge is how to fit all that into a life that seemed pretty busy even before classes started.

Stephen Covey's book *The 7 Habits of Highly Effective People* (1989) offers a way to think about how we spend time. Covey suggests that all activities can be put into four categories, depending on how important they are and how urgent they are. Look at the chart on the next page.

Time-Management Matrix

	Urgent	Not Urgent
Important	**Quadrant I—Emergencies and Crises** *Examples:* Death, illness, accidents Spending the entire weekend in the library finishing a term paper Completing add/drop procedures on the last allowable day	**Quadrant II—Takes Planning: You, Relationships, School, Work, Maintenance of Material Things** *Examples:* Filling in all test dates, assignment due dates, academic deadlines, breaks, holidays, and special days on a semester planner Keeping a file of all the financial information needed for FAFSA (Free Application for Federal Student Aid) and other grant/ scholarship applications
Not Important	**Quadrant III—Other People's Problems** *Examples:* Rushing to a last-minute meeting with your roommate about a project that has nothing to do with you Getting to the student center for free pizza before the party ends Giving your little brother your last $20 for a haircut and driving him to the barber shop	**Quadrant IV—Time Wasters** *Examples:* Surfing the Internet for travel deals when you don't have the time or money to travel Reviewing course material that you are already knowledgeable about Watching reruns on TV

Note. Adapted from *The 7 Habits of Highly Effective People* (p. 151), by S. R. Covey, 1989, New York, NY: Simon & Schuster. Copyright 1989 by Simon & Schuster.

Covey tells us that the best place to be most of the time is Quadrant II, where the activity is important, but not under the pressure of time. There is time to think and plan and create and organize. Quadrant I activity is important too, but it's under the stress of a deadline or consequence. If you don't take care of things that belong in Quadrant II, they end up being emergencies in Quadrant I, as in the case of two of the examples above. In Quadrant III, the activities are usually about someone else's priority that you got pulled into; it needs to be done now, but it's not going to help you particularly. Quadrant IV … well, those are activities that don't get us very far. We all do them: watching TV, doing stuff on the computer/Internet, sitting around, playing with the dog. The unimportant and non-urgent activities are time wasters unless you intentionally plan for "you" or "relationships," etc. If you plan for these activities because they're impor-tant to you, they go into Quadrant II. In that case, the activities have a place in your life: It's called relaxation, fun, entertainment, or down time. But if you're watching TV five hours a night every night, maybe it's going to put most coursework into Quadrant I—last-minute, high-pressure, and high-stakes.

V. A. Activity: Becoming More Effective

Time: 20 minutes

Materials: Time-Management Matrix Worksheet on next page and your completed Time Monitor sheets from previous week

Procedure:

1. Refer to open chart on next page.

2. Analyze your Time Monitor sheets:

    a. Where does each activity fall in relation to the four quadrants?

    b. Assign each activity to a quadrant. If the activity occurs often (for example, talking on the phone) just put "hash" marks (or "ditto" marks) after you write it once.

    c. Might some activities appear in more than one quadrant?

3. Finally, make a new plan for how you'll spend your time in the week to come. Set aside certain blocks of time to study certain courses. Look for blocks of time you spent in Quadrant III and IV. Can you redirect that time? Are there "natural" spaces in your schedule, such as between classes, when you can find a quiet spot to study?

Time-Management Matrix Worksheet

	Urgent	Not Urgent
Important	Quadrant I—Emergencies and Crises	Quadrant II—Takes Planning: You, Relationships, School, Work, Maintenance of Material Things
Not Important	Quadrant III—Other People's Problems	Quadrant IV—Time Wasters

Note. Adapted from *The 7 Habits of Highly Effective People* (p. 151), by S. R. Covey, 1989, New York, NY: Simon & Schuster. Copyright 1989 by Simon & Schuster.

V. B. Discussion/Journal

1. What did you discover that you didn't realize the first time you looked at your Time Monitor sheets?

2. Think of one or two persons you know who have achieved great things, changed their life, "succeeded." Think about how they spent time while they were making their changes. Where (in what quadrant) do you think they spent the most time?

3. Look at your chart and at the activities you wrote in the four quadrants. Put a check mark (✓) by the ones that, a year from now, will have made a positive difference in your life.

4. Look at your chart again and make a different mark beside any activity that involved an-

other person or persons. Write their name(s) outside the chart—and draw a line from their name to the activity they are involved in with you. What conclusions can you draw from this exercise?

5. Go to *http://www.literacynet.org/icans/ chapter06/time1.html* and take two quizzes on saving time and wasting time. What does your score tell you?

6. What are some specific steps you can take today to use your time more effectively? Make a list.

Readings

Bowling Alone: The Collapse and Revival of American Community by Robert D. Putnam. "Economic sociologist Mark Granovetter has pointed out that when seeking jobs—or political allies—the 'weak' ties that link me to distant acquaintances who move in different circles from mine are actually more valuable than the 'strong' ties that link me to relatives and intimate friends whose sociological niche is very like my own. *Bonding* social capital is, as Xavier de Souza Briggs puts it, good for 'getting by,' but *bridging* social capital is crucial for 'getting ahead' (p. 23)." From Chapter 19, "Economic Prosperity," found on pages 319–325.

Building Communities from the Inside Out: A Path Toward Finding and Mobilizing a Community's Assets by John Kretzmann and John McKnight. "The development strategy concentrates first of all upon the agenda building and problem-solving capacities of local residents, local associations, and local institutions. Again, this intense and self-conscious internal focus is not intended to minimize either the role external forces have played in helping to create the desperate conditions of lower income neighborhoods, nor the need to attract additional resources to these communities. Rather, this strong internal focus is intended simply to stress the primacy of local definition, investment, creativity, hope, and control. If a community development process is to be asset-based and internally focused, then it will be in very important ways 'relationship driven.' Thus, one of the central challenges is to constantly build and rebuild the relationships between and among local residents, local associations, and local institutions" (p. 9).

Management of the Absurd: Paradoxes in Leadership by Richard Farson. "People tend to be much smarter about their own situations than we give them credit for. After all, a full grasp of any problem is only in the hands of the people who have experienced it … In the early 1940s when Carl Rogers claimed that people with problems might be in the best position to know what to do about them, the professional world responded with disbelief and ridicule. How could the very people who were suffering from a problem know how to solve it? This idea was heresy to professionals trained to think that problems could be solved only by bringing to bear their own analytic ability and therapeutic skills" (p. 77).

Modello: A Story of Hope for the Inner City and Beyond by Jack Pransky. "It is a story of discovery, of profound yet simple truths, of how a 'new' understanding of the human mind changed lives in one of the most violent and dangerous low-income, inner-city housing projects in South Florida. What is this understanding? Put simply, it is that everyone has an innate capacity for health and well-being, for wisdom and common sense, and this health, when brought to light, when truly realized, once unleashed, can create the 'miracle' of change" (p. 13).

Motivational Interviewing: Preparing People for Change (second edition) by William R. Miller and Stephen Rollnick. "Intrinsic motivation for change arises in an accepting, empowering atmosphere that makes it safe for the person to explore the possibly painful present in relation to what is wanted and valued. People often get stuck, not because they fail to appreciate the downside of their situation, but because they feel at least two ways about it. The way out of that forest has to do with exploring and following what the person is experiencing and what, from his or her perspective, truly matters" (p. 12).

Narrative Therapy: The Social Construction of Preferred Realities by Jill Freedman and Gene Combs. "We can also ask how the emerging new story influences a person's ideas about the future. As people free more and more of their pasts from the grip of problem-dominated stories, they are able to envision, expect, and plan toward less problematic futures" (p. 101). From Chapter 4, "Story Development," found on pages 77–112.

Pedagogy of the Oppressed by Paulo Freire. From the foreword by Richard Shaull: "He came to realize that their ignorance and lethargy were the direct product of the whole situation of economic, social, and political domination—and of the paternalism—of which they were victims. Rather than being encouraged and equipped to know and respond to the concrete realities of their world, they were kept 'submerged' in a situation in which such critical awareness and response were practically impossible … Coupled with this is Freire's conviction (now supported by a wide background of experience) that every human being, no matter how 'ignorant' or submerged in the 'culture of silence' he or she may be, is capable of looking critically at the world in a dialogical encounter with others. Provided with the proper tools for such encounter, the individual can gradually perceive personal and social reality as well as the contradictions in it, become conscious of his or her own perception of that reality, and deal critically with it" (pp. 12–14).

Synchronicity: The Inner Path of Leadership by Joseph Jaworski. "Bohm had shared with me in London an explicit mental model of the way he believed the world works and the way he believed human beings learn and think. To Bohm it was clear that humans have an innate capacity for collective intelligence. They can learn and think together, and this collaborative thought can lead to coordinated action. We are all connected and operate within living fields of thought and perception. The world is not fixed but is in constant flux; accordingly, the future is not fixed, and so can be shaped. Humans possess significant tacit knowledge—we know more than we can say. The question to be resolved: How to remove the blocks and tap into that knowledge in order to create the kind of future we all want?" (p. 109).

MODULE 4
The Rich/Poor Gap and How It Works

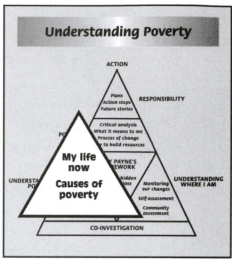

Understanding Poverty

ACTION

Plans
Action steps
Future stories

RESPONSIBILITY

Critical analysis
What it means to me
Process of change
to build resources

My life now
Causes of poverty

PAYNE'S FRAMEWORK

hidden class

UNDERSTANDING WHERE I AM

Monitoring our changes
Self-assessment
Community assessment

CO-INVESTIGATION

Learning Objectives

WHAT'S COVERED

You will:

Understand the range of causes of poverty—from personal to systemic

Establish that there is a need for strategies to reduce poverty that come from all four areas of research

Investigate the rich/poor gap and learn how it works

Establish a strategy to protect yourself from predators—defined as people and businesses that profit by taking advantage of people in poverty and other low-wage workers

Make mental models for what life is like for people in middle class and wealth

Introduce the concept of sustainability

Learn how to think about what you want to do, and "plan backwards" to reach the goal

WHY IT'S IMPORTANT

It's important to know how the economic system works so we can consider what hurts *and* helps people at the bottom of the economic ladder.

It's important to know that poverty is not just about the choices of the poor. Community and system issues also must be addressed.

We need to see the abstract, bigger picture before we can make good decisions. There's an important connection between understanding abstract information and making informed decisions.

Concrete problems need concrete solutions informed by abstract information. Backwards planning is a concrete method for making such plans.

HOW IT'S CONNECTED TO YOU

We established information about the reality of living in poverty when we made the Mental Model of Poverty. Now we are investigating additional information about income and wealth.

Having mental models about poverty, middle class, and wealth helps you understand other people's motivation and behavior—and how they think and reason.

We need to have a plan for ourselves and our community's political/economic systems if we're going to build economic stability and sustainability.

In college, you have to manage many new demands on your time. Concrete plans will help you to get work done, pass courses, and graduate.

Learning Process

- You will review the four categories of poverty research.

- You'll make a short-term plan to protect yourself from predators.

- You'll do some activities that demonstrate the "rich/poor gap."

- You'll use case studies to investigate and label aspects of life in middle class and wealth, then use that information to create two new mental models.

- You'll review information about the concept of sustainability.

- You'll make a concrete plan to accomplish a specific future goal.

Lexicon for Module 4

Adjusted gross income
Assets
Capital gains taxes
Community Sustainability Grid
Deindustrialization
Downward pressure on wages
Economic disparity
Espoused theory
Estate taxes
Exploitation
Free-market economies
Globalization
Household wealth
Human and social capital
Human capacity development
Income and wealth disparity
Individual income tax
Institutional discrimination
Liabilities
Macro economics

Mental Model of Middle Class
Mental Model of Wealth
Middle-class flight
Negative wealth
Organisation for Economic
  Cooperation and
  Development (OECD)
Planning backwards
Political/economic structures
Predator
Predatory lending
Research Continuum
Return on political investments
  (ROPI)
Revolving door
Situational poverty
SMART plans
Sustainable communities
Tacit knowledge
Wealth-creating mechanisms

I. Research on Poverty

David Shipler, author of *The Working Poor* (2004), says that in the United States we are confused about the causes of poverty—so we're also confused about what to do about it. Much research has been done on poverty in the U.S. The author of *Poverty Knowledge* (2001), Alice O'Connor, says there's a "research industry" (p. 6) just on poverty. That industry—made up of universities, governmental organizations, foundations, institutes, and think tanks—studies poverty from every conceivable angle. Research on poverty can be organized into four areas, giving us a way to label and analyze the information. The Research Continuum below shows the four major clusters of poverty research, as well as sample topics.

Causes of Poverty—Research Continuum

INDIVIDUAL BEHAVIORS AND CIRCUMSTANCES	COMMUNITY CONDITIONS	EXPLOITATION	POLITICAL/ ECONOMIC STRUCTURES
Definition: Research on the choices, behaviors, and circumstances of people in poverty	Definition: Research on the resources and human and social capital in the city or county	Definition: Research on the impact of exploitation on individuals and the community	Definition: Research on political, economic, and social policies and systems at the organizational, city/county, state, national, and international levels
Racism Discrimination by age, gender, disability, race, sexual identity Bad loans Credit card debt Lack of savings Skill sets Lack of education Alcoholism Disabilities Job loss Language experience Child-rearing strategies Bankruptcy due to health problems Street crime	Racism Discrimination by age, gender, disability, race, sexual identity Layoffs Middle-class flight Plant closings Underfunded schools Inadequate public transportation Weak safety net Criminalizing poverty Employer insurance premiums rising in order to drop companies with records of poor health Charity that leads to dependency	Racism Discrimination by age, gender, disability, race, sexual identity Payday loans Lease/purchase outlets Pawn shops Subprime mortgages Sweatshops Human trafficking Drug trade Wages and benefits theft Some landlords Day labor	Racism Discrimination by age, gender, disability, race, sexual identity Globalization Deindustrialization Increased productivity Creativity and innovation Return on political investments (ROPI) Corporate lobbyists Bursting economic "bubbles" Property rights Access to markets Free-trade agreements Recessions Lack of wealth-creating mechanisms

(continued on next page)

(continued from previous page)

INDIVIDUAL BEHAVIORS AND CIRCUMSTANCES	COMMUNITY CONDITIONS	EXPLOITATION	POLITICAL/ ECONOMIC STRUCTURES
White-collar crime Dependency	High rates of illness leading to high absenteeism and low productivity Brain drain City and regional planning Wealth-creating mechanisms Mix of employment/ wage opportunities, career pathways Access to high-quality education		Downward pressure on wages Stagnant wages Minimum wage, living wage, self-sufficient wage

In the U.S. we are most familiar with two of these four research areas: individual behaviors and political/economic structures. That's because the major political parties and the media focus most on these two causes. Conservatives tend to favor research about individual behavior; progressives tend to focus on systemic issues. Conservatives say, in effect, "If you want to get out of poverty, get motivated, get a job, keep the job, be punctual and sober, have a good work ethic, and pull yourself out of poverty through your own initiative. Do not blame the system." Progressives say, in effect, "Don't blame the individual. There are lots of people who are working more than one job, who are playing by the rules, and who are still in poverty. If you want to get out of poverty, change the system that moves well-paying manufacturing jobs overseas, puts downward pressure on wages, and provides few wealth-creating mechanisms for the shrinking middle class." It's fairly common for special-interest groups and in-

dividuals to have a bias or a preference for one particular way of looking at poverty.

Governmental policy and anti-poverty programs, therefore, do not come directly from pure research; they are filtered by how policymakers think about the research, along with their political and philosophical biases. Federal and state policies concerning workforce development and social services are felt at the local community level. National and state organizations—such as churches, synagogues, mosques, the United Way, Chambers of Commerce, and charitable foundations—also set policies and design programs that address poverty. And, of course, local agencies and organizations do the same.

Unfortunately, the talk about poverty and what to do about it has gone from discourse to diatribe, from discussing to ranting. This means neither side is listening to the other, which isn't helpful at the community level where the problems of poverty have to be solved. The "it's either this or that" approach will not help communities solve problems. Our communities need ways to have realistic discussions so they can develop a "both/and" approach. Poverty is caused both by the choices and circumstances of the individual *and* by political/economic structures and everything in between. There's good information from all four clusters of research; we need strategies to cover all four areas. The Research Continuum allows us to see that poverty isn't an "either/or" proposition as it's being presented now in the media—and often in the halls of government.

For a community to be healthy it's vitally important for people from all economic classes to have a shared understanding about economic class—and ways to analyze and use research, then build strategies that will help people get out of poverty. Many communities across the U.S. and Canada are using this information and these ideas to build a more sustainable future.

A Closer Look at the Research Continuum

Causes of poverty that cross all four clusters of factors: Before we look at individual clusters of research, we need to know that some issues don't fit into a single category. Racism and discrimination, for example, contribute in complex ways to the causation of poverty. You don't get to choose your race. However, discrimination that keeps a person from getting a job or building assets (such as buying a house) is experienced at the *individual* level. In *communities,* "redlining" makes buying a house or insurance difficult or even impossible for certain groups of people. Racial *exploitation* may take the form of steering a person of color toward subprime loans even

when the individual's credit rating is fine. After World War II, the GI Bill was 10 times less likely to benefit people of color than whites. This affected many people; it is considered a *systemic* political/economic cause of poverty. There are other causes of poverty as well that span more than one cluster.

Individual behaviors and circumstances: People make choices or experience circumstances that contribute to their poverty. There is a correlation between choices like dropping out of school, teen pregnancy, and single-parent families and higher rates of poverty. There is also a correlation between circumstances, like having a disability or disease and poverty. People make choices that contribute to their prosperity. This is sometimes referred to as *human capacity development.*

Most of the work in *Investigations* is focused on you, the individual: your situation, your thinking, your investigations, your self-assessment, and your plans—in large part because that's what is under your control in the short term. Therefore, this particular module will not focus on you but rather provide background on the other three areas of research.

Community conditions: In the literature this is often described as *human and social capital in the community.* In a slightly broader sense this category is about whether the community is one that contributes to the development of prosperity or one that has trouble helping its citizens build resources. It's somewhat easier to get out of poverty in a community that has employers offering well-paying jobs, schools that deliver a good education, facilities that provide high-quality healthcare, and banks that offer fair credit. Conversely, it's harder to get out of poverty in a city that has lost most of its manufacturing jobs or in a rural community that is losing family farms.

In *Investigations* we work on two themes: (1) that of you the individual and (2) that of the community in which you live, including your role in that community. In this class we focus on what poverty is like in the community and the places we go to build resources. We will do an assessment of the community just as we will do one for ourselves.

Exploitation: This refers to people in poverty being taken advantage of *because* they are in poverty. Regardless of the cause, once a person is caught in the debt cycle it's very hard to get out. There seem to be endless ways to exploit people who have little money or power and are trapped in the tyranny of the moment. A Getting Ahead group in Indianapolis explained that some predators operate like this: Your family needs food. The meat man comes to the door with pre-seasoned, vacuum-packed chicken, pork, and beef. You would love to buy it but your food stamp card is empty. He says, "No problem. Keep the meat, cook it up right now. I understand. I'll just come back next week and swipe your card." He has offered a concrete solution to a concrete problem, right now. He does it with respect, or at least a show of respect. He's banking on the fact that your family is in the tyranny of the moment. Who's going to read the fine print on the meat man's contract? Who's got the interest or energy to work out the math to figure out that chicken is going to cost you $8 a pound? The meat man knows you don't have the time or energy, he exploits this, he preys on this, and he is a predator. That's the basic business plan for exploitation: an immediate concrete problem; an

immediate, concrete, and overpriced solution; a phony show of respect; complicated fine print; and the tyranny of the moment. Many payday lenders, bail bondsmen, and debt consolidators also use some of these techniques. Following this section, there's a quick exercise about predators.

Political/economic structures: Systemic issues are the most complex causes of poverty. The research in this cluster is focused on macro-economic and systemic issues. To understand the importance of this area of research, imagine what it must be like to be at the bottom of the economic ladder in one of the poorest countries in the world. In Zimbabwe, for example, the economic situation in 2008 was such that 80% of the population was unemployed. Corruption was so bad that the *government* was confiscating money designated for humanitarian projects. Almost 2 million people were living with HIV and receiving no treatment because the healthcare system had collapsed. Just since 1990 the life expectancy declined from 60 years to 37 years for males and 34 years for females. These causes of poverty are so deeply ingrained in the system that getting out of poverty through individual initiative and effort would be almost impossible.

In North America, of course, the political/economic conditions are much more stable. The United States by most measures is one of the 10 wealthiest nations, but systemic issues still matter. For example, since 1979 inequality in income and wealth has grown steadily. The divide between the richest 10% and the poorest 10% is so great that the U.S. ranks third in disparity, according to the Organisation for Economic Cooperation and Development, a group of 30 nations that adhere to democratic principles and free-market economies. The following chart shows

OECD Rankings—How the U.S. Standard of Living Compares with Canada and Slovakia

Indicator	Canada	Slovakia	United States
Population Living Below 50% of Median Income, 2000–04	10	24	2
Income Ratio of Richest 10% to Poorest 10%, 1994–2004	21	24	3
Child Poverty Rate, % in 2000	10	NA	2
Unemployment Rate (% of those 15 years of age and older), 2005	21	2	18
Long-Term Unemployment (% of total employment), 2005	25	1	24

Note. Adapted from *The Measure of America: American Human Development Report, 2008–2009* (p. 196), by S. Burd-Sharps, K. Lewis, & E. B. Martins, 2008, New York, NY: Columbia University Press. Copyright 2008 by Columbia University Press.

that the U.S. has the second highest rate of poverty and child poverty among the 30 OECD nations. The U.S. ranks 18th in unemployment for people 15 years of age and older and 24th for those in long-term unemployment.

This means that we North Americans experience life and society very differently from one another, according to our economic class. This in turn results in the development of class distinctions—or what we call the *hidden rules* of class that will be examined later in *Investigations*. People in the U.S. who are trying to get out of poverty have to do so at a time when the middle class is shrinking, the working class is sliding into situational poverty, and the downward pressure on wages is making it more and more difficult to establish solid financial footing. These realities, most caused by political/economic structures and policies that are more abstract than the research on individual choices and behavior, have a very concrete impact on individuals—and must be addressed.

Examining some of the political, economic, and social policies that created the middle class in the United States is an excellent way to illustrate the power of systemic policy as it applies to prosperity and a high quality life. In his article "Are We Still a Middle-Class Nation?" Michael Lind (2004) lists seven factors in describing how the middle class in the U.S. was created.

1. The U.S. was able to create the middle-class farmer. The economic stability farmers enjoyed, the wealth they created and passed on to their children, and their prosperity did not come from their labor alone. It also came from government policies and sponsorship, such as the 1862 Homestead Act, which gave farmers 60 acres from which to make a start. Slave labor created wealth for many of the owners; in 1850 the income of the average slave owner in South Carolina was 10 times that of the average income of other whites in the state. In 1848 Mexico lost half its territory to the United States, and in 1851 the

Sioux tribe had to give up the entire state of Iowa to the U.S. All these policies and governmental actions created wealth for the agricultural middle class.

2. The industrial middle class did not earn its stability, prosperity, and wealth through its paycheck alone. Government policies protected workers by cutting off "Oriental" immigration and, after World War I, immigration from Europe. Additionally, children were removed from the workplace by child-labor laws, and the "family wage" increased income for married men. Henry Ford improved wages because he wanted employees to be able to own the cars they made. Later, unionization helped introduce the 40-hour work week, higher wages, and job security. With government support, employers provided employer-based health insurance.

3. Building on these gains, the white-collar middle class benefited from tax codes that encouraged employers to provide employer-based health insurance and employer-based pensions. After World War II, the GI Bill provided education, student loans, and home mortgages. Government policies also created Social Security and Medicare—and paid for the roads, highways, and infrastructure that supported manufacturing, home ownership, and the growth of the suburbs.

4. The wealth that was created by these policies and that was passed down to subsequent generations did not extend to all. In *The Color of Wealth,* published by United for a Fair Economy in 2006, the authors explain the wealth divide in the United States. The farming middle-class opportunities just described were reserved almost exclusively for whites—and often at the direct expense of

people of color. During the 1850s the land made available to whites was taken from Native Americans in a series of battles, appropriations, and treaties. And while whites accumulated wealth from slave labor, Mexicans lost their land to the U.S. Only whites were eligible for California land claims during the Gold Rush; the "Foreign Miner's Tax" of 1850 stopped Mexicans from participating in the Gold Rush. In 1852 this policy was extended to exclude the Chinese as well.

5. Industrial and white-collar, middle-class opportunities also were largely limited to white workers. Black colleges couldn't accommodate all the returning black veterans wanting to use the GI Bill, which left most of the African American veterans with no place to go for higher education, as most colleges were still segregated. From 1930 to 1960 only 1% of all mortgages were issued to African Americans, who comprised about 10% of the U.S. population during that era. Japanese Americans who lost property while interned received just 10 cents on the reparation dollar. In Puerto Rico (a territory of the U.S.) most locally owned businesses were crowded out by U.S. companies when Operation Bootstrap gave the companies tax incentives in 1947. During World War II, Mexicans were brought to the U.S. to fill labor shortages, then deported in Operation Wetback. In the 1950s Congress terminated recognition of certain Native American tribes, thus throwing the prosperous Menominee and Klamath tribes, among others, into poverty.

6. The legacies of wealth and poverty still persist—and, despite the civil rights laws of the 1960s, discrimination still exists in the United States. Racism may not seem overt, and

institutional racism has abated somewhat, but there's still a huge benefit to being white and a cost to being of color. Those who think we don't need to talk about color, race, and diversity are expressing a color-blindness not supported by the facts. For example, the *racial wealth gap* continues to grow. According to the U.S. Federal Reserve Bank, the median net worth (assets minus debts) of families of color dropped 4.5% to $17,000 from 1998 to 2001. During the same period the median net worth of white families grew 17% to $120,900.

7. Finally, it should be noted that the middle class is shrinking for the first time in U.S. history. The very policies and structures that made the middle class are disappearing, including employer-based healthcare, employer-based pensions, the 40-hour work week, wages, student loans, mortgage assistance, and Social Security.

We undertook this discussion about the middle class to emphasize the importance that policy has on our lives. Laws passed by Congress and the states, along with decisions by judges, have an impact on the economy. Policies can work for people at the bottom of the ladder, for low-wage workers, and for the middle class—and they can work against them. The free market and the economy do not operate in a vacuum. They are molded by policy, which is important to the creation of sustainable communities.

"The nearly uniform advantages received by the children of the college-educated professionals suggest the evolution of an increasingly distinct subculture in American society, one in which adults routinely transmit to their offspring the symbolic thinking and confident problem solving that mark the adults' economic activities and that are so difficult for outsiders to acquire in mid-life. A trend toward separation into subcultures jeopardizes the upward mobility that has given this nation greatness and presages the tragedy of downward mobility that produces increasing numbers of working poor. If this trend is to be reversed, a beginning must be made now. The issue is no longer one of eradicating poverty or of putting welfare recipients to work but of reversing a trend, the downward drift of the working class."

—Betty Hart and Todd R. Risley, *Meaningful Differences in the Everyday Experience of Young American Children*

I. A. Activity: Identifying and Detaching from Predators

Time: 10 minutes

Materials: Worksheet, mental model of "My Life Now" from Module 2

Procedure:

1. As a group, list on the subsequent worksheet all the predators you can think of in your community.

2. Privately, not as a group exercise, mark an "X" in the middle column for every predator with whom you have some association.

3. Again as a group, brainstorm how to get out from under the control of a predator. What might a person have to do?

4. Privately, write down a quick plan for what *you* might do about each predator in your life.

5. Finally, if you have some connection with one or more predators, go back to your "My Life Now" mental model and add each predator.

PREDATORS		
List the predators in your community	Are you involved with this predator? If so, how?	How can someone get out from under a predator's control? How long might it take?

I. B. Discussion

1. What do (or did) you need that caused you to become associated with a predator?
2. What alternatives to using the "services" of the predator existed in the community at that time?
3. Was there ever a time when you didn't have to relate to predators? When was that? What were your circumstances at that time?
4. What would it be like for you if you didn't need to have any involvement with predators?

II. The Rich/Poor Gap: Economic Disparity

In the United States the past 30–40 years the rich (top 10%) have been getting richer, while the bottom 90% have been getting poorer. This is the fourth time in U.S. history that the gap has widened in a statistically significant way. The first was in the Gilded Age, the 1870s; the second was during the Roaring Twenties; the third was the Nifty Fifties; and the most recent growing divide was fueled by the "bull markets" of the 1980s, '90s, and the "bursting bubbles" of the first decade of the 21st century.

The following material—up to and including the chart titled "Family Median Net Worth by Race, 2004"—is provided by United for a Fair Economy (*The Growing Divide,* 2009).

A Note on Statistics and Sources

Whenever possible, we use government sources, such as the U.S. Census Bureau (e.g., family income), the Federal Reserve Bank (e.g., household wealth), the Bureau of Labor Statistics (e.g., unionization rates), etc. Even with their well-documented flaws, government statistics are generally the most comprehensive, frequently updated, and widely cited (*The Growing Divide,* 2009, p. 4).

II. A. Activity: Real Family Income Growth by Quintile and for Top 5%, 1946–79 and 1979–2006

Time: 15 minutes

Materials: Five income placards

Procedure:

1. Review the tables on the following three pages.

2. The group investigates the information presented by the facilitator and five volunteers.

Real Family Income Growth by Quintile & for Top 5%, 1979 - 2006

We Grew Apart

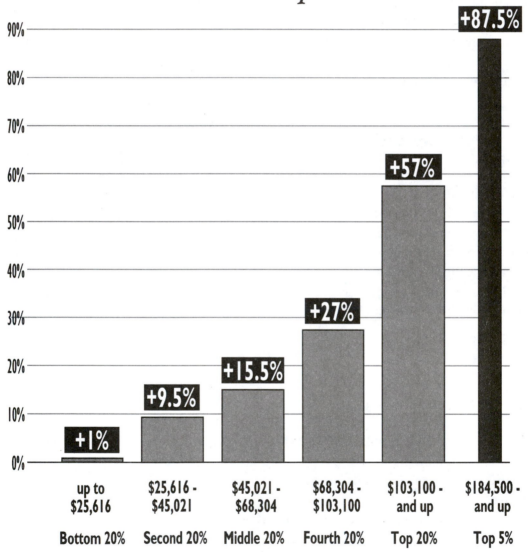

	up to $25,616	$25,616 - $45,021	$45,021 - $68,304	$68,304 - $103,100	$103,100 - and up	$184,500 - and up
	Bottom 20%	Second 20%	Middle 20%	Fourth 20%	Top 20%	Top 5%
Growth	+1%	+9.5%	+15.5%	+27%	+57%	+87.5%

Note. From *The Growing Divide: Inequality and the Roots of Economic Insecurity,* 2009, Boston, MA: United for a Fair Economy. Copyright 2009 by United for a Fair Economy.

Real Family Income Growth by Quintile & for Top 5%, 1947 - 1979

We All Grew

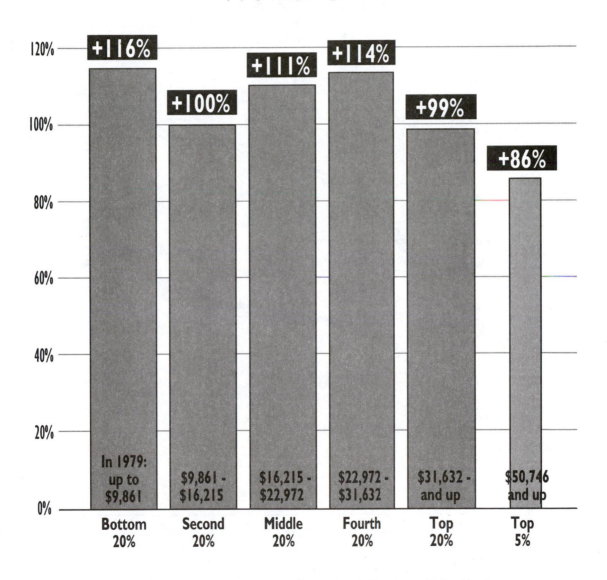

	Bottom 20%	Second 20%	Middle 20%	Fourth 20%	Top 20%	Top 5%
Growth	+116%	+100%	+111%	+114%	+99%	+86%
In 1979	up to $9,861	$9,861 - $16,215	$16,215 - $22,972	$22,972 - $31,632	$31,632 and up	$50,746 and up

Note. From *The Growing Divide: Inequality and the Roots of Economic Insecurity,* 2009, Boston, MA: United for a Fair Economy. Copyright 2009 by United for a Fair Economy.

Median Family Income by Race, 1947-2006

Racial Income Inequality Persists

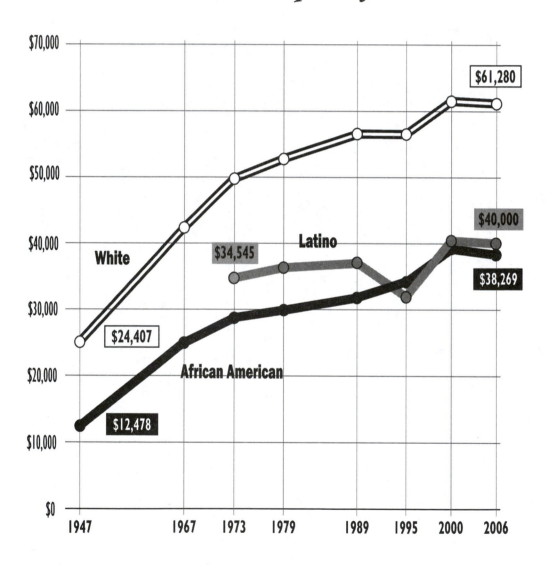

Note. From *The Growing Divide: Inequality and the Roots of Economic Insecurity*, 2009, Boston, MA: United for a Fair Economy. Copyright 2009 by United for a Fair Economy.

 **II. B. Discussion**

What conclusions do you draw about family incomes? What questions do you have?

II. C. Activity: CEO Pay as a Multiple of Average Worker Pay, 1960–2007

Time: 15 minutes
Materials: Six placards
Procedure:

1. Review the table.

2. Investigate the information presented by the facilitator and six volunteers.

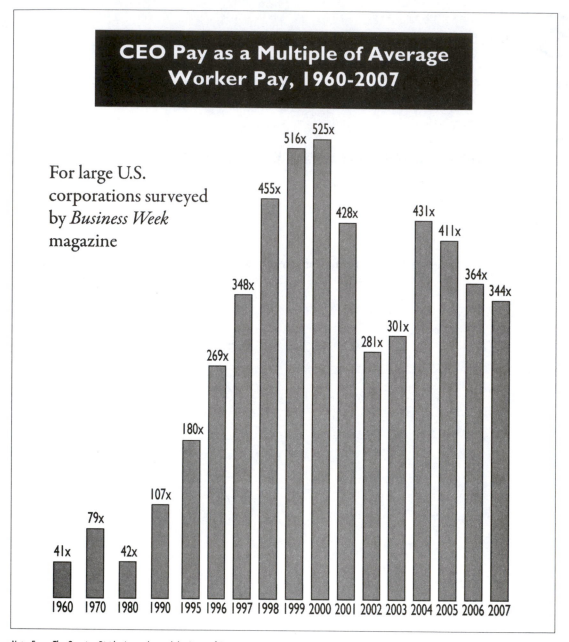

CEO Pay as a Multiple of Average Worker Pay, 1960-2007

For large U.S. corporations surveyed by *Business Week* magazine

- 1960: 41x
- 1970: 79x
- 1980: 42x
- 1990: 107x
- 1995: 180x
- 1996: 269x
- 1997: 348x
- 1998: 455x
- 1999: 516x
- 2000: 525x
- 2001: 428x
- 2002: 281x
- 2003: 301x
- 2004: 431x
- 2005: 411x
- 2006: 364x
- 2007: 344x

Note. From *The Growing Divide: Inequality and the Roots of Economic Insecurity,* 2009, Boston, MA: United for a Fair Economy. Copyright 2009 by United for a Fair Economy.

 II. D. Discussion

What strikes you about the income comparison between CEO pay and average worker pay?

II. E. Activity: Ownership of Household Wealth in 2007—'The Ten Chairs: the Difference Between Wealth and Income'

Time: 10 minutes

Materials: 10 chairs

Procedure:

1. Review the charts.

2. Investigate the information presented by the facilitator and 10 volunteers.

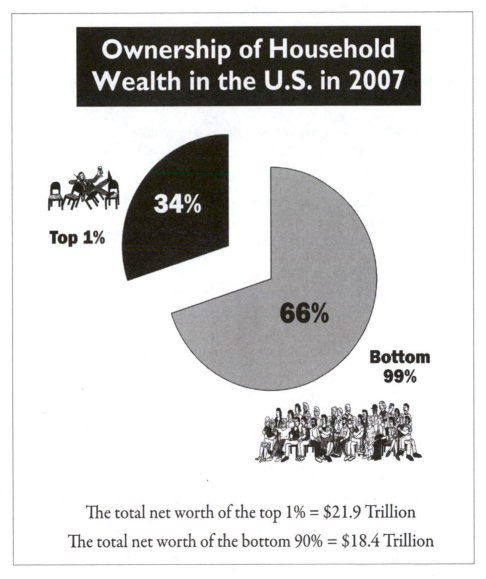

Ownership of Household Wealth in the U.S. in 2007

Top 1% — 34%

Bottom 99% — 66%

The total net worth of the top 1% = $21.9 Trillion

The total net worth of the bottom 90% = $18.4 Trillion

Note. From *The Growing Divide: Inequality and the Roots of Economic Insecurity,* 2009, Boston, MA: United for a Fair Economy. Copyright 2009 by United for a Fair Economy.

What Is Wealth?

Question: How is wealth different from income? What is wealth?
Answer: Wealth is private assets minus liabilities (debt). Simply put, wealth is what you own minus what you owe. Income is your paycheck or government benefit check or dividend check—or your profit from selling an investment. Wealth is what you have in the bank and the property you own.

Question: Is it possible to have negative wealth?
Answer: Yes. Seventeen percent of the U.S. population in 2004 had no assets, or they had negative assets: They owed more than they owned.

Question: What are examples of assets that lower income people might have?
Answer: Cash (checking and savings accounts), furniture, a car.

Question: What are examples of assets owned by middle-income people?
Answer: Cash (checking and savings accounts), equity in a house, a small business, some stocks, and/or a retirement fund.

Question: What are examples of assets owned by the top 1%?
Answer: Real estate, large stock and bond holdings, businesses, and paintings and other collectibles.

II. F. Discussion

1. Notice the circumstances you are in and your own feelings about this. How are you feeling at the top? How about in the bottom 90%?

2. Who in North American society gets pushed off the chairs? How does that work?

3. What conclusions do you draw about the focus of public policy discussions—looking up the chairs (at the top 1%) or looking down the chairs at the disadvantaged?

4. What questions do you have?

5. Did you find yourself directing your anger at the person representing the top 1%? Why or why not?

III. The Intersection of Race and Economic Class

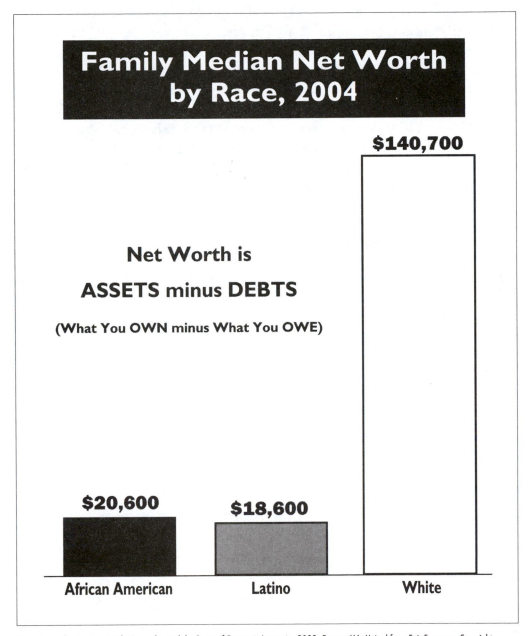

Family Median Net Worth by Race, 2004

$140,700 — White

Net Worth is

ASSETS minus DEBTS

(What You OWN minus What You OWE)

$20,600 — African American

$18,600 — Latino

Note. From *The Growing Divide: Inequality and the Roots of Economic Insecurity*, 2009, Boston, MA: United for a Fair Economy. Copyright 2009 by United for a Fair Economy.

The chart on the preceding page examines the amount of net worth (assets minus liabilities: "what you own minus what you owe") by race. This includes home ownership, savings, investments, and all other forms of assets. The chart looks at median net worth—or the experience of households in the middle. If we lined up all the white families by net worth, the family in the middle would have $140,700 in net worth, if vehicles are included. The African American family in the middle would have $20,600. The Latino family in the middle would have $18,600.

White households have nearly seven times as much wealth as African American households and nearly eight times as much as Latino households.

There were also vast differences along racial lines when examining households with zero or negative net worth. For example, in 2004 thirteen percent of white households had zero or negative wealth compared with 29.4% of African American households (*The Growing Divide,* 2009).

Journal Reflections

Write or draw an example of ways that economic/political policies or specific institutions discriminate against people in poverty.

"A broad spectrum of African-Americans have used education ... Malcolm X, Martin Luther King, Jr., Maya Angelou, Carter G. Woodson, W. E. B. DuBois, Cornel West, and many others. All these men and women hold the road map for change. They tell us in every way that education is essential to any movement toward freedom. Even in our most desperate hours—during slavery—we understood one fundamental truth: that we must become educated to make progress in this culture."

—Carl Upchurch, *Convicted in the Womb*

IV. Who Pays the Most Taxes? What Does It Mean to the Community?

Most people feel that taxes are pretty complicated and are happy if they can just get their own income taxes filed correctly each year. But there is key information about taxes that applies to our investigation into the causes of poverty and the development of sustainable communities.

Corporations vs. Individuals: The share of federal revenue being paid by corporate income tax has been declining since the 1950s. In 1962 it was 21% of the federal revenue; in 2007 it was 14%. This is the result of lower rates and loopholes. The share of federal revenue paid by individuals (including income tax, Social Security, and Medicare taxes) rose from 72% to 83%. (The percentages do not add up to 100% because excise taxes are not included.) This means that much of the tax burden is being shifted to the middle class.

Note. Adapted from *The Growing Divide: Inequality and the Roots of Economic Insecurity*, 2009, Boston, MA: United for a Fair Economy. Copyright 2009 by United for a Fair Economy.

Estate and Capital Gains Tax on Individuals: Estate taxes, sometimes called inheritance tax or death tax, are paid on assets that pass on to the next generation upon a person's death. The laws are changing: In 2009 the federal rate was 45%; the amount exempted was $3.5 million. In 2010 there is no estate tax, but in 2011 the rate will be 55%, and the exempted amount could be anywhere between $1 million and $7 million.

Note. Adapted from *"Taxes Are More Certain Than Death?"* by E. Istook, 2009. Copyright 2009 by E. Istook.

Capital gains taxes are paid on profit realized from the sale of stocks, bonds, precious metals, and property. In the U.S. the wealthiest 10% own 75% of stocks and mutual funds. Since 1980 estate taxes decreased by 46%, capital gains taxes by 31%. Meanwhile, payroll tax on work has increased 25%. Again, the tax burden is being shifted to the individual.

Note. Adapted from *The Growing Divide: Inequality and the Roots of Economic Insecurity*, 2009, Boston, MA: United for a Fair Economy. Copyright 2009 by United for a Fair Economy.

Individual Income Tax on Adjusted Gross Income: The U.S. Internal Revenue Service figures show that the top 10% of individuals paid 71.22% of all federal income taxes in 2007. The bottom 50% paid 2.89% of taxes.

Note. Adapted from "Summary of Latest Federal Individual Income Tax Data," by G. Prante, 2009. Copyright 2009 by Tax Foundation.

This information on taxes, as another indication of how great income disparity is in the U.S., is important to the long-term stability of communities. When a community loses high-paying jobs because of business closings or relocations, or the people with those jobs move to better school districts and safer communities, their contributions to the community are lost.

Middle-class flight to the suburbs continues to strip the budgets of cities that are losing population. Without a sustainable tax base, cities cannot remain viable. Services are cut, infrastructure isn't maintained, people are laid off, and wages are reduced. These factors contribute to the downward trend experienced by many U.S. cities today.

The inability of a community or school system to raise taxes is a sign of a weakening community. Schools that give up extracurricular activities (such as band, art classes, and sports) or turn to the "pay to play" strategy are depriving children of resources that build their bodies and minds—and create social connections that can last a lifetime. The community itself suffers when families leave in order to put their children in schools that can offer extracurricular activities. Those who are least able to move are people in poverty and low-wage workers.

IV. A. Discussion

1. What has happened to the tax base in your community?

2. How much difference is there in extracurricular activities and educational achievement among the school districts within an hour drive of your home?

3. What businesses employ the most workers in your community? Where do the workers in those businesses live?

4. Discuss local current events in terms of taxes collected in the community. Are school levies being passed? How are city/county governments doing in respect to service provision? What's being cut and what's being saved?

V. Wealth and Access to Power— Disparity in Wealth as a Cause of Poverty

The disparity in wealth shapes the way people experience life. People in wealth experience life in the U.S. very differently from those in middle class and poverty.

With extreme wealth comes greater access to power. That power can be used to support the structures that make accumulating more wealth and power possible. Access to political leaders, having a voice in planning, being heard on issues that matter to you are advantages that wealthy people and those who run corporations benefit from. This occurs at the international, national, state, and local levels and is supported to varying degrees through the following types of political structures:

Campaign contributions: Individuals may support and help elect candidates who support their interests. Corporations influence politicians by using lobbyists, think tanks, campaign contributions, and the media to advertise their messages.

Return on political investments (ROPI): In February 2006 *Fortune* magazine reported that Lockheed Martin spent $55 million lobbying Congress since 1999, during which time it won roughly $90 billion in defense contracts for a ROPI of 163,536%. This was not regarded as particularly high compared with other sectors (Miller, 2006, p. 36).

Meanwhile, average citizens investing in the stock market consider investment returns of 12% to be extremely good by any standard. By comparison, certificates of deposit (CDs) at local banks in late 2009 would yield 1% for a 21-month deposit, 1.98% for 42 months, and 2.71% for 59 months.

The revolving door: In this situation, high-level executives get jobs with the government regulating the industry he or she came from. When their term expires or they lose an election, many of them go back to work in that industry. Corporate leaders will often have the opportunity to make decisions and regulate the very sectors they used to work in. Meanwhile, elected officials join corporations that contributed to their campaigns and whose work they supported while in the government.

This sort of power can give voice to some people and make others invisible. It supports its own system as it becomes more embedded in the power structure.

Globalization has generally worked to narrow the gap between the poor and rich nations. The middle classes in India and China, for example, are growing quickly. On the other hand, in countries with advanced economies, globalization is widening the gap between rich and poor. With globalization and deindustrialization putting middle-income and low-wage U.S. workers in direct competition with workers in other countries, the downward pressure on wages is going to be hard to halt, then reverse. Likewise, income and wealth disparity also is going to be hard to reverse.

 V. A. Discussion

1. Considering the causes of poverty, which is your personal "favorite" category or personal bias: individual choices, community conditions, exploitation, or political/economic structures?

2. How might having a bias about the cause or causes of poverty affect your relationships with others?

3. Given that welfare programs are largely based on the bias that poverty is caused by the choices of the poor, what does this mean to people who are on the receiving end of the programs?

4. What, if anything, does your community do that helps people get out of poverty?

Investigate This!

In some places, local banks provide fair loans to low-income people so they didn't have to go to predators.

If banks in your area don't seem to do that, some help may be found by learning how to use the Community Reinvestment Act (CRA). Congress passed the CRA in 1977. It states that "regulated financial institutions have continuing and affirmative obligations to help meet the credit needs of the local communities in which they are chartered."

Community groups can be involved in the plans developed by local banks and can offer their comments on the CRA performance of banks to examiners prior to the evaluation of the bank. What groups are working on accountability issues together with local banks in your community?

For more information, contact:
National Community Reinvestment Coalition
Suite 540
733 15th St., NW
Washington, DC 20005
(202) 628-8866

VI. More About Mental Models

Peter Senge (1990) says, "The problems with mental models lie not in whether they are right or wrong—by definition, all models are simplifications. The problems with mental models arise when the models are tacit—when they exist below the level of awareness" (p. 176).

If you aren't aware of your mental models, you can't challenge them, and so they become a barrier to learning. They keep you frozen where you are. On the other hand, intentional mental models create ways to accelerate learning. Skillful users of mental models can do these things:

1. Make fast and large jumps between concrete observations of things (behaviors, situations, people, environments, relationships, activities) and abstract generalizations (analysis, labels).

2. Say what is not normally said—articulate the tacit knowledge behind the observations and generalizations.

3. Investigate honestly by balancing inquiry and advocacy.

4. Expose the differences between what we say (espoused theory) and what we do (theory-in-use).

We have already created a Mental Model of Poverty. Now we're going to create a mental model for the middle-class experience and for wealth.

This will help us understand how people in all three classes live, think, and make decisions. After all, no single economic group is responsible for causing poverty, and no single economic group can create sustainability.

VI. A. Activity: Mental Models of Middle Class and Wealth

Time: 1 hour and 15 minutes
Materials: Chart paper, markers
Procedure:

1. Read the following case studies of a family from middle class and a family from wealth.

2. Discuss what life is like in middle class; create a Mental Model of Middle Class.

3. Discuss what life is like in wealth and create a Mental Model of Wealth.

4. Review the Mental Model of Poverty that was created in Module 2.

5. Compare and contrast the three environments for:

    a. The types of businesses in the neighborhood that people access

    b. People's relationships with institutions (schools, courts, agencies)

    c. The level of stability in daily life

    d. The degree of vulnerability and fear

    e. The time horizon (how far ahead people think and make plans)

    f. How much access to power people have

    g. What types of problem-solving skills people have

6. Put these mental models on the wall at the beginning of each session, along with all the other mental models the group creates. Add information to them as it arises in group discussions.

Middle Class

Mark and Donna were both raised in middle-class families. Mark's father worked in an insurance company. His mother ran the house and was active in the community. Donna's father was an accountant, her mother a teacher. Donna has a bachelor's degree and is a certified respiratory therapist (CRT). She works for a company that provides in-home health services. Mark has a bachelor's degree and is a mid-level manager in a food distribution company. He was in the military for four years. They are in their early 40s and recently bought a house in a new development in order to have their children in a better school system. This is the second marriage for Donna. They have three children: a 15-year-old daughter from Donna's first marriage and two sons they had together; the boys are 13 and 11 years of age.

Mark's salary of $50,000 and Donna's salary of $33,000 were sufficient when they lived in the older section of the city, but when they moved to the new development the mortgage payments and the longer commutes to work became burdensome. They have excellent healthcare benefits, but their employers are increasingly shifting the cost of premiums to the employees. Mark was just diagnosed with Type II diabetes, and their eldest son has asthma. Donna's first husband hasn't been able to retain jobs because of a drinking problem, and he rarely pays child support. Mark and Donna bought their cars new. Donna drives a minivan; Mark drives an SUV.

Everyone in the family has a cell phone, and there are three computers in the home. They have a family tradition of visiting different states and Major League Baseball stadiums in the summer. These sports/camping trips are not working out so well now the children are older and involved in more summer activities. Mark is a member of Kiwanis. Donna and her friends go shopping together and like home decorating. She goes to the YWCA to exercise and is active in the PTA.

The children are very busy. The girl has been in dance and singing classes from the time she was little, and now she's on the volleyball and swimming teams. Mark coaches baseball for his sons' teams, and they enjoy playing golf together. The younger boy is in his school's chess club, and the older boy is in Boy Scouts. Moving to the new school district has given the children more to do, which is becoming increasingly expensive. In order maintain their active lifestyle, Mark and Donna have stopped saving money for emergencies and for college. Their credit card debt has grown to $30,000.

Mark and Donna are worried about the future because their financial situation is worsening, and Mark's diabetes is progressing. They realize they won't be able to help their children much with the cost of college. They have had a number of arguments about money but haven't made any significant changes in spending or saving habits.

Thanksgiving, Christmas, and other holidays have to be scheduled very carefully because their daughter goes to her father's house. Mark's parents live close by, so the family sees them regularly. About the only time they see aunts, uncles, and cousins are at Thanksgiving and a summer picnic.

Old Money

Olen is 24 years old and in generational wealth, also known as old money. The original fortune was made 150 years ago. A trust fund was established at his birth, but Olen also was named in other funds as "future progeny," so he has several trust funds. He was registered for private boarding school at birth and went there at age 6. He graduated from Yale University, as did his father and grandfather. At 21 he began receiving a monthly check from the interest his trust funds generate, but he won't control the principal until he's 35. Twice a year Olen meets with his trust adviser to be updated on his trust funds.

Olen's allowance is $10,000 a month. He doesn't have bills, because he lives in one of the many staffed and furnished residences his family owns around the world. He doesn't pay for the utilities, upkeep, or staff. He has no debt. Additionally, two houses were given to him as gifts. His club memberships are paid for by his mother, and one of his cars was a gift at college graduation. In the garage Olen has several cars and vehicles, all of which have been fitted to one key so a last-minute choice of cars can be made.

Olen divides his year among Palm Springs, California; Aspen and Vail, Colorado; Europe; and New York City. He flies first class or, more often, in either the corporate or the family jet. There is domestic help at all the houses who take care of everything, including his clothing, cleaning, and meals. A tailor makes his clothes and often selects both fabric and style, as he knows Olen's personal tastes. At one of the family estates, one person is hired full time to take care of the pool area and another to polish the brass. Because there is always staff around, privacy becomes a huge issue. Staff members have been fired for not being discreet.

Olen's hobbies are sailing, golf, ballooning, flying, skiing, and the theater. He spends a great deal of time in social activities but, in part, Olen uses his social and financial connections to further his career as a playwright. Olen is a bit unusual for his social group in that he wants to be an acclaimed writer. He is welcome in theater, film, and television circles because of his name and wealth; creative people are welcome in his circles because of their achievements. He knows he can be published—he has enough connections to do that—but he wants to be respected and renowned "in his own right."

It is expected that by age 30 Olen will participate in one of the family businesses. Besides social functions he is expected to take part in business meetings, foundation board meetings, and political fund-raising events. He spends considerable time with the family's law firm on a complex lawsuit he filed to protect his property rights. Most of his time is spent with family members, old-money friends, or friends from the theater. Olen doesn't need to worry that the theater people will make fun of him for his tastes in clothes or art—or that they will want to use him for his money. He has learned to guard his privacy by picking his friends carefully.

VI. B. Discussion

1. What is tacit knowledge? Where do you think your mental models of economic classes came from?

2. Discuss whether this information on the economy and economic classes changed your thinking or feelings about poverty in general.

3. How might this new information change how you see your future, or what you think you might do in the future?

4. What, if anything, do the associations, agencies, institutions, and businesses in the community do well in terms of helping end poverty? What might they do more of? What things might they do differently?

5. What kinds of things might people in middle class and poverty do *together* if they decided to work with one another? What might happen if wealthy people also came to the table?

6. What are some things that people from all three classes can do to make a more stable community—to develop sustainability?

Journal Reflections

Write or draw your thoughts and ideas about economic differences.

VII. Putting All These Ideas Together to Develop Sustainability

In this module we've reviewed the causes of poverty, examined economic disparity, looked at who pays the most taxes, and learned what it means when taxpayers leave the community. All this causes us consider the effect of economic disparity on our town, city, or county. What does it mean to you? What does this mean to our children and to their children? It seems this pattern cannot go on if we want to provide a decent life for them.

Making a stable life for ourselves *and* future generations is called sustainability. Creating sustainability may well be the biggest issue facing our generation. Some say it will require revolutionary changes in everything from where we get energy to how we live in our communities. The first major revolution that our human ancestors faced was moving from a hunter-gatherer way of life to farming—or an agricultural economy. It required people to develop new knowledge and skills, to build permanent homes, to store food, and to organize communities in new ways. The second revolution was the change from farming to industry, often called the Industrial Revolution (in the 1700s and 1800s). Again, new skills, knowledge, and tools were used to spur development. The third revolution is the development of the knowledge economy the last 20–25 years. Two things—intellectual capital and virtually instantaneous access to information—are still relatively new realities that are changing economies, societies, and cultures worldwide. The fourth revolution may well be the development of sustainability. The question we must answer is how can we use the earth's resources and yet have enough for future generations?

This question may not seem very important to someone living in survival mode. After all, if you can't find an affordable or safe place to live, are you going to be worrying about whether your home is "green," much less the problems of future generations? Not likely, but here's the thing. Thomas Sowell (1997), a historical and international researcher, said that none of our towns, cities, or counties can develop a sustainable future if they allow any group to be disenfranchised or left out for any reason (economic class, race, religion, etc.) because the entire community will become economically poorer. Consider poverty, for example. When the percentage of people in poverty reaches 35–40%, the community becomes alarmed, and when it reaches 60%, most of the top 10% move out (Sowell). That's obviously not sustainable. The children left in that community won't be better off if this pattern continues. One can argue that the wealthy children suffer too because they see and encounter little diversity, economic or otherwise.

These political and economic issues and the concept of sustainability are very complex. If we get confused by all the details of complex issues, we can refocus ourselves by coming back to the macro questions:

- How well will future generations of all groups live if this trend continues?
- Will the decisions we are making (whatever they are) create long-term economic stability for all groups now and into the future?

It would seem that creating sustainability is something all economic groups will have to pay attention to because we're all in this together. For that reason, all three economic groups will need to cooperate and work together.

VIII. Utilizing the Four Areas of Research to Bring People from All Political Persuasions and Economic Classes to the Planning Tables

We began this module talking about the extreme either/or arguments that come from political debates and personal bias. By recognizing that there's good information from all four areas of research it's possible to bring people from both ends of the political continuum together to solve community problems. Instead of designing programs and policies to address poverty from one narrow perspective, this approach takes the best of all thinking to create a holistic approach. In our view, poverty is caused by the choices of the poor and by political/economic structures and by everything in between (community conditions and exploitation).

For example: In St. Joseph County, Indiana, there's a Bridges Steering Committee that formed to address poverty in a comprehensive way. Committee members have the support of the mayor of South Bend who is a Democrat and the mayor of twin city Mishawaka who is a Republican, as well as the support of county commissioners from both parties in an initiative that provides long-term support for Getting Ahead graduates who are entering the workforce. (Remember that *Getting Ahead* is the name of a workbook like this, as well as a program that has been used successfully in a number of communities since 2005.)

The Community Sustainability Grid: a Planning Tool for Addressing All Causes of Poverty

The idea for the Community Sustainability Grid came from people in Burlington, Vermont, who also are using the *Getting Ahead* workbook. The Community Sustainability Grid (see next page) is a mental model that presents two themes:

1. We must develop strategies that cover all four areas of research on the causes of poverty. These are listed across the top of the grid as column headings.

2. Creating a sustainable community will require the active engagement of individuals, organizations (agencies, schools, healthcare providers, courts, etc.), and the community (elected leaders, business sector, faith-based entities, and cultural groups), along with changes in policies. These label the rows on the left-hand side.

Bridges Steering Committees, such as the one in Indiana, use the Community Sustainability Grid as a planning tool. It helps planners find four strategies to address the barriers that people encounter as they build resources to get out of poverty. For example, if predatory lending were the barrier for people in a community who were trying to stabilize their environment and get out of poverty, this is how the table would be used. In fact, the chart on the next page illustrates how it was used in Clark County, Ohio.

How Clark County, Ohio, Used the Community Sustainability Grid to Address the Problem of Predators

	Individual Behaviors and Circumstances	Community Conditions	Exploitation	Political/ Economic Structures
Individual Action				
Organizational Action				
Community Action	Financial literacy classes available	Credit union loans to compete with predatory lenders	Attorney to take on predatory practices	Educate elected representatives and work to pass laws limiting the interest rate that can be charged
Policy				

Acting in the "Community Action" row (see table above), the Bridges Steering Committee in Clark County addressed "Individual Behaviors and Circumstances" by initiating financial literacy classes so that everyone had a way to learn the rules of money.

The steering committee in that setting also addressed "Community Conditions" by asking the local credit union to offer loans to low-income people with poor credit at a fair interest rate. The credit union developed a product to compete with predatory lenders.

To address "Exploitation" they hired an attorney to take on predatory practices by businesses.

To address "Political/Economic Structures" or systemic issues, they educated elected representatives by meeting with them and going to the state capital to advocate for laws that would limit the interest rates that payday lenders could charge. Those laws eventually passed in Ohio.

This approach addressed a broad range of factors, brought people together across class lines to solve problems, and attracted people from different political persuasions to take concrete action.

Earlier in this module, you thought about what you could do personally to get out of or avoid interactions with predators; those examples would go into the top left box. Now think about what you as an individual can do to impact community conditions, the exploiters themselves, and political/economic structures or policy. Those items would finish out the top row.

IX. Time Management and Planning—Setting a Goal and Working a Plan

Having investigated how you really spend your time and thought about how you can find enough time to study, the next step is learning to make a plan to get bigger assignments done. Sometimes it's hard to know where to start—or maybe you get started all right, but then you don't have time to put the finishing touches on the project before it's due. Whatever the case, you aren't alone. It takes time and practice before it feels natural to work a plan and manage a project. Managing a project means knowing what the end result will look like (maybe a homework assignment, a re-search paper, or a completed degree program)—and knowing what needs to happen, in what order and by when, for the result to be achieved. It's having a vision, then working the plan.

In this activity, you'll practice the steps of "backwards planning" as it relates to one of your assignments coming due. Stephen Covey in *The 7 Habits of Highly Effective People* (1989) says one of those seven habits is "Begin with the End in Mind." Please follow the steps below.

IX. A. Activity: Backwards Planning

Time: 1 hour, probably outside of class time
Materials: Paper, your workbook or syllabus, and an academic calendar
Procedure:

1. **Set the goal:** Make notes as you ask yourself the following questions:

    a. What do I want to accomplish (for example, a final term paper about how welfare reform affected single-parent households)?

    b. What will be different when you achieve your goal?

    c. What motivates you to achieve this goal?

    Now write the goal and check to see if it is a SMART goal.

    d. **S**pecific—Is it specific? What will be created or changed?

    e. **M**easurable—Is it measurable? How many? How often? How long?

    f. **A**ttainable—Is it attainable? Do you have the ability to do the things that need to be done to accomplish the goal?

    g. **R**ealistic—Is it realistic? Is it doable? Is it something you want to do (or have to do so you can get what you want)?

    h. **T**ime-specific—When will it be completed? Short-term goals are days, weeks, or months in the future, while long-term goals are a year or more into the future.

2. **Set the objectives:** Big goals and long-term goals may require you to accomplish several shorter term objectives. What are the major things that need to happen before you will completely accomplish the goal? Work backwards from the goal. *For example, if the final term paper is due December 7:*

   - What date would you set to have completed a final draft?

   - If you want the instructor (and/or someone else) to review that draft, when would that need to happen?

   - When should your library research be completed?

   - How much time do you need to do the research? When would your research start, and how many hours on what days will you do the research?

   - And, planning backwards, the first thing you need to do is decide the topic of the paper and get the instructor's OK on it. When will you do that?

3. **Determine the steps:** What are the actions you will take, what will you do to get to your goal? Be as specific as possible and write out all the details. You might get partway though a list of steps and think of something that must get done first; go back and add that in.

4. **Add a timeline:** Use an academic calendar. Starting from the end (for example, paper due December 7) make sure the goal has an end date in it (December 7), then work your way backwards, assigning dates to all the objectives and calculating how much time each step will take.

5. **Make a daily list of "To Do Today":** What are the 10 most important things for you to get done today? Some of them will be in the "Steps" section of your plan, while some won't. Keeping a daily list of things that need to be done, then crossing them off as you go along, helps you stay focused and keep track both of what has been accomplished and what still needs to be done.

IX. B. Discussion for Next Class Period

Look at the results of your work in Module 3, "Becoming More Effective." Here you assigned your activities to four quadrants, depending on how urgent and important they were.

1. How many of the activities or steps in your backwards plan fit into Quadrant II?

2. As you planned backwards with a calendar, did you foresee Quadrant I, III, and IV activities?

3. Can you make mini-plans to account for any of the Quadrant I, III, and IV activities?

Readings

American Dream: Three Women, Ten Kids, and a Nation's Drive to End Welfare by Jason DeParle. Describes how policy shapes the poverty experience.

"Are We Still a Middle-Class Nation?" by Michael Lind. Information on how the middle class was created.

An Atlas of Poverty in America: One Nation, Pulling Apart, 1960–2003 by Amy K. Glasmeier. An atlas that provides a comprehensive portrait of poverty in the U.S., from the beginnings of Lyndon Johnson's Great Society to the present.

The Color of Wealth: The Story Behind the U.S. Racial Wealth Divide by Meizhu Lui, Barbara Robles, Betsy Leondar-Wright, Rose Brewer, and Rebecca Adamson. Describes the intersection of race and poverty.

Culture Matters: How Values Shape Human Progress edited by Lawrence E. Harrison and Samuel P. Huntington. "He [Alan Greenspan] assumed that capitalism was 'human nature.' But he has concluded, in the wake of the Russian economic disaster, that it was 'not nature at all, but culture'" (p. xxv). Harrison's introduction, "Why Culture Matters," is found on pages xvii–xxxiv.

The Divine Right of Capital: Dethroning the Corporate Aristocracy by Marjorie Kelly. See "The Six Principles of Economic Aristocracy" and "The Six Principles of Economic Democracy" on pages 14–15.

From Poverty to Prosperity: Intangible Assets, Hidden Liabilities, and the Lasting Triumph Over Scarcity by Arnold Kling and Nick Schulz. The authors describe the positive forces of creativity, innovation, and advancing technology that propel economies forward. They also describe the forces that hold economies back: bad governance, counterproductive social practices, and patterns of taking wealth instead of creating it. See especially pages 1–50.

The Impact of Inequality: How to Make Sick Societies Healthier by Richard G. Wilkinson. The author answers these questions: "Why do people in more unequal societies have worse health and shorter lives?" and "Why are levels of violence higher and community life weaker where there is more inequality?"

An Inquiry into the Nature and Causes of the Wealth of Nations by Adam Smith. "A man must always live by his work, and his wages must at least be sufficient to maintain him. They must even upon most occasions be somewhat more; otherwise it would be impossible for him to bring up a family, and the race of such workmen could not last beyond the first generation" (p. 77). From Chapter VIII, "Wages of Labor," pages 73–99.

"Make 150,000% Today!" by Matt Miller. Information on the ROPI (return on political investment).

The Measure of America: American Human Development Report 2008–2009 by Sarah Burd-Sharps, Kristen Lewis, and Eduardo Borges Martins. Introduces the American Human Development Index, which provides a single measure of well-being for all Americans, disaggregated by state and congressional district, as well as by gender, race, and ethnicity.

The Mystery of Capital: Why Capitalism Triumphs in the West and Fails Everywhere Else by Hernando de Soto. How property law established a way to acquire assets. See Chapter 3, "The Mystery of Capital," found on pages 39–68.

Polarized America: The Dance of Ideology and Unequal Riches by Nolan McCarthy, Keith T. Poole, and Howard Rosenthal. The authors study political polarization and argue that it is linked to economic inequality.

Poverty Knowledge: Social Science, Social Policy, and the Poor in Twentieth-Century U.S. History by Alice O'Connor. A must-read for those who are going to take this course of study to a deeper level.

"Race, Culture, and Equality" by Thomas Sowell. Offers a global view of how income and wealth disparities occur.

The Rise of the Creative Class—and How It's Transforming Work, Leisure, Community, and Everyday Life by Richard Florida. "The basis of the Creative Class is economic. I define it as an economic class and argue that its economic function both underpins and informs its members' social, cultural, and lifestyle choices. The Creative Class consists of people who add economic value through their creativity" (p. 68). From Chapter 4, "The Creative Class," found on pages 67–82.

The Trouble with Diversity: How We Learned to Love Identity and Ignore Inequality by Walter Benn Michaels. "The trouble with diversity, then, is not just that it won't solve the problem of economic inequality; it's that it makes it hard for us even to see the problem. If we're on the right, of course, it's not clear that there is a problem. The right tends to regard economic inequality less as a political issue than as something like a fact of nature—maybe temporary … maybe permanent

... and either way, not that big a deal. The left ... insists on giving poor people identities; it turns them into black people or Latinos or women and treats them as victims of discrimination as if in a world without discrimination, inequality would disappear. The debate we might have about inequality thus becomes a debate instead about prejudice and respect, and—since no one's defending prejudice and no one's attacking respect—we end up having no debate at all" (pp. 172–173). From Chapter 6, "Religion in Politics: The Good News," found on pages 171–190.

The Tyranny of Dead Ideas: Letting Go of the Old Ways of Thinking to Unleash a New Prosperity by Matt Miller. The author asks, "Can middle-class societies be sustained in wealthy nations in an era of globalization? Can democracy survive the emergence of extreme inequality? How will these trends affect our posture toward the hopes of the developing world? Can Americans build secure and happy lives amid this tumult?" (p. 8). From the author's introduction, "Trapped," found on pages 1–13.

The War on the Poor: A Defense Manual by Randy Albelda, Nancy Folbre, and the Center for Popular Economics. Refutes assertions that poverty is chiefly caused by people in poverty themselves.

The Working Poor: Invisible in America by David K. Shipler. "Breaking away and moving a comfortable distance from poverty seems to require a perfect lineup of favorable conditions. A set of skills, a good starting wage, and a job with the likelihood of promotion are prerequisites. But so are clarity of purpose, courageous self-esteem, a lack of substantial debt, the freedom from illness or addiction, a functional family, a network of upstanding friends, and the right help from private or governmental agencies" (pp. 4–5). From the introduction, "At the Edge of Poverty," found on pages 3–12.

World Development Report 2006: Equity and Development by the World Bank. "The main message is that equity is complementary ... to the pursuit of long-term prosperity ... Greater equity is thus doubly good for poverty reduction: through potential beneficial effects on aggregate long-run development and through greater opportunities for poorer groups within any society" (p. 2). From the overview found on pages 1–17.

MODULE 5
Hidden Rules of Economic Class

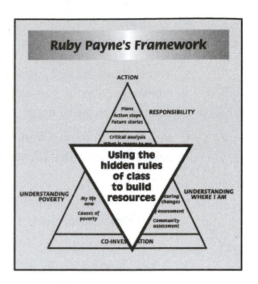

Learning Objectives

WHAT'S COVERED

You will:

Define the hidden rules of class that arise from the economic environments

Understand the key points that underlie this perspective on economic class

Apply the hidden rules to your own situations on campus and in the community

Learn how and when to use the hidden rules to help you in different situations

WHY IT'S IMPORTANT

This information is abstract and provides new ideas on how to solve problems and be able to navigate new situations more skillfully.

Knowing this information can help develop economic security.

HOW IT'S CONNECTED TO YOU

Earlier we found that poverty is about being stuck in the tyranny of the moment.

In the Process for Change module, we learned that abstract information provides options for how to think and act.

This information is at the core of Payne's theories and provides, from a less emotional level, a way to understand your personal experience and how other people react. When you can detach emotionally, you can make decisions that are more helpful to your goals in the long term.

Learning Process

- You will use the key points to understand the perspective, or frame of reference that this theory is based upon.

- You'll find examples from your past or current situation that illustrate the hidden rules.

- You'll investigate the hidden rules of college, financial aid, and college social life.

Lexicon for Module 5

Generational poverty
Hidden rules
Legacies
Lens of economic class
Mutual respect
Noblesse oblige
Normalize
Poverty is relative
Social *faux pas*

I. Defining the Hidden Rules of Economic Class

In this module we begin to explore Ruby Payne's ideas on poverty and economic class. Her work is very different from most others who have written about poverty. The large majority of studies focus on race, ethnicity, gender, age, sexual orientation, or disability when describing poverty. Payne's longitudinal study of a low-income neighborhood offers a new way to understand the impact of poverty that "clicks" with those who hear it, especially with those who live in poverty or grew up in poverty.

What are the hidden rules? Hidden rules are the unspoken cues and habits of a group. If you know the rules, you belong; if you don't, you don't. If you know the rules, you can navigate the group and its systems skillfully.

How do you know when you belong? When you don't have to explain what you say or do to the people around you. To fit in like that you have to know the unwritten and unspoken cues and habits of the group. When you know the hidden rules, you don't have to worry about being understood.

Wherever we go we're surrounded by hidden rules because all groups of people and all cultures have their own rules. We have hidden rules for nationality, neighborhoods, clubs, gangs, race, age, gender, ethnicity, the workplace, and, yes, economic class.

How do people learn hidden rules? We normally learn the rules from living in our environment, not by taking lessons. If you were raised in wealth, you learned how to belong in your world. The same is true if you were raised in poverty or middle class. Children learn by interpreting the tone of voice, the looks, the reactions, and, finally, the words used by their caregivers and the people closest to them. Seldom are these rules explicitly taught.

Where do the rules of economic class come from? They come from disparity in income and wealth. The greater the economic disparity between/among the rich, the middle class and those in poverty, the greater the difference in the economic environments in which people live, the more distinct the hidden rules of economic class. In earlier modules we investigated economic disparity and developed mental models of poverty, middle class, and wealth. It is from those environments that our hidden rules of class arise. Unstable worlds in which things break down frequently require different hidden rules to survive than settings that are more stable.

 I. A. Discussion

- What groups do you and the others belong to?

- Name a group you belong to and explain one hidden rule a new person would need to know in order to fit in.

- Have you ever broken a hidden rule? How did you know when you broke it? How did people in the other group react?

II. Key Points to Provide Perspective on the Hidden Rules

The key points below are definitions and core concepts that underlie this understanding of and approach to poverty.

1. Poverty, middle class, and wealth are all *relative*. The 2008 Current Population Survey (conducted jointly by the U.S. Bureau of Labor Statistics and the Census Bureau) tells us that a household with an annual income of $100,000 or more is in the top 20% of American households as ranked by income, which leads the other 80% to consider them rich. However, if you asked households making that amount if they are rich, few would say that they are. They would think of others—acquaintances, friends, family—who make more money as a basis for comparison. The point is that perception of economic class is relative in comparison to how others live (Pfarr, 2009, p. xii). In Africa and Asia there are countries where people are in absolute poverty, where people don't have enough resources to secure basic life necessities, such as food, shelter, and clean drinking water. Using that metric makes most of us in the United States rich by comparison.

2. Poverty occurs among people of all races and in all countries.

3. There are many lenses through which to view poverty issues, all of which are important: race, ethnicity, gender, age, sexual orientation, disabilities, and culture, for example. This work uses the lens of economic class to focus and address poverty. *Without a clear understanding of how income and wealth affect the environment we live in, it will be difficult for our strategies against poverty to be effective.*

4. Economic class is a continuous line, not a clear-cut distinction.

5. *Generational* poverty, middle class, and wealth mean that individuals have been in that socioeconomic class for two generations or more. People in a generational class are more likely to exhibit the patterns associated with that class than are people whose families haven't been in it for two or more generations.

6. *Situational* poverty, middle class, or wealth means that one spends only a portion of one's life in that class. For example, if you grew up in middle class and maintained middle-class status into adulthood but then experienced poverty due to, for example, an illness, death, divorce, or plant closing, this would be considered situational poverty. You wouldn't bring the same lenses and mindset

to the experience of poverty as would some-one who has never experienced anything else.

7. This work is based on patterns. All patterns have exceptions. People sometimes choose not to talk about the different ways economic groups operate because they fear being accused of stereotyping. We are not asserting that if you live in one community or the other you are guaranteed to be or act a certain way; that would be absurd and, yes, stereotypical. Still, it is equally absurd to state that no differences exist between the different economic environments. We must have the courage to talk about the differences in a way that is respectful and constructive to all (Pfarr, 2009, p. xi). Observe, discuss, and learn, as opposed to prejudging and judging.

8. Individuals bring with them the hidden rules of the class in which they were raised.

9. Schools and businesses operate largely from middle-class norms and tend to use the hidden rules of middle class.

10. Understanding the hidden rules of economic class with which we were raised allows us to own our societal experience—be it poverty, middle class, wealth, or a journey that covered two or more class experiences. Understanding our own history helps us explore the hidden rules of other classes without being judgmental. Knowledge of the hidden rules can help people navigate diverse environments more skillfully, resolve conflicts, and build relationships of mutual respect across class lines.

11. In order to move from poverty to middle class or middle class to wealth, an individual must usually give up relationships for achievement (at least for a period of time).

12. As there are many reasons for poverty, we must have a wide array of strategies to address poverty comprehensively.

 ## II. A. Discussion

- Which of the key points are most interesting to you?

- Which of the key points might someone disagree with?

- What perspectives do you bring to the discussion that support or conflict with the key points?

- Why might it be important to "suspend judgment" when studying issues of economic class?

A Closer Look at Key Point 11

This key point could read, "In order to achieve *anything* an individual must give up relationships at least for a period of time." Achievements (regardless of class) tend to come at the cost of relationships. This suggests that for someone to become an outstanding singer or dancer or athlete he or she would have to give up some relationships for a period of time. To do investigative research for a book might mean that the researcher has to be away from his or her spouse and children for the duration of the research phase. All the time spent practicing or researching is time not spent with others. This doesn't mean that the authors of this workbook are expecting investigators to leave their friends or family behind. But it does recognize the fact that relationships usually change when someone pursues achievement. Virtually every person who has left poverty has a story to tell about the relationships that were changed, as well as the relationships that were lost and those that were added.

Earning a degree in higher education is an accomplishment that takes a lot of time and energy; we can almost guarantee it's going to affect some of your relationships for a while.

 II. B. Discussion

1. How much time does attending classes and doing coursework take in a day?

2. Who in your life first noticed that you had less time for them?

3. What sacrifices have to be made? Have you talked specifically about this with the people close to you?

4. How do your friends and family react to your pursuit of a college degree?

5. What relationships do you *gain* when you attend college?

6. How might this key point be experienced differently according to a person's economic class? How might going to college be harder for a student from an unstable environment or from poverty?

III. Suggestions on How to Study the Hidden Rules

Before we look further at the hidden rules of economic class, it's important to be clear about what we are and are not investigating. We will be studying the hidden rules of *economic class only.* Middle-class people of all racial and ethnic groups share some rules of economic class; the same is true for people in poverty and wealth. We are *not* studying the hidden rules of race, religion, ethnicity, gender, etc., though these factors sometimes enter the discussion because they are related to class issues.

- Understanding the hidden rules of economic class can help you *if* you don't think of them as *right and wrong, good and bad*—as if you have to be *for* or *against* them. It's more helpful to think of them as "rules" that children learn almost unconsciously when they're growing up. Naturally, they will keep using many of them in their adult life.

- Understanding the hidden rules can help you *if* you don't think of them as your *identity.* If you cling to your hidden rules as the definition of who you are, it will be much harder to use them to help yourself and others.

- Think of the hidden rules as a *choice* or as *the rules of a game.* The more rules you know, the more games you can play. For example, if you want to play basketball, you have to know the rules; you can't tackle people like in football. And you can't play poker if you don't know the rules; without the rules it's just a deck of cards. So ... if you want to do well at work and school, you'll need to know and use middle-class rules. That doesn't mean the rules of poverty are wrong. Use the rules of each class when and where you need to. A woman who is a supervisor in a government agency said, "When I'm at work I use the middle-class rules. When I'm at home with my friends, I use the poverty rules."

- Understanding the hidden rules can help you *if* you don't use them to judge others or to compare yourself to others.

- Judgments and comparisons happen in all classes. We tend to measure how we're doing compared to our neighbors and friends. Those kinds of comparisons are about social snobbery. People who get too caught up in constant comparisons live on the "knife's edge" between envy and contempt. We prefer to think in terms of economic security, something we wish for everyone.

- Breaking hidden rules of the other classes is pretty easy especially when you're doing new things and starting to meet more people from other classes. You know you've broken a hidden rule when the other person suddenly gets quiet, avoids you, or gives you *"the look."*

- Unfortunately, people get into conflicts all the time over the hidden rules. One of the best things about this theory is that it gives us a different, less personal, way to understand the conflicts. Once we know there are hot spots, we might choose to handle ourselves differently. This will improve our ability to notice and name the conflicts as they happen.

- Taking responsibility for our own societal experience and our hidden rules is the first step to understanding others. If we do not "own" *our* experiences and hidden rules, we tend to be judgmental and negative about others who are not like us. Another way of putting this is to think about how people "normalize" their own experience and assume that others see the world in the same way. People from the dominant culture, race, or class are most likely to nor-

malize their experiences because to them the power and status they enjoy can be invisible.

Here's an example of a conflict over hidden rules:

In the first hidden rule, "Driving Forces" (see chart on next page), you will learn that, for the middle class, the driving forces tend to be work and achievement and, for people in poverty, they tend to be survival, relationships, and entertainment. One conflict that arises out of this difference is the judgmental attitude of many middle-class people toward the big-screen TVs that some people in poverty own. It's often expressed like this: "I can't believe they have a big-screen TV! They should be using that money to pay the bills." This attitude shows little understanding of what life is like for people at the bottom of the economic ladder. Learning about the impact that poverty has on individuals through the Mental Model of Poverty and learning the hidden rules of class give this middle-class person awareness that slows the leap to judgment—and also a choice about his or her attitude. On this topic Fred Keller, CEO of Cascade Engineering, a Michigan firm that created a successful "Welfare to Career" program, said, "We learned that not only did we need to understand the life situation of our employees who are on welfare, *we needed to change* from judging their actions to meeting their needs."

III. A. Activity: Studying the Hidden Rules

Time: 1 hour
Materials: Chart below, pencil
Procedure:

We suggest that you use the same pattern for studying each of the hidden rules.

1. **Information:** First, make sure you understand them. Investigate why the rules make sense for each class.

2. **Activity:** Find examples of the rules being used or broken by others. Using the forms provided, give examples of how you have seen the hidden rules used.

3. **Discussion:** Discuss what you have learned from this investigation.

4. **Reflections:** Make the information personal to you. Write notes or draw in order to put your thoughts on paper.

Hidden Rules of Economic Class

	POVERTY	MIDDLE CLASS	WEALTH
Driving Forces	Survival, relationships, entertainment	Work, achievement	Financial, political, social connections
Power	Power is linked to respect; must have the ability to fight; people respond to personal power; there is power in numbers; people in poverty can't stop bad things from happening	Power is separated out from respect; must have the ability to negotiate; power is linked to taking responsibility for solutions; people respond to positional power; power is in institutions; people in middle class run most of the institutions of the country	Power is linked to stability; must have influence, connections; people respond to expertise; power is information; people in wealth set the policies that direct business, corporations, and society
Time	Present most important; decisions made for the moment based on feelings, emotions, or personality	Future most important; decisions made against future ramifications	Traditions and history most important; decisions made partially on basis of tradition and decorum

HIDDEN RULE	YOUR EXAMPLES

	POVERTY	MIDDLE CLASS	WEALTH
Destiny	Believes in fate; cannot do much to mitigate chance	Believes in choice; can change future with good choices now	*Noblesse oblige*
World View	Sees world in terms of local setting	Sees world in terms of national setting	Sees world in terms of international setting
Language	Casual register; language is about survival	Consultative and formal register; language is for negotiation	Formal register; language is about networking

HIDDEN RULE	YOUR EXAMPLES

	POVERTY	MIDDLE CLASS	WEALTH
Education	Valued and revered as abstract but not as reality	Crucial for climbing success ladder and making money	Necessary tradition for making and maintaining connections
Money	To be used, spent	To be managed	To be conserved, invested
Family Structure	Tends to be matriarchal	Tends to be patriarchal	Depends on who has the money
Possessions	People	Things	One-of-a-kind objects, legacies, pedigrees

HIDDEN RULE	YOUR EXAMPLES

	POVERTY	MIDDLE CLASS	WEALTH
Personality	Is for entertainment; sense of humor is highly valued	Is for acquisition and stability; achievement is highly valued	Is for connections; financial, political, and social networks are highly valued
Social Emphasis	Social inclusion for personally likable people	Emphasis is on self-governance and self-sufficiency	Emphasis is on social exclusion
Love	Love and acceptance conditional, based upon whether individual is liked	Love and acceptance conditional, based largely upon achievement	Love and acceptance conditional, related to social standing and connections

HIDDEN RULE	YOUR EXAMPLES

	POVERTY	MIDDLE CLASS	WEALTH
Humor	About people and sex	About situations	About social *faux pas*
Food	Key question—did you have enough? quantity important	Key question—did you like it? quality important	Key question—was it presented well? presentation important
Clothing	Clothing valued for its individual style and expression of personality	Clothing valued for its quality and acceptance into norm of middle class; label important	Clothing valued for its artistic sense and expression; designer important

HIDDEN RULE	YOUR EXAMPLES

IV. The Hidden Rule of Power

Most of the United States' institutions (schools, business, courts, and service providers) operate according to middle-class rules and norms. This gives middle-class individuals power that they may not be fully aware of. As noted earlier in this module, power that is normalized is often invisible to the dominant group that enjoys the benefits. It's those who don't have power who are most sensitive to power issues, to their own powerlessness, and to their invisibility. In addition, information is power, and the institutions generally hold the information (this is changing somewhat in the era of the Internet, but middle-class institutions still hold "most of the cards"). Those seeking resources or services from the institutions must access them through the middle-class people working there.

Most middle-class employees know how to navigate institutions and systems. Members of the middle class who are familiar with power structures within the organization and wish to maintain their careers—and a stable environment for their families—will show respect for the position a person holds even when they don't respect the person. This makes it possible for the middle-class employee to separate respect from power, thereby preserving their jobs even when there are disputes with a superior.

"In poverty, power and respect are directly linked," states Pfarr (2009). "If a worker in poverty does not respect a supervisor, then that worker may find it extremely difficult to take direction from that supervisor. In poverty, because your survival depends upon other people, it is hard to grant power to those for whom you have no respect" (pp. 29–30).

Disputes with supervisors often arise from the power/respect dynamic. The supervisory role, as an achievement and as status, doesn't necessarily command respect. People in poverty often hold low-wage, entry-level positions and are the first to be laid off. Low-status jobs are hard on an individual's sense of self-worth, and any show of disrespect can be seen as an affront to one's dignity. One way to maintain personal dignity is to walk off the job; many people have given up jobs because they have felt disrespected.

When people in poverty join the middle class and wealthy at the decision-making table there is a shift in power. The dominant classes are required to make physical space at the table, to share time with other speakers, to listen to the information that is provided by people in poverty, and even take direction from people who once were not at the table; they were invisible. *Investigations* is designed to prepare students from poverty to take a seat at the table, prepared to interact by providing valuable information, new insights, and the tools to analyze problems and proposed solutions.

Before we leave hidden rules and move on to the next module, let's explore how our knowledge of the hidden rules can help us figure out what is happening at the national policy level. Can we use this information to understand, analyze, and predict decisions and actions of wealthy and middle-class people?

IV. A. Activity: Power and Public Policy

Time: 5 minutes
Materials: Chart below, pencil
Procedure:

1. Draw an arrow from the economic class that creates national anti-poverty and social service policies to the economic class that runs the social service institutions.

2. Draw an arrow from the economic class that runs the social service institutions to the economic class that most often uses the institutions.

POVERTY	MIDDLE CLASS	WEALTH

IV. B. Discussion

1. How much influence do people in poverty have to shape policies and program designs, as opposed to the influence of the middle class?

2. To what extent does economic stability influence the time and resources needed to solve problems and pursue personal interests?

V. Hidden Rules of College

As one student put it, *"College is a whole 'nother world."* He was talking about the culture, expectations, rituals, values, norms, etc., that students encounter on campus. Some students seem comfortable already in the college setting; maybe they visited siblings in college and got a feel for the place. Maybe their parents coached them on what to expect, how to act, what to do, and what not to do. Most students, though, even if they are relatively familiar with college, feel a little uneasy about the whole experience.

Learning how to navigate the college environment can take a little time, but the pay-off can be huge. Colleges are miniature communities (actually, big universities are larger than some towns!); many have their own versions of government, social service agencies, retail stores, restaurants, coffee houses and bars, religious organizations, social clubs, health and wellness facilities, athletic fields and sports complexes, libraries, entertainment, and so on.

Besides learning about all the opportunities on campus, it's also helpful to be aware of the hidden rules of the college culture so you can feel comfortable. The middle-class hidden rules are very, very strong in higher education. Here's a sample of hidden rules for the academic side of college life:

a. Most professors cover a lot of material quickly, and students are expected to study outside of class, turn in assignments on time, and show respect for the professor and their classmates.

b. Sit in class where you can best focus on what is important—sitting in the front of the room helps some students stay focused and helps build a relationship with the professor. In classes where there is much class discussion, it might be better to sit along the edge, somewhere where you can see and hear as many of your classmates as possible.

c. If you are in a clinical setting, internship, or other hands-on learning environment and there's an opportunity to practice a skill, now is the time to step up. Now is the time to practice and learn.

d. The responsibility for success is yours and yours alone.

e. Ask questions in class, and schedule meetings with your professor during office hours if you have a lot of questions or need extra help.

f. If you know you will be absent or late—or need to leave early—inform the professor in advance. Be as quiet as possible if you have to arrive late or leave early.

g. Turn in assignments on time or talk to the professor if you are having trouble meeting the deadline.

h. Your professors, generally, will treat you like an adult, and you are expected to do the same.

i. Talk one on one to your professor, *especially* if you are having trouble in the class.

j. If you can't understand the professor—or feel insulted or offended—again, the first step is to talk to the professor. If you and the professor can't work things out, then talk to the department chair, then the dean, then the provost or vice president of academic affairs. It's not like in high school when your mom called the principal.

k. While some classes might have attendance policies, many do not. It's really your responsibility to attend class and be accountable for making up materials you missed.

l. If you want to withdraw from a class because you're afraid you might fail it, you have to fill out official paperwork by a certain deadline. If you just stop going to class, you will fail the course *and* have to pay for it.

m. If something terrible happens, like a major illness or injury, talk to your professor about taking an "incomplete" for the course. Read the handbook for the rules about incompletes.

n. Cell phones, text messaging, and headphones need to be turned off during class. Really, it's a major mistake to use your devices during class. The same is true for other distracting behavior, such as talking to your friends in class, cracking gum, and so on.

o. Keeping paperwork organized can save you from academic disasters. Colleges lose things too, so keep a file for registrations, tuition paid, and transcripts, as well as scholarship information, financial aid letters, and other official documentation.

p. You'll need to get organized about your coursework too. If there isn't an area at home where you can organize and store your things, investigate getting a locker on campus and using the library or other quiet place to study. If you live on campus and share a room with someone, make sure an area of the room is clearly designated for your use and storage of important items. Likewise, respect their bounders, their "space," and don't use their things without asking.

q. Most schools provide access to computer labs for student use. If you don't have your own computer, you'll want to think about how to plan time in the labs to write up and print out your assignments.

r. A lot of campus correspondence is done by e-mail. Once again computer labs on campus provide access to the technology. But it will be up to you to make the time to use the computers.

s. College lexicon: These are words and phrases that describe people, places, and things associated with higher education.

College Lexicon			
Postsecondary Institutions	Titles and Staff	Academics	Procedures and Documents

College
Community college
Graduate school
Junior college
Technical school
University
Vocational school
	Academic adviser
	Bursar
	President
	Provost
	Registrar
	Student
	  government
		Academic freedom
		Academic standing
		Clinical
		Course load
		General education
		  requirements
		GPA (grade-point
		  average)
		Intellectual property
		Internship
		Major
		Minor
		Practicum
		Work/study
			Appeals process
			College catalog
			Exemptions
			Grievance process
			Incompletes
			Prerequisite
			Probation
			Reinstatement
			Syllabus
			Transcripts
			Withdrawals

NOTE: In the next three sections we look at hidden rules—of college in general, of financial aid, and of social life. Most colleges have a number of rules and guidelines, including behavioral expectations, in writing in the student handbook. What we're dealing with here are the hidden rules—those unwritten cueing mechanisms that go a long way in determining how positive or negative a student's college experience will be.

V. A. Activity: Hidden Rules in College

Time: Variable, usually an out-of-class assignment

Materials: List of categories of hidden rules

Procedure:

1. Assign the items in the list of hidden rules at college (see listing on preceding two pages) into the categories of hidden rules. For example, "g." is an example of the hidden rule of *time*.

2. Observe. Analyze the behaviors of instructors, staff, and fellow students in relation to the hidden rules of economic class.

3. Document examples of hidden rules in action on campus.

4. *Draw a mental model* of how the hidden rules of college relate to college success. Label the elements in the model with words from the college lexicon (chart on previous page) and hidden rules.

 ## V. B. Discussion

1. How do you think about life on campus now? Did this exercise change your perception of some of your fellow students or the college staff? How so?

2. What examples did you observe of people breaking each other's hidden rules?

3. What difference does it make if a person does or does not follow the hidden rules of the dominant group?

4. Who in your *Investigations* class has the most knowledge about the hidden rules of college and the college lexicon?

5. What is most difficult about adjusting to college life?

V. C. Activity: Hidden Rules of Financial Aid

Time: Variable, usually an out-of-class assignment

Materials: Varies from campus to campus but may include student handbook(s) and publications distributed by the financial aid office

Procedure:

1. Go to *www.fafsa.ed.gov.* Write in your planner the date you will submit your application for federal student aid.

2. Working backwards, note in your planner other tasks you must do—and information you must gather—before you can complete the FAFSA form.

3. Find the answers to the following questions from your school:

    a. The location, hours, and counseling procedures for the school's financial aid office.

    b. The financial aid assistance available, including federal, state, local, private, and institutional financial aid programs.

    c. The procedures and deadlines for submitting applications for each available financial aid program.

    d. The school's criteria for selecting financial aid recipients.

    e. The school's process for determining your financial need.

    f. The school's process for determining the type and amount of assistance in your financial aid package.

    g. The method and timing of financial aid payments made to you.

    h. The school's basis for determining whether you're making satisfactory academic progress—and what happens if you're not. (Whether you continue to receive federal student aid depends, in part, on whether you make satisfactory academic progress.)

    i. If you're offered a federal work/study job, the nature of the job, the hours you must work, your job duties, the pay, and the method and timing of payment to you.

    Note. From http://studentaid.ed.gov/students/publications/student_guide/2009-2010/english/eduafterhighschool.htm; accessed August 22, 2009.

V. D. Activity: Hidden Rules of Campus Social Life

Time: Variable, usually an out-of-class assignment

Materials: None

Procedure:

1. Think back to your first visit to the campus. Did you feel comfortable when meeting other students? Did you feel like you belonged? Were there students who seemed to belong and others who didn't? What made the difference between those who "belonged" and those who didn't?

   a. Were there times when you broke hidden rules? How did you know you had broken a rule? Did anyone help you learn the rules? Did the orientation provided by the campus cover the unwritten/hidden rules?

   b. What are the rules for meetings, greetings, dating, and partying?

   c. What are the rules about clothing, backpacks, footwear?

   d. What are the rules for sororities and fraternities?

   e. What are the rules for traditional students and adults/returning students?

   f. What are the rules for athletes and non-athletes?

   g. What other rules are there?

2. Make a list of hidden rules about campus social life that incoming students could benefit from.

 V. E. Discussion

1. What was the funniest hidden-rule story you heard?

2. Which hidden rule for academic life was the most important to you?

3. Which hidden rule for dealing with finances was the most important? For social life?

4. How can knowing the hidden rules help people develop better relationships on campus? Resolve conflicts? Solve problems?

Journal Reflections

Write or draw your thoughts and ideas on the hidden rules of economic class.

- Which rules were you raised with? Which rules do you use now? To what extent does your usage of hidden rules change depending on the setting in which you find yourself?

- Is it important to learn—and sometimes use—rules from other economic groups? Why or why not?

Investigate This!

Bring newspaper articles about the economy, housing, jobs, layoffs, plant closures, and corporations to the next session and discuss how the hidden rules shape the thinking and behavior of the people involved.

Readings

The Absolutely True Diary of a Part-Time Indian by Sherman Alexie. Arnold goes to a white school off the reservation to get a good education and plays basketball against his friends. See in particular pages 179–198.

All Over but the Shoutin' by Rick Bragg. Bragg writes about growing up dirt poor. See in particular the piece titled "White Tuxedoes" found on pages 143–147.

Bobos in Paradise: The New Upper Class and How They Got There by David Brooks. Describes the social codes of etiquette and morality of the educated classes. See in particular pages 43–53.

Class: A Guide Through the American Status System by Paul Fussell. Identifies nine classes on page 27.

The Lone Ranger and Tonto Fistfight in Heaven by Sherman Alexie. "Your past is a skeleton walking one step behind you, and your future is a skeleton walking one step in front of you. Maybe you don't wear a watch, but your skeletons do, and they always know what time it is" (p. 21). Read more about "Indian time" on pages 21–22 of this book.

People Like Us by Louis Alvarez and Andrew Kolker. Video clips and narrative stories about socioeconomic class, individuals, and communities. See http://www.pbs.org/peoplelikeus/resources/index.html

Thinking Class: Sketches from a Cultural Worker by Joanna Kadi. Working-class view of the upper classes. See in particular the section titled "Stupidity 'Deconstructed'" found on pages 39–57.

Upside Down: A Primer for the Looking-Glass World by Eduardo Galeano. Describes "top, bottom, and middle" classes in Latin America. See in particular pages 11–20.

Where We Stand: Class Matters by bell hooks. See in particular Chapter 8, "Class and Race: The New Black Elite," found on pages 89–100.

MODULE 6
Language Rules and Resources

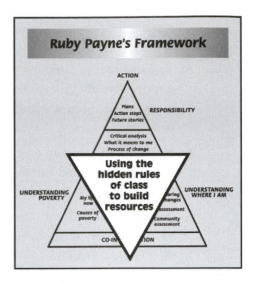

Ruby Payne's Framework

ACTION

Plans
Action steps
Future stories

RESPONSIBILITY

Critical analysis
What it means to me
Process of change

Using the hidden rules of class to build resources

UNDERSTANDING POVERTY

My life now

Causes of poverty

UNDERSTANDING WHERE I AM

CO-INVESTIGATION

Learning Objectives

WHAT'S COVERED

You will:

Learn about the registers of language and discourse patterns

Learn about code switching between language patterns of the community and Standard American English

Understand how the "voice" (parent, child, adult) and body language change the meaning of what is said

Explore the connection between story structures and a child's readiness for school

Investigate the meaning of the Hart/Risley research on economic class and how children learn to talk

Apply the mediation strategy to assist children's learning and to prepare them for school

Learn how to use language to resolve differences and to discipline children

Apply the language of negotiation

Do a self-assessment of negotiation skills

WHY IT'S IMPORTANT

Being able to use language skillfully and flexibly, according to the situation, is important for relationship building, resolving conflicts, and negotiating, as well as for overall college success.

In addition, understanding how language develops and is used will help you teach language to your children—if and when you have them!

HOW IT'S CONNECTED TO YOU

Find out what areas of language you might improve.

Your success in college, academically and socially, is inextricably linked to your language skills.

The way we use language can make or break the way we get along with others. There are several layers to this section that build up to useful information that can help us and our children.

Learning Process

- You will read summaries and overviews of information about various aspects of language, then discuss it to learn more from each other.

- You'll analyze your writing for patterns showing casual and formal register and determine the need for code switching.

- You'll learn relatively easy ways to help children (yours or someone else's) develop their language skills.

- You'll negotiate for something important that you must have.

- You'll assess your own skill in negotiating.

Lexicon for Module 6

Code switching
Discourse and story patterns
Intentions
Knowledge sector
Language experience
Mediation
Negotiation
Penance/forgiveness cycle
Registers of language (frozen, formal, consultative, casual, intimate)
Service sector
Voices (parent, child, adult)

I. Registers of Language

Becoming skillful in using language is important because language is used to form relationships, exchange information, solve problems, and make connections with others in the community. In his book *The Five Clocks: a Linguistic Excursion into the Five Styles of English,* Martin Joos (1967) defines the following registers of language. Knowing about the registers gives us flexibility in the way we choose to talk about relationships and how we communicate across class lines.

Registers of Language

REGISTER	EXPLANATION
Frozen	Language that is always the same. For example: Lord's Prayer, wedding vows, etc.
Formal	The standard sentence syntax and word choice of work and school. Has complete sentences and specific word choice.
Consultative	Formal register when used in conversation. Discourse pattern not quite as direct as formal register.
Casual	Language between friends and is characterized by a 400- to 800-word vocabulary. Word choice general and not specific. Conversation dependent on nonverbal assists. Sentence syntax often incomplete.
Intimate	Language between lovers or twins. Language of sexual harassment.

Note. From *Under-Resourced Learners* (p. 40), by R. K. Payne, 2008, Highlands, TX: aha! Process. Copyright 2008 by aha! Process.

The formal register is often called Standard American English. The formal and consultative registers are typically used in middle-class settings like work and school. Formal register also is used to negotiate settlements. Think of the civil courts and processes for resolving disputes. The more words one has the easier it is to understand the finer points of the arguments and to understand another's point of view. People in generational middle class tend to use the formal and consultative registers because they help maintain a stable environment in which they can pursue their goals. It's not exaggerating to say that formal register is used for *survival* in middle-class environments.

The casual register or informal English is a powerful and creative form of speech. It often generates new terms that make their way into mainstream culture and dictionaries. Musicians, poets, and activists enrich and invigorate language and culture through casual register. Informal or casual register is common in settings with friends and family, and it's frequently used by people in generational poverty. Because it usually involves the use of nonverbal communication, facial expressions, tone of voice, gestures, and body language, casual register is very important for "reading" a person's intention, something that is an absolute necessity for people who are living in a less stable environment. In other words, casual register is used for *survival* in poverty environments.

Vocabulary size is linked to registers in that the frozen and formal registers require a large vocabulary. Think of frozen register in terms of the court system and legal documents. Formal register is used in most elementary and secondary schools, professional occupations, and jobs in the knowledge sector, as well as in government departments and nonprofit agencies. In colleges and universities it's utilized to instruct students in all disciplines; the deeper one goes into a particular field the more specific and detailed the vocabulary becomes. Casual register has a much smaller vocabulary but many more nonverbal prompts and skills.

Language skills are linked in many studies to economic class and to success in school and work. The investigators in one of the first groups to use Getting Ahead found that formal register can be a way out of poverty. It helps if you have the *language* of school (formal register) before you arrive at school. The investigators also said, "When we go to that agency and start talking (using casual register), they look at us like we're stupid."

One register is not "better" than another; each has its value and uses. However, ignorance about language registers and other topics covered here can lead to broken relationships, misperceptions, and missed opportunities. This happens whether that ignorance is on the part of the student or the instructor. The reverse also is true; knowledge of this information can lead to new and respectful relationships based on a more accurate understanding of a person's ability.

 I. A. Discussion

1. Relate this information to the people in your life. Can you identify people who use one register considerably more than another?

2. When have you seen people get into conflicts over the way they use these registers?

3. Which register are you most comfortable using?

4. Do you know people who are bilingual, meaning they can "code switch" and move back and forth between registers easily?

5. Which register is needed for construction jobs? Manufacturing jobs? Service sector (fast food, discount stores, gas stations, convenience stores, hotels) jobs? Knowledge sector (nurse, lab technician, teacher, accounting, technology, finance) jobs?

6. Which of the sectors mentioned above require the ability to write in the formal register?

7. How far can a child or young person go in school and be successful with casual register?

8. Which hidden rules are behind the fact that most people in middle-class institutions like schools, work, and agencies prefer the formal register?

9. What registers are used much of the time in e-mails, instant messages, and social networking sites?

10. What are the implications of those personal web pages being accessible to future employers?

11. Discuss who holds the power in frozen, formal, and casual register settings.

II. Discourse Patterns

Another aspect of language is called discourse patterns. This refers to the way a group of people will carry on a conversation. For example, in some groups it's OK—even expected—for people to talk over each other. In other words, before one person is done speaking another begins talking. In other societies and cultures, where the rule is to wait at least one or two seconds after a person has finished talking to begin speaking oneself, it would be considered rude to break in, to "step on" someone's sentences, or to "interrupt."

The discourse pattern for people who use formal register tends to be quite direct. They usually present the story or information in chronological order—the sequence of how it happened. The speaker often uses abstract terms to present ideas and information. They go directly to the point and say things like, "Let's get down to business." Listeners are not expected to add information, but they might ask questions to clarify something that has been said.

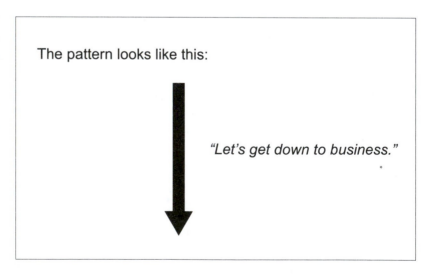

The pattern looks like this:

"Let's get down to business."

The discourse pattern for people who use casual register, on the other hand, tends to be circular. They go around and around before coming to the point and may jump into the story just about anywhere, not necessarily the "beginning." Instead, they may start where the story is most interesting or funny. This pattern relies on the use of common words and an ability to tell what people mean by the way they move their eyes, hands, and body (nonverbal communication) or by tone of voice. Hosts of late-night talk shows often speak in casual register, using body language and "reading" the social situation, while conversing with their guests. Circular story patterns take much longer to tell than stories in the formal-discourse pattern. Listeners might even be expected to contribute information and side remarks to the story as it is told.

 II. A. Discussion

1. Which hidden rules are behind the circular story pattern?

2. How do discourse patterns—casual and formal—lead to misunderstandings? Give examples.

3. How would it help someone to know how to use both formal and casual registers? How would it help to be able to use both discourse patterns? In what jobs would this be especially useful?

The pattern looks like this:

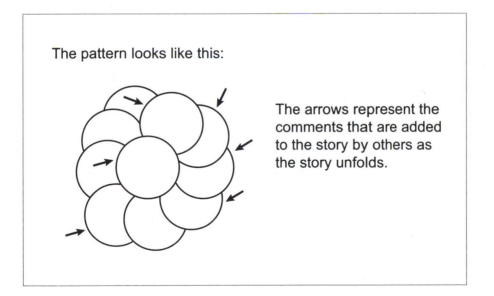

The arrows represent the comments that are added to the story by others as the story unfolds.

III. Code Switching

We've been using economic class as a lens through which to analyze personal experiences. Language is often used as a similar lens by teachers (and others) to judge intelligence. Rebecca Wheeler (2008) writes about how the traditional language arts lens used by many teachers misdiagnoses students as needing special education for learning disabilities because the students use the patterns of speech in casual register. Her research shows that, in fact, the students are not learning disabled, but rather the teachers don't understand casual register. Wheeler explains that the students' use of casual register is not *wrong;* it is simply *different* from Standard American English (SAE). Students using casual register are "not making errors, but instead are speaking or writing correctly using the language patterns of their community" (p. 55). She also suggests that to be successful in school, and eventually work, students do need to master SAE in formal register. Wheeler uses a method called *contrastive analysis* that makes this much easier to understand. Wheeler and Swords' (2010) work addresses the most common informal English grammar patterns that crop up in students' work: In each chart, there are examples in casual or informal English and formal or SAE, and then the pattern is spelled out, so you can see the difference.

SHOWING POSSESSION	
Informal	**Formal**
We went to my <u>aunt house</u>.	We went to my <u>aunt's house</u>.
A <u>giraffe neck</u> is very long.	A <u>giraffe's neck</u> is very long.
My <u>dog name</u> is Princess.	My <u>dog's name</u> is Princess.
I made <u>people beds</u>.	I made <u>people's beds</u>.
Be good for <u>Annie mom</u>.	Be good for <u>Annie's mom</u>.
THE PATTERN	**THE PATTERN**
owner + what is owned	owner + *'s* + what is owned

Note. From *Code-Switching Lessons: Grammar Strategies for Linguistically Diverse Writers* by R. S. Wheeler and R. Swords, 2010, Portsmouth, NH: Heinemann. Copyright 2010 by Heinemann.

PAST TIME PATTERNS	
Informal	**Formal**
<u>Yesterday</u> I trade my MP3 player.	Yesterday I trad<u>ed</u> my MP3 player.
We walk all around the school <u>last night</u>.	We walk<u>ed</u> all around the school last night.
<u>Last Saturday</u> we watch that movie.	Last Saturday we watch<u>ed</u> that movie.
I call my grandma <u>two days ago</u>.	I call<u>ed</u> my grandma two days ago.
Martin Luther King talk to the people.	Martin Luther King talk<u>ed</u> to the people.
THE PATTERN	**THE PATTERN**
time words and phrases common knowledge	verb + *-ed*

Note. From *Code-Switching Lessons: Grammar Strategies for Linguistically Diverse Writers* by R. S. Wheeler and R. Swords, 2010, Portsmouth, NH: Heinemann. Copyright 2010 by Heinemann.

PLURAL PATTERNS

Informal	Formal
I have <u>two</u> dog and <u>two</u> cat.	I have two dog<u>s</u> and two cat<u>s</u>.
Three <u>ship</u> sailed across the ocean.	Three ship<u>s</u> sailed across the ocean.
<u>All</u> of the boy are here today.	All of the boy<u>s</u> are here today.
Taylor loves cat.	Taylor loves cat<u>s</u>.
THE PATTERN	**THE PATTERN**
number words	noun + -*s*
other signal words	
common knowledge	

Note. From *Code-Switching Lessons: Grammar Strategies for Linguistically Diverse Writers* by R. S. Wheeler and R. Swords, 2010, Portsmouth, NH: Heinemann. Copyright 2010 by Heinemann.

A VERSUS *AN*

Informal	Formal
He is <u>a excellent</u> student.	He is <u>an excellent</u> student.
It was <u>a old</u> door.	It was <u>an old</u> door.
He tries to send <u>an positive</u> message.	He tries to send <u>a positive</u> message.
Nas is <u>an rapper</u>.	Nas is <u>a rapper</u>.
THE PATTERN	**THE PATTERN**
V - V (<u>a e</u>xcellent, <u>a o</u>ld)	*C - V (<u>an e</u>xcellent, <u>an o</u>ld)*
C - C (<u>an p</u>ositive, <u>an r</u>apper)	*V - C (<u>a p</u>ositive, <u>a r</u>apper)*

Note. From *Code-Switching Lessons: Grammar Strategies for Linguistically Diverse Writers* by R. S. Wheeler and R. Swords, 2010, Portsmouth, NH: Heinemann. Copyright 2010 by Heinemann.

SUBJECT-VERB AGREEMENT

Informal	Formal
<u>I work</u> quickly.	<u>I work</u> quickly.
<u>You work</u> quickly.	<u>You work</u> quickly.
<u>He work</u> quickly.	<u>He works</u> quickly.
<u>She work</u> quickly.	<u>She works</u> quickly.
<u>Bobby work</u> quickly.	<u>Bobby works</u> quickly.
<u>It work</u> quickly.	<u>It works</u> quickly.
The <u>printer work</u> quickly.	The <u>printer works</u> quickly.
<u>We work</u> quickly.	<u>We work</u> quickly.
<u>They work</u> quickly.	<u>They work</u> quickly.
THE PATTERN	**THE PATTERN**
any subject + bare verb	*he/she/it* subject + verb + *s*
	any other subject + bare verb

Note. From *Code-Switching Lessons: Grammar Strategies for Linguistically Diverse Writers* by R. S. Wheeler and R. Swords, 2010, Portsmouth, NH: Heinemann. Copyright 2010 by Heinemann.

III. A. Activity: Code Switching in Personal Writing Samples

Time: 1 hour, outside class time

Materials: Samples of your own writing—such as journal entries, papers

Procedure:

1. Try to find one or more examples of each of the five grammar patterns described in the previous charts. They might be examples of casual register or formal register—or both.

2. Mark your papers in some way so you can find your examples easily. For example, use symbols (C for casual, F for formal) and numbers (1–5) for the preceding patterns.

3. Analyze your papers.

    a. Do you consistently use either the casual patterns or the formal patterns?

    b. If you switch back and forth, are you aware of the difference in the patterns now?

4. In any example where you used the casual patterns, revise the sentence using the formal pattern. If your papers have no examples of the casual pattern, switch some of the formal patterns to casual.

When you revised your sentences from casual to formal or formal to casual, you practiced *"code switching."* You can consciously choose which register to use, depending on the time and place, whom you are speaking or writing to, and the purpose of your communication. This tool is similar to the hidden rules of economic class (see Module 5). Understanding the rules of more than one class provides you with more choices, more opportunities, and more options.

IV. 'Voices': Parent, Child, Adult

How people talk to each other makes all the difference between getting along and not getting along, between respect and disrespect. When we learn about the registers of language and discourse patterns, we have a way to understand where other persons are coming from and what they expect to hear. Another helpful tool is to understand the "voices" that we use: the parent, the child, and the adult voices. Eric Berne, a therapist who developed Transactional Analysis, says all three voices exist in every person's mind. They are self-talk, like recorded messages that play back from our childhood—sometimes put there by others, sometimes what we have created. These inner voices reflect our concept of what we were taught, of relationships, of how life feels, and of how we think about the world.

Parent Voice

The "internal parent" is ingrained in us by our *real* parents, teachers, and caregivers. It is the *taught* concept of life. The parent voice is made up of many messages that come out in phrases like these (at right):

- You shouldn't (should) do that …
- That's the wrong (right) to do.
- That's stupid, immature, out of line …
- Do as I say.
- Don't lie, cheat, steal …
- Life isn't fair; get busy.
- You are worthless …
- If you weren't so _____, this wouldn't happen to you.
- Why can't you be like _____)?
- You must never …

Note. Adapted from *A Framework for Understanding Poverty* (p. 84), by R. K. Payne, 2005, Highlands, TX: aha! Process. Copyright 2005 by aha! Process.

The body language that goes with the parent voice is often angry, with impatient gestures, finger pointing, and a loud voice. These phrases tend to be dictatorial, authoritative, directive, judgmental, evaluative, demanding, punitive, and threatening.

These are things we say to ourselves and to others. When we use the parent voice in our self-talk, sometimes it "keeps us in line," but often it reinforces feelings of inadequacy. When we use the parent voice on others, it frequently causes conflict because people usually don't like being told what to do or talked down to. It isn't easy to change the way we talk to ourselves or others, but it's possible.

Child Voice

Our "internal child" is how we react to what we see, feel, and hear from the world around us. It is the *felt* concept of life. When our internal child is angry or afraid, it can dominate our thinking; the child is in control. Our self-talk child voice expresses itself in phrases like these (at right):

The body language that often accompanies the child voice is rolling eyes, shrugging shoulders, temper tantrums, and a whining voice. These phrases tend to be defensive, victimized, emotional, and exaggerated.

The child voice still comes out in how we communicate with ourselves and others, even though we are adults now. When we use the child voice in our self-talk, we are usually avoiding responsibility for our own situation. When we use the child voice on others, it can invite the parent voice in response from them. The child voice can

- If you liked (loved) me …
- If you respected me, you would …
- Things never go right for me.
- You don't trust me.
- You make me sick.
- It's your fault.
- I don't care.
- This is the worst day of my life.
- Don't blame me.
- I don't trust you.
- You make me mad.
- You made me do it.
- You must never …

Note. Adapted from *A Framework for Understanding Poverty* (p. 83), by R. K. Payne, 2005, Highlands, TX: aha! Process. Copyright 2005 by aha! Process.

117

be very manipulative and thus powerful, but it becomes annoying and tiring to others and harmful to relationships.

Adult Voice

Our "internal adult" begins to form around 10 months of age, according to Berne. We develop the ability to think and determine our behaviors and actions. The adult is the *thinking* part of who we are, which gives us a way to control our parent and child. This is the voice that is needed for learning. We use it to discover how other people think and feel. We use this voice to resolve conflicts. The adult voice is heard in phrases like these (below):

▪ What are the options in this situation?	▪ What factors will be used to determine the quality of _____?
▪ When you _____ I feel _____.	▪ These are the consequences of that choice or action.
▪ What did you mean by _____?	▪ In what ways could this be resolved?
▪ I realize, I see, I think, in my opinion …	▪ We agree to disagree.
▪ I would like to recommend …	

Note. Adapted from *A Framework for Understanding Poverty* (pp. 84–85), by R. K. Payne, 2005, Highlands, TX: aha! Process. Copyright 2005 by aha! Process.

The body language that goes with the adult voice is attentive, leaning forward, not threatened or threatening—and the voice is calm. The phrases tend to be respectful, comparative, informative, and reasoned. Questions might include: What, when, where, who, how?

There are no hard-and-fast rules about the use of the three voices. In some situations the parent voice might be the most effective—for example, if there is a fire, and you want people to leave the room quickly and calmly. Being directive would be necessary. "Quiet, everyone! Use the doors at the back of the room, and do not push!"

But the parent voice (and/or body language) can be insulting and disrespectful. The parent voice pushes the listener into the child role. It can break relationships and is not effective when trying to teach. A way of salvaging a situation could be responding to the parent voice with the adult voice.

The child voice, when teasing playfully, can defuse angry and potentially dangerous situations. Some people use it to manipulate and get what they want. Again, the adult voice in response might help.

As noted, Berne would suggest that we use the adult voice to control our internal child and parent, as well as in relating to others. Speaking adult to adult can be used for building relationships, learning, resolving conflicts, and negotiating. In short, the adult voice is respectful, which enhances the chances that real communication and connection will happen.

 IV. A. Discussion

1. What "recorded messages" do you have in your mind, and where did they come from (yourself or other people)?

2. Share examples of the "voices"—how they worked for people and when they didn't. How do you react to the voices that you carry with you?

3. How do you tend to react when you hear the child voice or parent voice in others? How about the adult voice? Is there anything about the adult voice that also can be annoying or disconnected from reality? Why?

4. What happens to "voices" when we write? Examine some e-mail messages and discuss how the voices might be misunderstood.

V. Story Structure

Most children learn to talk by the time they are 3 years old, and their experience with language depends almost entirely on their immediate family. The register and discourse pattern of their family will become *their* register and discourse pattern. All families have their own "culture of talk." Some families talk more than others. Some encourage children to join in the conversation, while others don't, saying explicitly or in effect that children should be "seen but not heard."

During the first three years of life, the brain is building neural pathways for thinking. The more words a child hears from family members, the more pathways are created. The more stories a child hears, the more a family explains how things work, the more pathways are created. Research tells us that children need to hear stories and fairy tales several times a week in order to build thinking pathways.

The typical story pattern in books for children looks like this:

PLOT

BEGINNING **END**

The formal-register story structure starts at the beginning of the story and goes to the end in a chronological or accepted narrative pattern. The most important part of the story is the plot.

Goldilocks and the Three Bears

Remember the story of *Goldilocks and the Three Bears*? Take a minute to talk about the story in the group, then answer these questions:

1. What happened first?

2. When Goldilocks got to the house, she did three things. What were they, and in what order did they happen?

3. Each time she tried something in the bears' home she tried them in a certain order. What was that order?

4. Have you ever noticed what happens when you read a fairy tale to a child but skip a page or try to change the story?

The above story pattern is much more than just a story. It is a storage/retrieval system that children use for remembering the information in the story. In their brain they put the porridge first on the "plot curve" (previous page), the chair second, and the bed last. Putting these items into the thinking pattern of the story allows them to go back to those places to find the details of the story.

There are other patterns—or mental pictures—that children will rely on too. For example, they will recall that each time Goldilocks tries things in the bears' house, it's in this order: "Papa Bear, Mama Bear, then Baby Bear."

The reason children like to hear the story again and again is to gain mastery over the story. They like and want to be able to anticipate and predict what will happen. This is why children don't like it when adults "mess" with the story by skipping a page or making up different events. Children need to hear a story multiple times to embed this

neurological thinking pathway, this *cognitive structure,* in their brain. They can use this pathway again and again.

 ## V. A. Discussion

1. Notice the difference between the circular story pattern (described in Discourse Patterns earlier in this module) and the linear fairy tale structure (left). How might it be argued that the circular story structure gives children a less reliable or memorable thinking pathway than a linear story structure?

2. Imagine youngsters going to their first day of kindergarten, meeting their teacher, spending their day doing things with other kids, and learning the rules of school. How important is it for them to feel like they fit in, like they belong? What part does language play in their feeling of belonging?

3. What does all this have to do with poverty?

VI. Vocabulary

Betty Hart and Todd Risley researched how children learn to talk. They studied youngsters in professional, working-class, and welfare homes. Researchers went into the homes as a child was approaching his or her first birthday and studied the language experience of the child for nearly three years. The families in the study were all considered healthy and loving; there were no addiction issues or mental illness in any of the families, and all of the families had stable housing. Hart and Risley published their findings in *Meaningful Differences in the Everyday Experience of Young American Children* (1995).

In all of the homes the children learned to talk, but there was a big difference in language experience and development by economic class. The following findings illustrate the principal differences.

Working vocabulary: The more words children learn, the easier and faster they can learn more words. For example, learning the word "bird" can lead to naming different birds, then learning the categories of birds, and perhaps even discovering the various life patterns of birds.

Research About Language in Children, Ages 1 to 4, in Stable Households by Economic Group

Economic Class	Number of Words Children Exposed To	Encouragements vs. Prohibitions		Working Vocabulary
Professional	45 million	6	1	1,200 words at 36 months
Working Class	26 million	2	1	No information
Welfare	13 million	1	2	900 words for adults

Definitions

Number of words that children are exposed to: As noted previously, the research tells us that the more words children hear from their parents (TV and radio don't count) in the early years of life, the more neural pathways are developed in the brain.

Encouragements (affirmations/"strokes") vs. prohibitions (criticisms/reprimands): An encouragement is when an adult responds to a child's interest in something and encourages him or her to explore and talk about it. A prohibition is when an adult stops a child with a "Be quiet," "Shut up," or "Don't do that." The more encouragement the child receives, the more words he or she has—and the more learning structures are built.

 ## VI. A. Discussion

1. Standardized tests typically place children from poverty two years behind their peers from middle class and wealth—and thus not ready for school. How does the information above explain part of the reason why?

2. Hart and Risley say it's impossible to suddenly make up 20 million words when a child is 4 or 5, but we also know that it isn't "over" for children who come to school with weak language background. What are some things families can do right away to help their children? Make a list on the chart paper.

3. How does this information relate to you?

VII. Mediation: the *What*, the *Why*, the *How*

There are many things parents can do to help their children develop learning structures in the brain. One of the most effective strategies is called mediation, and it means "bringing significance to things, events, or situations, thereby transferring values" (Becker, Krodel, & Tucker, 2009, p. 41). This idea comes from Reuven Feuerstein, an educator who used mediation to help both adults and children develop values by considering the meaning of events and objects—or, in other words, to think abstractly.

When parents are encouraging their children, as we discussed above, they need to give them three steps: the *what,* the *why,* and the *how.* The "what" is when you point out to children the *content* of their actions or words, the "why" is when you explain the *meaning* of it, and the "how" is when you suggest *alternative strategies* or behaviors for them.

Here's how it looks in a table. In this example, a little boy is standing on the seat of an airport shuttle bus, looking out the window. It's late at night, and everyone on the bus is bleary-eyed and tired—except this 4-year-old boy. The dad says:

WHAT	WHY	HOW
"Hey, you're standing up in your seat."	"When the bus takes off, you might fall down."	"So … why don't you kneel down or sit on my lap."

The boy, who obviously was used to his dad talking to him in this way, knelt down on the seat and happily counted the airplanes as the bus moved along.

In this mediation, the father offers the boy a *choice* between two strategies: to kneel down or sit on his lap. Given a choice, the little boy was less likely to feel forced to do something and, at the same time, could practice taking responsibility for his choice.

This is much different from another travel experience. In this case another father and 4-year-old boy were in an airplane traveling across the country—a very long flight. The boy was fidgeting, fussing, and asking a lot of questions. The dad says:

WHAT	WHY	HOW
		"Shut up. Be quiet. Settle down. Stop that" (repeated dozens of times over the next several hours).

In mediation, all three steps are necessary to instill thinking structures. If this father had mediated the situation for his son, what might he have said?

In the space at the top of next page write your mediation for the little boy on the airplane. Hint: Don't leave out the "why." Without the *why,* the thinking piece is missing.

Mediation takes time but, when used frequently and well, kids are easier to manage, and discipline is more about learning than punishment.

WHAT	WHY	HOW

VII. A. Activity: Mediation in the College Classroom

Time: 20 minutes

Materials: None

Procedure: Most college courses are designed using the process of mediation.

There's *what* you learn—what the course is about:

- *Investigations* is about the impact of economic class on you personally, as well as on the larger community and society. It's also about building personal and community resources for greater economic stability.

There's *why* it's important:

- *Investigations* provides a means of understanding oneself, individuals, and society through the lens of economic class. It develops cognitive skills and other resources that enable students to experience college success and envision a new future story for themselves.

- *Investigations* enables students to transfer their life experience to the college campus, and it teaches students to translate, at times literally, based on the needs of the setting.

- Learning about the causes of poverty, hidden rules of economic class, resources for a stable life, and an intentional process of change supports personal growth and engagements in the learning process. The knowledge can be used within the campus, the larger community, and/or within other social, political, and economic structures.

There's *how* you learn:

- *Investigations* uses mental models, mediated learning experiences, a distinct lexicon, and assessment/planning processes to discover new information and understand its relevance—and understand how it might be utilized to achieve and maintain change.

- Through a process of co-investigations and assessments, students learn to utilize the framework of economic class, as well as to analyze and support their reasoning with new information and meaning. The group process of co-investigations, assessments, discussion/debate, and reflection builds peer support and language skills. Creation of mental models develops abstract thinking and analysis, concrete planning, and future stories.

And finally, there's *how* you and the facilitator decide how successful you have been:

- Assessments and plans result in problem solving that is *informed, proactive, and differentiated*. Students learn to define and predict problems—and to seek the relationships and support necessary to address them.

 ## VII. B. Discussion

1. The description of the course is written in formal register. Translate it into language most students are comfortable with. When you can explain something in your own words, it can prove you understand it.

2. How well can you describe the mediated learning process at work in your other courses? How might you go about talking to your instructors about your questions?

VII. C. Activity: Getting Time to Study Through Mediation

Time: 5–10 minutes
Materials: None
Procedure:
Working with one other person, pretend that one of you is a child who won't leave his or her mother or father in peace and quiet so that they can study for an upcoming test. How would you do mediation? Write out the three steps, then try them on the child. Now switch and let the other person try his or her mediation on you.

 ## VII. D. Discussion

Think about your own children, younger brothers and sisters, or other young children in your life. What are some circumstances where mediation could be added? What are some of the reasons people don't use mediation with children?

1. Describe the mediation strategies used at work? At agencies? In court?

2. Talk about the voice (parent, child, adult) and discourse pattern (circular vs. linear) used in mediation.

VIII. Using Language to Resolve Differences

Discipline and Change

How we develop self-discipline and how we discipline our children is based in part on our hidden rules for destiny. In a stable environment where families have a lot of resources, children get to practice making choices. Children can choose what to eat, what to wear, which after-school activities they want to pursue, and how to behave. As they grow older and prove they're responsible by making good choices, children can be given more freedom to try new things. Mediation is a tool for developing the hidden rule that *your choices make a difference*. The man who used mediation with his son who was standing on the seat in the bus was disciplining his son—but in a way that subtly helped his son learn a life lesson about cause and effect. If parents do this form of mediation regularly, children will get a sense that their choices can change things. The understanding that our choices make a difference is empowering.

In an unstable world where resources are low, there are fewer choices to be made. There may only be one brand of cereal to eat and one shirt to wear. When children don't practice making choices or when they do make choices but don't have the resources to turn a choice into a reality, they are more likely to feel *fated*. A common statement might be: "No matter what I do, things stay the same."

Parents who believe that choices matter tend to discipline their children using the choice-and-consequence approach. This, coupled with a future orientation, allows a parent to base discipline on the choices a child makes with the expectation that he or she will change the behavior in the future. Parents, of course, must hold the child—even a teenager—accountable for his or her choices: "You chose to drive too fast, so I'm taking your keys away for two weeks. I expect you to drive safely, and I expect you to change this behavior. If this happens again, you won't be allowed to drive for a month."

Parents (or grandparents) who feel controlled by fate, or fated, tend to use the penance/forgiveness approach. Using the diagram on the next page, imagine a man in his early 30s who has had a series of service-sector jobs, none of which he kept very long. He lives with his grandmother who cooks and cleans for him. When he decides he needs a truck for a job, he gets her to cosign on a loan for him. Before long she's making the truck payments. Later he decides he's going to get married and asks his grandmother for her credit card so he can get things he needs for the wedding and new apartment. He maxes out her card at $10,000. His grandmother is pushed by other members of the family to kick him out and demand he repay the money. After he has been gone for a week, he calls and says he's living in his truck and has no place to stay or money to live on. He says he will get a job and help pay the rent, so she takes him back.

In summary, the grandson felt there was nothing he could do differently from what he was already doing, so he took money from his grandmother. He didn't want other members of the family to

Penance/Forgiveness Cycle

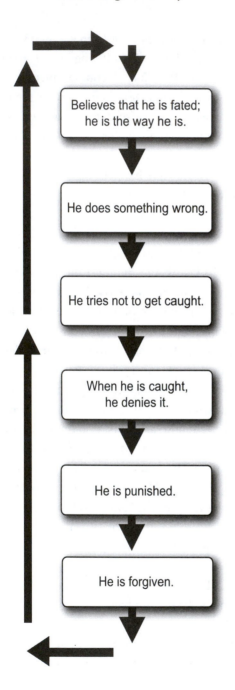

Believes that he is fated; he is the way he is.

He does something wrong.

He tries not to get caught.

When he is caught, he denies it.

He is punished.

He is forgiven.

catch him using her money and made excuses when they found out. When he was finally caught, and they pressured Grandma to kick him out, he took his punishment. For a week. And then the cycle repeated itself.

What is more important to the grandmother than the truck payments and the $10,000? The relationship with her grandson.

In poverty, the penance/forgiveness cycle is about maintaining relationships and almost never about any long-term changes in behavior; it's about the relationship returning to the way it was. In middle class, on the other hand, discipline is about consequences and change. If you don't change your behavior, you may lose the relationship. Middle-class people often do "tough love" better than people in poverty because there's more of a history in middle class of living with the consequences of decisions.

VIII. A. Discussion

1. Someone once said, "No matter what economic class, we all strives to earn the respect of our peers." How might that attitude make it difficult for us to change the way we do things?

2. What is it about poverty and its impact on families that makes it difficult for people to change?

3. Which aspects of language (discussed in this module) have caused you problems at college? What might you do to reduce the problem or improve the situation?

4. If you have seen examples of parents who use the choice/consequence approach and other parents who use the penance/forgiveness approach, describe the differences you observed in their children's behavior and in the parents' relationship with the child.

5. What might happen when someone who is part of the penance/forgiveness cycle gets into trouble with the law or with school officials?

IX. Using the Language of Negotiation

Negotiating is about getting what you want and need from others. Being good at negotiating can help you navigate life on campus, as well as at work and in the community. Negotiating skills also can help with disciplining children and preparing them to be successful at school. Being able to negotiate can help you and any children you may have maintain healthy family relationships and resolve conflicts.

Whether we think much about it or not, we negotiate every day with family members, co-workers, fellow students, teachers, supervisors, neighbors, and banks. How much should we spend on Christmas presents this year? How should we divide up the chores? Who's responsible for the various aspects of a project? How can we get the best price for a product? What's the best mortgage or healthcare deal you can get?

Negotiations can look and feel very different, depending on the skills of the people involved. It isn't a negotiation when threats are involved; that's more like a mugging. One step up from a mugging is manipulation and coercion—when one person has a lot more power and informa-

tion than another. True negotiation feels different; you don't walk away from it feeling angry or used, and neither does the other person. You both got something out of it. There's a feeling of mutual respect.

IX. A. Activity: Negotiating for Ugli Oranges

Time: 30 minutes
Materials: Story sheets for Dr. Roland and Dr. Jones

Procedure:

1. Divide the class into two groups.

2. Half the class will be Dr. Roland, while the other half will be Dr. Jones.

3. Read the information on your sheet carefully. Do not give your sheet to "the other side" to read. Your company has told you to get the best deal possible and warned you not to reveal too much information.

4. Have one member of the Roland group pair up with one Jones member and ask each pair to discuss the conflict and try to negotiate a solution.

 ### IX. B. Discussion

Your facilitator will probably stop the negotiation before you have finished and lead a discussion of what happened and why.

The Basics of Negotiating: Things We Need to Know and Account For

Economic class matters: The information we have already covered in *Investigations* will help you as a negotiator. In fact, it is information that most experts on negotiation do not cover and may not have as part of their thinking. When negotiating, class matters. How comfortable are you with the idea of issues around economic class and using them in your life? For example:

- Language use can be different for people in poverty, middle class, and wealth. This applies to the five registers, discourse patterns, story structures, and vocabulary. Can you think of a time when casual register was used during a negotiation? How did that work for the people involved?

- The environments we live in and the hidden rules we use to navigate are different and will affect the way that we negotiate. How does the hidden rule on power influence negotiations? What happens when someone feels disrespected?

- The resources we have or don't have will have an impact on negotiations too. The unstable environment of poverty that leads to the tyranny of the moment will affect negotiations. What does it do to someone's bargaining position if he or she is in the tyranny of the moment? How balanced is a negotiation going to be if one person has lots of resources (financial, emotional, social, physical, etc.) and the other person doesn't?

- The fact that most institutions and businesses operate on middle-class rules and norms matters too. How do negotiations work when one of the two negotiators had normalized the middle-class mindset and didn't know that the other person had experienced life in significantly different ways?

Intentions matter: John Barkai, in his paper "The Savvy Samurai Meets the Devil" (1996, p. 706), says that when negotiating we sometimes must change our perspective. Some people go into a negotiation thinking that on one side of the table is the devil backed up by two more devils while on the other side of the table is an angel backed up by two more angels: good against evil, right against wrong. To negotiate we must change our perspective to see that there is merit on both sides. Barkai is referring to more formal negotiations, such as those engaged in by attorneys and mediators, but many of these principles apply to everyday situations as well.

Feelings matter: We all know that we shouldn't drive under the influence of alcohol; we don't want a DUI. According to Barkai, negotiating under the influence (NUI) of strong feelings isn't a good idea either. When we're angry, hurt, or disgusted we're much less likely to keep listening. We might go into the parent or the child voice. We're also less likely to ask questions to discover the other person's point of view and more likely to pound away on our own points. We'll *want* a win-lose solution. Here are some things to know about emotions when negotiating:

- There will be both positive and negative feelings during negotiations.

- Expect to hear things that you may not like; determine before entering into a negotiation that you won't take them personally.

- Negative feelings reduce our capacity to think, learn, and remember; we can't afford to get stuck in negative feelings.

- Don't allow your feelings to be hijacked. Sometimes all it takes is a word or phrase; sometimes it's the tone of voice or a gesture—and our feelings take over.

- Try to stay in the adult voice. Find the calm spot by detaching, by being objective:

"How important is this issue to me?" Not every issue is a big one. Pick your battles.

- Recognize your feelings as you go into a negotiation and during the negotiation, then name them to yourself: "I'm beginning to feel tense, annoyed, angry, etc."

- Naming your feelings means that you are taking responsibility for them. Owning them means you can choose what to do with feelings.

- Find a way to briefly express your feelings—usually not to the other party—if that will help you return to the process of effective negotiation. Make a plan for dealing with strong feelings; ask for a break so you can walk or call someone.

- Look for the positive feelings; good things happen too, leading to good solutions.

- Appreciate the other side's point of view, finding value in their ideas.

- Remember, win-lose solutions, even the ones that go your way, can be expected to have an effect on your relationships into the future.

- Make personal connections with the other side; sometimes going through hard times, including conflicts, can lead to strong friendships.

 IX. C. Discussion

1. With whom do you find it hardest to negotiate? Your ex-husband or ex-wife? Your children? Sister or brother? Boss? Probation officer? Associates at work? In your role at work? How do you account for the differences?

2. How good are you at handling your emotions? Share with others what works for you.

Listening matters: Many experts in negotiation say that listening is *the* most important skill. If you aren't open to the merits of the other side's point of view, if you enter into negotiations with the intention of coming to a win-lose, and if you get emotionally hijacked, it isn't likely that you'll be able to catch the opportunity for a negotiated solution. Here are some things to know about listening:

- If you're primarily thinking about what you're going to say next, you aren't listening.

- If you ask questions skillfully, you might find out very important information about the other side's point of view and values.

- Barkai, a lawyer who knows the reputation that lawyers have for talking, reminds us of the old saying, "You were born with two ears and one mouth, and that is the proportion in which you should use them" (1996, p. 21).

- Emotional blocks (see "Feelings matter") can keep us from listening.

- When we really listen we can rephrase in our own words what the speaker just said to his or her satisfaction.

- When we are actively listening we can encourage others to elaborate, explain, and clarify their points fully.

- Active listening means leaning forward, making eye contact, and having an open mind to learning. It *doesn't* mean frequently interrupting, though occasionally a question can be asked "midstream" for clarification.

- How to negotiate by asking questions:

  - Prepare some of your questions before-hand.

  - Can you tell me about that _____? (This is called an open-ended question. It encourages a person to expand on his or her thoughts. A closed question gets a one-word answer: yes or no.)

  - What do you mean by that? (This is a follow-up question. Use it when you aren't sure you understand.)

  - Can you put that in other words? Could you state it another way? (These are clarifying questions. They can help you understand the answer more fully.)

  - How do you feel about that? (Questions about feelings are appropriate in some settings and not in others. Especially with family and friends, it's important to know how people feel.)

  - *What, where, when,* and *how* are good questions.

  - Asking *why* usually isn't a good question; it sounds like a challenge and tends to make people defensive.

IX. D. Discussion

1. Thinking back to the Ugli orange negotiation, how hard was it to listen to the other person? Did the other person listen carefully to you?

2. What questions did you ask? What questions did the other person ask?

3. How might listening more carefully and asking more questions have helped the negotiation?

Information matters: Information is power. Think about the predators whom we investigated earlier. Individuals selling mortgages have a lot more information about the products, processes, fees, and interest rates than a customer ever will. Selling mortgages is something they do every day, all day. They take classes to learn more about the business. They see hundreds of customers in a year and can categorize and name the "types" of homebuyers within minutes of their coming through the door. They know which tricks to use on a customer to sweeten the deal for themselves. Most people buying a house go through the process only a few times in their lives. So who has the power in this situation?

- When negotiating, the person with the best information about the issue has most of the power.

- Do your homework, know the facts.

- Get help from experts.

- The information the other side has is important to you and can be discovered by asking questions.

IX. E. Discussion

1. Thinking back to the Ugli orange negotiation ... Who had the best information—you or the other side?

2. Thinking back to the last dispute you had with a family member, business, or employer, who had the best information?

3. Thinking ahead to the next time you negotiate a pay increase at your place of work, what information do you think you would need to have in order to be successful?

Communicating matters: Negotiating is all about communicating, but communicating is about more than words. A study by Albert Mehrabian of UCLA on ways people communicate found that there's much more to sending and receiving information than just the words that are used, especially when emotional content is important. In that context his findings show that when communicating, words count for 7%, the tone of voice 38%, and body language 55%. Style, expression, tone of voice, facial expression, and body language convey a great deal of the meaning (Mehrabian, 1981, pp. 43–44). How does this information fit with what we've covered in *Investigations*? Consider these points:

- In this module we've learned that when using the casual register we rely heavily on nonverbal (tone of voice and body language) communication.

- Casual register is a very powerful register for this reason.

- The "voices" we use can come from our internal parent, child, or adult. People will react to us depending on the voice we use.

- Feelings are expressed through our choice of words, tone of voice, and body language. If we can't manage our feelings in a healthy or skillful way, we'll have trouble communicating and negotiating.

- Our mindsets or mental models about different topics change the way we communicate. If individuals think that poverty is caused only by the choices of the poor, their mindsets will become apparent through their words, tone of voice, and body language.

- Knowing all of this can help us negotiate more skillfully—whether are home, in the neighborhood, at work, or at college … in short, wherever we are.

IX. F. Activity: Self-Assessment of Negotiating Skills

Time: 10 minutes

Materials: Self-assessment chart on next page

Procedure: In the following table rank yourself by drawing a circle around the number that applies to you on the 1–5 scale.

> 1 = Don't understand the concept/don't have the skill
>
> 2 = Need a lot of work to understand it/to use it
>
> 3 = Getting the idea/starting to use the idea
>
> 4 = Understand the idea/can use it when I think about it
>
> 5 = Got it/can do it automatically with very little thought

Self-Assessment of Negotiating Skills

Concept	Understand Concepts					Ability to Use Concepts				
Hidden rules of economic class	1	2	3	4	5	1	2	3	4	5
Identifying intentions	1	2	3	4	5	1	2	3	4	5
Managing feelings/ emotions	1	2	3	4	5	1	2	3	4	5
Skillful listening and questioning	1	2	3	4	5	1	2	3	4	5
Gathering important information	1	2	3	4	5	1	2	3	4	5
Verbal and nonverbal communication	1	2	3	4	5	1	2	3	4	5

 IX. G. Discussion

1. What negotiations are going on right now in your life?

2. Where are your negotiating strengths?

3. Where are your negotiating weaknesses?

Conclusion

This module touched on many ideas and fields of study; think of it as a crash course in language and communication *through the lens of economic class*. Language is a resource that you can use to build other resources; it is central, for example, to building relationships across class and race lines. Reflecting on everything covered here, where are your strengths? Are you bilingual, meaning *Are you able to use both casual register and formal register skillfully?* Can you express yourself well both orally and in writing? Are you good at resolving conflicts and negotiating? Are there areas within this module that you want to strengthen? In the plans you make at the end of *Investigations,* you may choose to pursue some of the ideas we addressed here.

Journal Reflections

Write about your experience with language as a child—and now as a student.

Readings

"Becoming Adept at Code-Switching" by Rebecca S. Wheeler. Code-switching was introduced in this module; learn more about it here.

Class: A Guide Through the American Status System by Paul Fussell. Of special note is the chapter titled "Speak, That I May See Thee" found on pages 151–169.

Convicted in the Womb by Carl Upchurch. See pages 15–20 on early school experience and pages 81–95 on being introduced to the beauty of language.

Getting to YES: Negotiating Agreement Without Giving In by Roger Fisher and William Ury. Popular book on negotiation skills.

Ghettonation: A Journey into the Land of Bling and the Home of the Shameless by Cora Daniels. In Chapter 1, "Livin' Large," pages 23–44, Daniels claims that it is not only poor ethnic groups that have been brainwashed by the glitz and glam of the ghetto lifestyle but the nation at large. She uses examples of how this bling-infested hysteria has altered our speech, dress, and mindset but, more importantly, our standards.

Meaningful Differences in the Everyday Experience of Young American Children by Betty Hart and Todd R. Risley. A study about how children learn to talk and the dramatic differences in language development by economic class.

"Teaching Negotiation ADR: The Savvy Samurai Meets the Devil" by John Barkai. The Ugli orange exercise and more.

Unequal Childhoods: Class, Race, and Family Life by Annette Lareau. See Chapter 6, "Developing a Child: Alexander Williams," found on pages 108–133. See also Chapter 7, "Language as a Conduit for Social Life: Harold McAllister," found on pages 134–160.

MODULE 7
Eleven Resources

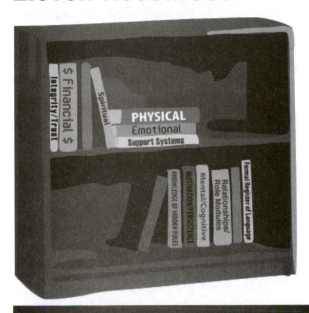

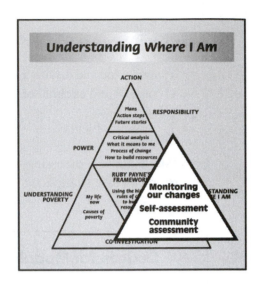

Understanding Where I Am

Learning Objectives

WHAT'S COVERED

You will:

Define poverty

Define the resources

Create your own Social Capital mental model

Use case studies to practice doing assessments of resources

Explore ways to use this information

WHY IT'S IMPORTANT

Resources are important because it is by building our resources that we can have economic security.

If we want a rich life in all areas, we need to build all resources.

Investigating our resources leads naturally to ideas for improving our life.

HOW IT'S CONNECTED TO YOU

Defining poverty as the extent to which an individual does without resources gives us something to do about it.

One way to accelerate the development of our resources and to build a well-rounded life is to develop bridging social capital.

The resources describe all areas of our life. When we're good at analyzing resources, we'll be ready to do a self-assessment of our own resources, then begin making our plans.

Learning Process

- You will read and discuss information about 11 internal and external resources.

- You'll create a mental model of your social capital.

- You'll practice assessing the resources of people in case studies.

Lexicon for Module 7

Auditory
Bonding social capital
Bridging social capital
Emotional intelligence
Financial literacy
Kinesthetic
Learned helplessness
Persistence
Poverty definition
Resources

I. Defining Poverty

The Federal Poverty Guidelines are most commonly used to define poverty in the United States (see Module 4). It is an income guideline that determines if someone is eligible for services or not. It was developed in the 1960s and was based on the percentage of income used for food. Minor adjustments have been made in the formula since then, but it doesn't take into account the things that cost the most today: housing, healthcare, and transportation. In 2009 a family of four living on less than $21,200 was considered to be in poverty. There are two failings of this defini-tion: (1) It undercounts poverty in the U.S. and (2) it is set so low that someone making considerably more than the guideline is still in poverty. So achieving an income of $21,200 would still leave a family in a very unstable and vulnerable financial situation.

The Organisation for Economic Cooperation and Development (OECD) is made up of 30 nations (including the U.S.) that subscribe to democracy and the free market. *The OECD defines poverty as those with incomes 50% below the median income of the country.*

In the U.S. the estimated four-person family median income from October 1, 2008, to September 30, 2009, was $70,354—50% of which would be $35,172 ("Estimated State Median Income," 2008).

Ruby K. Payne (1996) defines poverty as the degree to which a person or family does without resources—the 11 resources that we will be exploring in this module. The preceding definition gives the individual and community something to do about poverty: Build resources!

Given the investigations into the environments of poverty, middle class, and wealth—and knowing the importance of stability in family life—we could define the three economic classes this way:

- We are in poverty when our environment (our homes, neighborhoods, community) is so unstable that we're afraid for today. Not only is tomorrow not covered, we aren't even sure about today.

- We are in middle class when our environment is stable enough that we have today covered, but we're afraid for tomorrow.

- We are in wealth when our environment is stable enough that we have both today and tomorrow covered. However, we're afraid for our safety and that we'll lose our assets—and perhaps even the connections that have come along with the lifestyle.

Our experiences, of course, don't fall neatly into three perfect circles; they stretch across a continuum from instability to stability. In Module 1 you created the mental model of "My Life Now" that allowed you to define your own experience and environment along that continuum. This understanding of poverty allows us to build resources no matter where we are on the continuum.

II. Defining Resources

The 11 resources we have identified are financial, emotional, mental/cognitive, formal register of language, support systems, physical, spiritual, integrity/trust, motivation/persistence, relationships/role models, and knowledge of hidden rules. To be sure, money is an important resource. When people don't have enough money to meet their basic needs, they are in poverty. But money is only one of the resources. Being in poverty over generations can wear down other resources. The more resources a person has in all areas, the easier it is to make changes and to live well. In short, the resources are interconnected. By that we mean having high levels of some or many of the resources makes it easier to build the rest.

Eleven Resources

Financial	Having enough income to purchase goods and services and to save or invest money. Having an educated understanding of how money works—being financially literate.
Emotional	Being able to choose and control emotional responses, particularly to negative situations without engaging in self-destructive behavior. This is the "state of mind" that determines the way we think, feel, and behave at any given moment. This is a resource that shows itself through stamina, perseverance, and choice. This is about interpersonal skills like teamwork, teaching others, leadership, negotiation, and working with people from many backgrounds.
Mental/Cognitive	Having the mental ability and acquired skills (reading, writing, computing) to deal with daily life. This includes how much education and training individuals have in order to compete in the workplace for well-paying jobs or run their own business.
Formal Register of Language	Having the vocabulary, language ability, and negotiation skills to succeed in work and/or school environments.
Support Systems	Having friends, family, and backup resources available to access in times of need.
Physical	Having physical health and mobility.

Spiritual	Believing in divine purpose and guidance and/or having a rich cultural connection that offers support and guidance.
Integrity/Trust	Trust is linked to two issues: predictability and safety. Can I know with some certainty that this person will do what he or she says? Can I predict with some accuracy that it will occur nearly every time? The second part of the question is safety: Will I be safe with this person?
Motivation/Persistence	Having the energy and drive to prepare for, plan, and complete projects, jobs, and personal changes.
Relationships/Role Models	Having frequent access to adults who are appropriate, who are nurturing, and who don't engage in self-destructive behavior.
Knowledge of Hidden Rules	Knowing the unspoken cues and habits of poverty, middle class, and wealth.

A key goal of this workbook is to help you build resources, thereby becoming both successful in college and economically stable by improving all areas of your life. Building a solid balance of resources will free you from the tyranny of the moment.

These resources cover every aspect of life, and every one of them is important. This workbook will only scratch the surface of what there is to know about each resource because our purpose is to examine our whole situation, not just one resource or another. At the end of the workbook you will be invited to make plans for the resources you want to build up. Right now it's important to know that there are guidebooks and self-help books for almost every resource. It would be good to start thinking now about which resources you might want to build up.

III. Additional Information on Five Key Resources

Module 5 provided additional data regarding hidden rules, and Module 6 addressed language

issues in greater detail. Now we are going to investigate five other key resources.

1. Financial Resources

There are a number of workbooks and books about what is called "financial literacy." Another way of saying this is: Everyone needs to know how to play the money game. In the money game there are no fans in the bleachers and no cheerleaders; everyone is a player. The only question is: How well can you play? And, can you play it well at every stage of your life? What we needed to know coming out of high school was different from what we need to know when starting college, buying a house, planning to have children, or when preparing for retirement. Most schools don't teach this important information, and yet it's crucial to the economic security of each of us. That leaves the teaching about money to our parents who may or may not be very good at the game themselves—or we learn it ourselves. In Module 2 you did the calculations for three important measures of your financial resources (percentage of income that goes to housing, savings cushion, and debt-to-income ratio).

2. Emotional Resources

Our emotional resources help determine how successful we'll be with this workbook and this class, so we want to look at some key concepts that can help us right away.

Addiction, abuse, and other dangerous situations can create in us reactions and patterns of behavior that work against us. They can create thoughts, feelings, and behaviors that are weak. Learned helplessness is a behavior noticed among people who feel that their problems are permanent, pervasive, and personal (Seligman, 2002). A student feeling that way might say (or think): "I'll never pass, I mess up everything, I'm so stupid." Such individuals might feel sorry for themselves, useless, ashamed, angry, or self-destructive. They might blame others, whine, waste time, manipulate others, give up, hurt themselves, or hurt others. If this describes you more than you might like to admit, it will be hard to complete your plans and take the action steps necessary to get out of the trap of poverty.

In "Empowerment: A Course in Personal Empowerment" the writers say:

> The single most important skill of the Empowerment Skills Training is the ability to *regulate* what you think and feel inside yourself—meaning that you decide the content, nature, and intensity of what you think, feel, and do.

> Regulating what you think and feel inside yourself does *not* mean, "suppressing," "keeping the lid on," "putting up with it," "ignoring it," or "holding it in."

> To regulate feelings means to adjust the degree, intensity, and meaning of internal experiences. It works like an internal thermostat that keeps the temperature inside where you want it, regardless of the temperature outside.

Note. From *Empowerment: A Course in Personal Empowerment* (p. 25), by Twin Cities RISE!, 2009, Minneapolis, MN: Twin Cities RISE! Copyright 2009 by Twin Cities RISE!

For one man in a Getting Ahead group, it was his older brother who taught him how to regulate his own emotions. The following story illustrates that it's not so much what happens to us in life, it's how we respond to it that matters most, starting with our thoughts and attitudes. He said:

> For some reason, my older brother loved to beat me up. To get me mad, he would push my buttons. And believe me, he knew them all. I would explode and start swinging; then he could "defend" himself and happily twist me into knots. One day, in a rare moment of kindness [and candor], he said, "Why do you let me do that to you? You know I love to piss you off so I can beat you up. Why do you fall for it every time?" At that moment I realized that the control for what happened was in me, not in him. I had always said, "He makes me lose my temper. He made me do it." From that day forward my thinking changed. I never gave that power to someone else again, including my brother. The power over my thinking and feeling is in me.

Another way to look at emotional resources is to assess "emotional intelligence." Daniel Goleman (1995) first wrote about this and describes emotionally intelligent people as being very aware of their own feelings—and when they feel bad, they're usually able to reframe the situation to feel more positive. Because they can identify and manage their feelings, they also can rein in their impulses, stay focused, and control their actions. Emotionally intelligent people can relate to other people's emotions, and they can manage the emotions that come up in relationships in a positive way so that the relationships are healthy. It's interesting that one doesn't have to be educated academically to have high levels of emotional intelligence.

3. Mental/Cognitive Resources

Your mental resources aren't just about *what* you know, it's also about (1) *how* you learn and (2) how well you *use* what you learn. Learning to learn begins with understanding how your brain processes information. There are three major types of learning styles:

Visual: You learn best by watching someone else do it or looking at pictures. You write things down and look at pictures, colors, shapes, and books.

Auditory: You learn best by hearing the instructions. You talk and discuss, ask questions, connect sound patterns, and remember rhymes and songs.

Kinesthetic: You learn best by doing it, and the more active the task, the easier it is to learn. You have energy, move around a lot, use your hands to "talk." You can fix, build, and take things apart.

Visual and auditory learning is most common, and since people tend to teach the same way they learn, many teachers use visual and auditory teaching methods, leaving the kinesthetic learners behind. Plus, in school, you usually are supposed to sit quietly, which is not an effective strategy for kinesthetic learners.

There are many self-assessment tools that identify personal learning styles, along with study strategies that work best for the different styles (try *www.collegeforadults.org*). While it makes sense to play to your strengths when you're studying the subjects that are hardest for you to learn, you also might think about trying different strategies. For example, try auditory learning strategies if you're a visual or kinesthetic learner. This will actually increase your mental resource and your physical capacity to learn by building new thinking pathways and memory systems in your brain.

4. Support Systems

In *Bowling Alone* (2000) Robert Putnam describes social capital (or support systems) as something that is just as important as financial capital. He is talking about our connections with others, our networks, the things we do for each other with the trust and knowledge that they would do the same for us. Well-connected people feel a mutual obligation to help others; they have "favor banks." One man said, "It's like the golden rule. I'll do this for you now knowing that, down the road, you will return the favor."

Individuals have social capital, and so do communities. While individuals have a lot of connections with other individuals, their communities have a lot of clubs and organizations like bowling leagues, service groups, unions, religious organizations, and so on.

There are two important types of social capital: bonding and bridging. Bonding social capital is what we have with our tightest friends. It's exclusive, keeping others out. It's about belonging and identity. Others in our bonded group have many of the same resources and connections that we do. Some examples of bonding capital are ethnic fraternal organizations, church-based reading groups, and country clubs. Some bonding groups are harmful, such as gangs, the Ku Klux Klan, or certain neighborhood groups that form to keep other people out, those who have the NIMBY (not in my back yard) attitude.

Bridging social capital is what we have with people outside our usual circle; it is inclusive of people from different backgrounds. Examples of bridging capital are civil rights movements, youth service clubs, the chamber of commerce, United Way, and so on. When you have bridg-

ing capital, you may not have close friendships, but you do have many acquaintances and connections.

Putnam cites Xavier de Souza Briggs who says bonding capital is good for getting by, while bridging capital is good for getting ahead. By this he means that our bonding-capital friends will have the same contacts and knowledge of job opportunities as we have. But someone outside our normal circle will have a number of contacts that we don't have and might be able to give us good leads for jobs or other resources.

"By the end of the twentieth century the gap between the rich and poor in the United States had been increasing for nearly three decades, the longest sustained increase in inequality in at least a century, coupled with the first sustained decline in social capital in at least that long."

—Robert Putnam, *Bowling Alone*

III. A. Activity: Mental Model of Personal Social Capital

Time: 10 minutes

Materials: Paper and pencil

Procedure: Use a full sheet of paper to create a mental model. Draw a small circle inside a larger circle. The center of the circles represents you.

1. Thinking of the circles as a pie, draw eight pieces of pie and write the following labels around the outside of the larger circle: Household, Other Family, Friends, Work, Religious/Spiritual, Schools, Clubs, and Agencies.

2. In each section of the pie, put the initials of the people who are in your life. Those with bonding relationships will be in the inner circle, while those with bridging capital will go in the outside circle.

Social Capital Mental Model

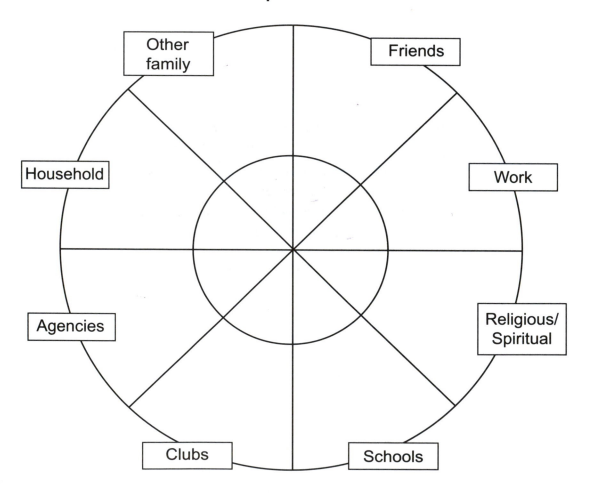

Investigate This!

The Circles™ Campaign uses bridging social capital to help under-resourced college students and others make the transition to economic stability. Allies from the middle class and upper middle class who are familiar with the concepts in this workbook join with students to overcome barriers that can interfere with earning a degree. How does the Circles Campaign work? Is there a Circles initiative on campus? If not, which campuses do have a Circles initiative? What would it take to start a Circles initiative on your campus?

Start the investigation by going to *www.movethemountain.org*.

III. B. Discussion

1. How many people did you name as bonding capital? Who are they, and why did you name them? How many people did you name as bridging capital? Who are they, and why did you name them?

2. What are the positive things you see in your relationships when you look at this mental model?

3. What are the negative things you see in your relationships?

4. If you decided to make a change in the future, how might this information help you?

5. How does this pattern today impact what you see in your future?

6. How might you strengthen your social support system?

7. Bonding social capital may be more important to people in poverty because of the value placed on relationships. Bridging social capital may be more valuable to people in wealth because of the value placed on connections. How does the social capital of different groups support or maintain their economic status?

8. How might students benefit from a Circles™ initiative on campus or in the community?

Journal Reflections

Write or draw your thoughts and ideas about your own bonding and bridging capital.

"Never mistake knowledge for wisdom. One helps you make a living; the other helps you make a life."

—Sandra Carey

5. Motivation/Persistence

Motivation and persistence are internal resources that an individual can make choices about; they are resources over which individuals have control. Here are some things we know about motivation, persistence, and change.

Change is always going to happen. Some changes we have no control over. Some we do. Change is not always easy. It takes wisdom, courage, and motivation to change. Let's investigate motivation by reviewing the work of William Miller and Stephen Rollnick, who wrote *Motivational Interviewing* (2002), and Steve Andreas and Charles Faulkner, who edited *NLP: The New Technology of Achievement* (1994). NOTE: NLP stands for neurolinguistic programming.

Wisdom and values: We need wisdom to know what we should and can change. And to figure out what we should change we need to understand our values.

Values describe what life means to us, what is important to us. They influence our motivation. We move toward the things that we value and away from things we don't. For example, if a woman values money highly, she will make decisions and take action toward things that make money. She will be motivated to make money or find ways to have money. If a woman dreams of and values a certain house in a certain neighborhood, she will make choices and take steps to get that house. She is motivated to get that particular house. If a woman values relationships highly, she will make choices and do things that maintain and enhance those relationships. She will be motivated by the importance to her of those relationships.

Some people become disconnected from their values. When that happens, they lose their motivation and end up sitting in front of the TV for hours, flipping through the channels. It's as if they've lost their purpose for living.

Miller and Rollnick (2002) describe motivation as being "willing, able, and ready."

Willing: When we first think about changing something, we tend to put the idea on a scale (consciously or unconsciously). On one side of the scale is what we have now, and on the other is what we could have—or what we want, what we value. For us to be *willing* to change, the scale has to be tipped toward the "what we want" side, toward the future. The scale tips back and forth while we figure out if the change is going to be worth all the effort it will take. Sometimes the change we want might be in conflict with other things we value. For example, we have already learned that to *achieve* we might have to give up some relationships, at least for a time. So ... if we want to go back to school (because we value education and because it's a means to a better job and more security for ourselves and our family), the scale may tip back and forth between going to school and our desire to be with our old friends.

The key to being willing is the size of the gap between what we have now and what we might have—the difference between what is and what could be. The bigger the difference, the more willing we tend to be to change.

Able: To be *able* to change, we must know the steps—and have the strength and/or skill and the resources to take action. But beyond that, we must imagine ourselves moving ahead and feel confident enough that we can do what it takes. We have to think positively and be persistent. When we want to change (when we're willing) but then aren't able—can't see a way to do it, or live in a community with very few opportunities and supports—we often shift back into thinking that we're fated, soon slipping again into living for the moment and thus losing our motivation.

Ready: To be *ready,* we have to move beyond the "I'll do it tomorrow" and the "yes, but" phase. This requires that we overcome our fear of failure *and* our fear of success and push through toward what we want.

Andreas and Faulkner (1994) say that motivation is a relatively simple mental strategy that we can learn to use ourselves. They point out that we are always motivated for something. In fact, sometimes we are *too* motivated. Some of us are too motivated for chocolate, sex, cigarettes, and so on. In that case, we have to learn some anti-motivation strategies, which includes self-control and impulse control.

But what happens when we see that big gap between what we have now and what we could have? What happens when the things we value seem out of reach? What do we need to do to get motivated?

Andreas and Faulkner also say there are two basic thinking strategies about motivation. Those who "move toward" what they want and those who "move away from" what they don't want.

Characteristics of "moving toward" thinkers
- Jump out of bed in the morning, ready to go!
- Plan ahead for things they want to do, such as meet friends, go fishing, etc.

- Pick friends who keep them going, who interest them
- Take advantage of opportunities when they arise

Pros of being "moving toward" thinkers
- Goal-oriented
- Get things done
- Get the jobs because they match what most employers are looking for

Cons of being "moving toward" thinkers
- Don't think through the problems carefully enough
- Rush into things, putting the "pedal to the metal"
- Have to learn things the hard way

Characteristics of "moving away from" thinkers
- Lie in bed until the threats of what will happen become too great
- Wait to change things until it gets really uncomfortable
- Pick friends who don't bother them
- Wait to change jobs until they just can't stand their job another minute

Pros of being "away from" thinkers
- Careful about getting into things
- Remember the bad times to stay motivated
- Good at identifying and fixing problems

Cons of being "away from" thinkers
- Afraid to try things
- Get fixated on problems

- When the pain and pressure to change are off, so is the motivation
- Motivation comes and goes with the threats
- Less attention is given to where they'll end up when they're looking back at the problem instead of looking ahead
- Much higher stress levels and risk of health problems

It's best if you learn to use both motivational strategies, with an emphasis on the "moving toward" strategy. You can do this by monitoring your motivational strategies and practicing new ways of thinking and acting.

Focus and persistence: Staying focused means you control your thinking, while being persistent means you control what you do. When you start hearing yourself think that your books or your teachers are boring or stupid, that you could be doing something more fun than being in school, or that maybe you'll take some time off and come back later, you've lost focus. If you combine that with negative emotions like "I'm not that smart and will never pass this anyway" you have the makings of a dropout. But if you persist in your actions, if you keep going to class and reading and turning in assignments, you still have a chance. Someone once said 90% of success is simply showing up.

Courage: The Serenity Prayer, attributed to Reinhold Niebuhr, has something to say about motivation:

> *"God, grant me the serenity to accept the things I cannot change, the courage to change the things I can, and the wisdom to know the difference."*

This can apply as much to what we are doing about poverty as it does to recovery from addiction.

When we think about change and motivation, we have to consider what we'll do with our own life, as well as what we'll do about poverty in our community. What can we change about ourselves? What can we change about our community? When we've answered these questions, we'll know what it will take in the way of courage to move toward prosperity. By the way, the prosperity we're talking about here isn't just financial, it's an overall sense of well-being, success, contentment, and (yes) happiness.

You know you're motivated when *you* are the one making the argument for change and not someone else.

III. C. Discussion

1. How does poverty impact what a person values?

2. What are some things that cause people to lose their motivation?

3. How will you know when you are willing to change?

4. What might help you feel confident about moving toward economic stability?

5. How will you know when you are ready for change?

6. Which motivational strategy do you tend to use the most?

7. What would it be like for you if you used the "moving toward" strategy more often?

Journal Reflections

Write or draw your thoughts and ideas about motivation and change.

III. D. Activity: Case Studies

Case studies give you a chance to practice analyzing a person's resources. Soon you'll do a self-assessment of your own resources.

Time: 30–90 minutes

Materials: Case studies provided by facilitator

Procedure:

1. Do one case study at a time.

2. Read and score each case study using the upcoming three-page table. You will notice that for each resource there are five levels: (1) = Urgent/Crisis, (2) = Vulnerable/High-Risk, (3) = Stable, (4) = Safe/Secure, (5) = Thriving/ Giving Back. Read the five descriptions of each resource and decide which description best matches the information in the two case studies.

3. Share your scores with others and discuss how you came to your decision. It is important that each person gets good at "tight thinking." One of the best ways is to hear what others think, so you can sort out and explain your own ideas. It's OK to build on the ideas of others. Try to be specific.

4. In each of the two case studies, look for the person's strong and weak resources. It's the strong resources that he or she will use to build the other resources.

Case Study—Carl

Carl's memories of his early family life are of an abusive and disturbed father who heard voices and had mental health problems that became progressively worse over time. His father taught his children to steal from malls. He also beat his wife and children. Carl's mother couldn't handle the beatings anymore and, taking her three children, left his father.

Carl's family moved frequently and went from having lots of toys and material things to being hungry and not having enough clothes. Every time they settled into a new place to live, his father would find them, and they would have to move again. They lived in dumpy apartments, shelters, and with family members and strangers. During this time Carl learned to protect himself from being hurt by building walls and isolating himself from others.

Carl has a vivid memory of his mother standing in front of a gas station looking at the children, trying to smile, but with tears rolling down her face as she told them they were going to live with a different family.

Carl and his siblings were taken from his mother and put into a foster home. The first foster placement was for three years, but then the children were split up. The second foster parents were Christians who went to church every Sunday and Wednesday and enrolled Carl in a Christian school. That was a good experience for him—

both for the religious foundation and academically. He was a good student and made good grades. The family lived on a farm where he was given chores.

His mother brought the family together again only to continue the life of moving from neighborhood to neighborhood with a series of men. She was heavily involved in drug use. As the oldest child, he protected his brother and sister as best he could.

When Carl was in high school he skipped school frequently and began experimenting with alcohol, drugs, and sex. He went to parties and was in lots of fights. He dropped out of school his senior year.

He moved from place to place, job to job, and girlfriend to girlfriend. Carl found it easy to find work and always learned the work quickly. If he had stayed at any of the jobs, he could have worked his way up quickly. But he was heavily into drugs, which took a toll financially and physically.

Toward the end of his drug use Carl was homeless and described himself as spiritually bankrupt. He had developed a terrible reputation and all kinds of enemies. At the time he went into treatment for drug addiction, his nose, cheekbone, eye socket, and hand were all broken. Carl said he had hit bottom. His recovery began with a renewal of his spiritual life.

He now has two part-time, low-wage jobs. His money goes to paying child support and rent, leaving very little for keeping his car running and food. He is basically healthy but doesn't have health insurance. His social life is centered around 12-step meetings and reconnecting with his family. He enjoys helping people with fix-it projects, moving, and giving them rides. He wants to get a GED, but is busy with his two jobs, along with helping family and friends. His mother is very ill and still using drugs; his brothers always need money. They are not supportive of his efforts to stay clean and sober.

Despite his conflicting feelings about his mother and the hard times they have lived through, Carl remembers some good times too. They would go for walks and to the park. He finds himself laughing over the silliest things they did. Carl has deep bonds with his brothers and maintains a relationship with them. He has learned to turn hard experiences into strengths; he has the ability to survive and find the humor in things. He is generally self-assured and able to make friends easily.

Case Study—Sandy

Sandy is the product of a one-night stand. Her father was Vietnam veteran and, for a short time, a member of the Black Panthers. Her mother was a white girl from Tennessee. He was married at the time of their encounter and went on to marry two other women. She was married twice; they both had several children from each of their marriages.

They were living in a small town in Indiana when, at the age of 8, Sandy's father took her to California, telling her that her mother was in jail for welfare fraud. Her father spent most of his time living with girlfriends and using drugs. He became addicted to cocaine and would leave her alone in motel rooms or with strangers for long periods of time. Before her mother was able to find her, Sandy experienced homelessness, spent her ninth Christmas living in a car, learned how to fend for herself, and got herself to school using the bus and rail system in San Francisco.

Sandy's mother also had a hard childhood. When she was 12 she was raising her 6-year-old sister and 14-year-old brother who had mental health prob-

lems. She didn't get along with Sandy's father or his family and had to fight to keep Sandy. After she got Sandy back from California, they lived in Chicago where she worked long hours and left Sandy to her own devices. Sandy joined a gang where she found love, support and acceptance. But gang life was a struggle, with frequent fights with members of other gangs; Sandy was hungry most nights and in almost constant pain from fighting. Soon she became pregnant.

Six months into her pregnancy Sandy was jumped by another gang and was spared from being killed by a girl who told the would-be shooter that the baby didn't deserve to die. That crisis led to them returning to Indiana. Sandy promised to go back to school and stay out of trouble. However, she dropped out of school and got involved in abusive relationships. When she was 17 she had an apartment and was the target of every hustler and drug dealer around. She was abused physically, sexually, and mentally on a daily basis. She had five children who were forced on her by men who wanted to keep her in a relationship. She

survived by doing what others did to her: exploiting and terrorizing others.

Eventually Sandy realized that she was starting to do to her children what had been done to her. She worked a series of low-wage jobs and went to school at the same time. She did well in school, getting a GED and going on to a community college. Her children have excelled at school; all five are on the honor roll. She figured that she had role models of "what not to do" and determined that it was more important to be a role model than to have one. It was having children that made her realize that she had to manage her emotions in a less destructive way.

Sandy's relationships with men have settled down considerably. There is no violence, but her life is complicated by relationships that have led to lost jobs, indebtedness, and moves to new apartments. She has borrowed money from payday lenders four times and now must pay them first on payday, leaving little money for necessities.

Sandy is now working 30 hours a week at a "big box" store; there are relatively few companies that pay good wages in her community, and she feels fortunate to have the job she does. At work she has always caught the eye of supervisors and has moved up quickly. Sandy thinks that being biracial has helped her learn to manage herself in different settings—both the 'hood and the workplace. She is quite verbal.

She uses food stamps and Medicaid. She has been diagnosed with diabetes and is trying to manage it with diet and exercise, but she is finding it difficult because of the crises that often interrupt her days and all the demands on her to manage her children, three of whom are now in high school. Her relationships with workers at local agencies generally are not good because she confronts those who don't treat her with respect as she is trying to improve her life.

Resources Scoring Table

	(1) Urgent/ Crisis	(2) Vulnerable/ High-Risk	(3) Stable	(4) Safe/ Secure	(5) Thriving/ Giving Back
Financial	Doesn't have enough income to purchase needed goods and services.	Has some, but not enough, income to purchase needed goods and services— and to save money.	Has enough income to purchase needed goods and services— and to have money saved for crisis.	Has enough income to purchase needed goods and services, to save for emergencies, and to invest for future.	Actively seeks to increase personal financial assets over time and help build community assets.
Emotional	Can't choose and control emotional responses. Often behaves in ways that are harmful to others or self.	Can sometimes choose and control emotional responses. Sometimes behaves in ways that are harmful to others or self.	Can almost always choose and control emotional responses. Almost never behaves in ways that are harmful to others or self.	Is good at choosing and controlling emotional responses. Engages in positive behaviors toward others.	Actively seeks to improve emotional health in self and others.
Mental/ Cognitive	Lacks ability, education, or skills to compete for well-paying jobs.	Has some ability, education, or skills to compete for well-paying jobs.	Has enough ability, education, or skills to compete for well-paying jobs.	Has plenty of ability, education, or skills to compete for well-paying jobs.	Actively seeks to improve on existing ability, education, or skills—and build mental resources in community.

	(1) Urgent/ Crisis	(2) Vulnerable/ High-Risk	(3) Stable	(4) Safe/ Secure	(5) Thriving/ Giving Back
Formal Register of Language	Lacks vocabulary, language ability, and negotiation skills needed for workplace settings.	Has some of vocabulary, language ability, and negotiation skills needed for workplace settings.	Has enough of vocabulary, language ability, and negotiation skills needed for workplace settings.	Has plenty of vocabulary, language ability, and negotiation skills needed for workplace settings.	Actively seeks to improve upon already strong vocabulary and language ability foundation—and works to develop language resources in community.
Support Systems	Lacks positive friends, family, and connections that can be accessed to improve resources.	Has some positive friends, family, and connections that can be accessed to improve resources.	Has enough positive friends, family, and connections that can be accessed to improve resources.	Has plenty of positive friends, family, and connections that can be accessed to improve resources.	Actively develops networks and social resources that can be accessed to improve personal and community resources.
Physical	Lacks physical health and mobility for workplace settings.	Has some physical health and mobility problems that could limit effectiveness in workplace.	Has physical health and mobility needed for workplace settings.	Consistently maintains physical health and mobility needed for self and others in workplace.	Actively develops physical resources for self, workplace, and community.
Spiritual	Lacks cultural connections or sense of spiritual purpose that offers support and guidance.	Has some cultural connections or sense of spiritual purpose that offers support and guidance.	Has sufficient cultural connections or sense of spiritual purpose that offers support and guidance.	Has plenty of cultural connections or sense of spiritual purpose that offers support and guidance.	Actively seeks cultural connections and/or spiritual growth.
Integrity/ Trust	Cannot be trusted to keep one's word, to accomplish tasks, and to obey laws even when under supervision.	Can sometimes be trusted to keep one's word, to accomplish tasks, and to obey laws when under supervision.	Can be trusted to keep one's word, to accomplish tasks, and to obey laws, without supervision.	Can invariably be trusted to keep one's word, to accomplish tasks, to obey laws, and to inspire others to do same.	Actively seeks to build integrity and trust—and sets high ethical standards at work and in community.

	(1) Urgent/ Crisis	(2) Vulnerable/ High-Risk	(3) Stable	(4) Safe/ Secure	(5) Thriving/ Giving Back
Motivation/ Persistence	Lacks energy or drive to prepare for, plan, and complete projects, jobs, and personal change.	Has some energy or drive to prepare for, plan, and complete projects, jobs, and personal change.	Has enough energy or drive to prepare for, plan, and complete projects, jobs, and personal change.	Has plenty of energy or drive to prepare for, plan, and complete projects, jobs, and personal change.	Actively seeks to maintain motivation and persistence— and to assist others in finding theirs.
Relationships/ Role Models	Lacks access to others who are safe, supportive, and nurturing.	Has limited access to others who are safe, supportive, and nurturing.	Has enough access to others who are safe, supportive, and nurturing.	Has plenty of access to others who are safe, supportive, and nurturing.	Actively seeks out others who are safe, supportive, and nurturing— and is safe, supportive, and nurturing of others.
Knowledge of Hidden Rules	Lacks knowledge of hidden rules of other economic classes.	Has some awareness of hidden rules of other economic classes but can't use them.	Knows rules of other economic classes and can use some of them in personal ways.	Knows rules of all three economic classes and can use most of them effectively in limited settings.	Actively seeks to understand rules of all three economic classes—and to use them effectively in variety of settings.

Note. Adapted from work of Jennifer Clay, Opportunities Industrialization Center of Clark County, Springfield, Ohio.

 ## III. E. Discussion

When the group has analyzed several case studies—enough to be able to do tight thinking about the resources—discuss these questions.

1. Which resources does poverty impact the most severely?

2. Which resources are the hardest to assess?

3. Which resources do you think are the most important in order to have a well-balanced life?

4. How are an individual's resources interconnected? What happens to other resources when someone has a sudden decline in health or loses a job?

5. As the group worked through the case studies, in what ways did the thinking about the resources get tighter?

Case Study—Dale (Resources in Action)

Dale is a 34-year-old man who was raised in poverty. He's still in poverty, but this story is about the beginning of his transition out. He's a high school dropout who has worked a series of jobs, the best one a manufacturing job in a mid-sized city in Ohio. He has moved frequently, living in a number of states with a number of different women. After a recent divorce, he returned to Ohio looking for work and is living with some friends. Dale wants custody of his daughter because his ex-wife has a serious mental health problem. The only way to get custody, though, is to establish a home. Dale's strongest resources are emotional, physical, and motivational. His weakest resources are financial, support systems, and knowledge of the hidden rules of middle class.

Dale applied at the manufacturing plant several times with no results before beginning Getting Ahead. He decided to try again, using what he had learned in the class about economic class.

He went to the plant to apply, this time not just dropping off the application and walking away, but staying to talk to the secretary taking the forms. He explained why he wanted the job (establish economic security, get custody of his daughter) and told the office worker that he had worked there before and knew how to do the work. He then asked about a man who had worked at the plant when he first worked there years earlier. It turned out that the man was now in management. The secretary made a call and arranged for Dale to see the manager right then.

When Dale went into the office he was fidgeting and stumbling over his language when he thought, *I've got to just go for it.* Again he explained himself, how he wanted to provide for his daughter, get and keep a good job, establish a home, and how he was at the point in his life where he knew he had to make a major change. The manager was impressed and told Dale he could have the job, but there was one thing he would have to do first. He would have to cut off his ponytail. The plant was under new management, and one of the rules that had changed was the one about ponytails. One man who had worked there for years quit his job rather than cut his hair. Dale recognized this as a conflict in hidden rules and chose to give up his ponytail for the job. The job pays a living wage and provides benefits. Dale moved to a small apartment near the plant so he could save money.

III. F. Discussion

1. What resources was Dale trying to build?

2. What resources did he use? How did he use them?

3. What hidden rules did he use? How did he use them?

4. How did Dale use mediation when talking with the manager?

5. How much did it matter that the manager had no idea about the hidden rules as they're taught here?

6. Which motivational strategy did Dale use?

7. What will Dale need to do to maintain his changes?

Journal Reflections

Write or draw your own thoughts about resources and finding a balance in life.

III. G. Activity: College Services

Time: 1 hour; may be outside class time

Materials: List of 11 resources, college handbook, student guide, phone directory, etc.

Procedure:

1. Working alone, in pairs, or in teams, list the departments, club programs, projects, etc., sponsored or supported by the college that are designed to help you build each resource.

2. Where does the college put most of its attention? Were there any surprises, good or bad?

3. How does this relate to hidden rules?

4. Assess your willingness, ability, and readiness to use these campus services.

5. Access one of these services. This might mean going to a student services department and requesting help with an issue, or it might mean attending a free art event or sports event. Stretch your comfort zone; do something you don't normally do.

Readings

The 7 Habits of Highly Effective People: Powerful Lessons in Personal Change by Stephen R. Covey. See the section titled "The Seven Habits—An Overview" found on pages 46–62.

An Angle of Vision: Women Writers on Their Poor and Working-Class Roots edited by Lorraine M. Lopez. From the back cover: "In a sense, these stories are the travel narratives of women who have journeyed beyond their family circumstances to cross class borders, aided by educational opportunities that encouraged their literary gifts to blossom."

Bowling Alone: The Collapse and Revival of American Community by Robert D. Putnam. About the importance of informal social capital. See in particular Chapter 17, "Education and Children's Welfare," found on pages 296–306, and Chapter 19, "Economic Prosperity," found on pages 319–325.

"College for Adults" by National College Transition Network (www.collegeforadults.org). Resource to discover your learning style.

Emotional Intelligence by Daniel Goleman. One of the popular books on managing emotions.

"Home" by WETA-TV (www.ldonline.org). Resources for students with disabilities.

The Illustrated World's Religions: A Guide to Our Wisdom Traditions by Huston Smith. A succinct description of spiritual and religious resources.

Outliers: The Story of Success by Malcolm Gladwell. Success is tied to when you were born, how many hours you practiced, and the community you came from—not just your personal attributes. Gladwell also discusses school achievement and what you did over your summer. See in particular Chapter 9, "Marita's Bargain: 'All My Friends Are Now from KIPP,'" found on pages 250–269.

Rich Dad, Poor Dad by Robert T. Kiyosaki and Sharon Lechter. Mental models of how people in poverty, middle class, and wealth think about money. See in particular pages 49–74.

Websites

American Psychological Association

http://www.apa.org/about/governance/council/policy/poverty-resolution.aspx

Resolution on Poverty and SES [socioeconomic status] adopted by The American Psychological Association, August 6, 2000

The following clauses are excerpted from the resolution to illustrate the concerns of the association: "WHEREAS, the income gap between the poor and the rich has continued to increase, with the average income of the poorest fifth of the population down 6% and the average income of the top fifth up 30% over the past 20 years (Bernstein, McNichol, Mishel, & Zahradnik, 2000); ...

"WHEREAS, poverty is detrimental to psychological well-being, with NIMH data indicating that low-income individuals are 2 to 5 times more likely to suffer from a diagnosable mental disorder than those of the highest SES group (Bourdon, Rae, Narrow, Manderschild, & Regier, 1994; Regier et al., 1993), and poverty poses a significant obstacle to getting help for these mental health problems (McGrath, Keita, Strickland, & Russo, 1990); ...

"WHEREAS, accumulating research evidence indicates that the greater the income gap between the poorest and the wealthiest in a society, the higher the death rates for infants and adults and the lower the life expectancy for all members of that society, regardless of SES (Kawachi & Kennedy, 1997);

"WHEREAS, the impact of poverty on young children is significant and long lasting, limiting chances of moving out of poverty (McLoyd, 1998), poverty is associated with substandard housing, homelessness, inadequate child care, unsafe neighborhoods, and under-resourced schools (Fairchild, 1984; Lott & Bullock, in press), and poor children are at greater risk than higher income children for a range of problems, including detrimental effects on IQ, poor academic achievement, poor socioemotional functioning, developmental delays, behavioral problems, asthma, poor nutrition, low birth weight, and pneumonia (Geltman, Meyers, Greenberg, & Zuckerman, 1996; McLoyd, 1998; Parker, Greer, & Zuckerman, 1988); ...

"WHEREAS, perceptions of the poor and of welfare—by those not in those circumstances—tend to reflect attitudes and stereotypes that attribute poverty to personal failings rather than socioeconomic structures and systems that ignore strengths and competencies in these groups (Ehrenreich, 1987; Katz, 1989; Quadagno, 1994), and public policy and anti-poverty programs continue to reflect these stereotypes (Bullock, 1995; Furnham, 1993; Furnham & Gunter, 1984; Rubin & Peplau, 1975) ..."

Learning Disabilities, Dyslexia, and Vision

www.ldonline.org

Excerpted from website: "Thanks to advances in imaging techniques and scientific inquiry, we now know much more about learning disabilities (LD), dyslexia, and the role of vision problems. The American Academy of Pediatrics, the Council on Children with Disabilities, and the American Academy of Ophthalmology published a joint statement that summarizes what is currently known about visual problems and dyslexia. The statement also covers what treatments are and are not recommended when diagnosing and treating vision problems, learning disabilities, and dyslexia."

College for Adults

www.collegeforadults.org

Excerpted from website: "This website will help you with career planning, college selection and the application process. We will also suggest ways to find money to pay for college, and direct you to resources to help you prepare for college-level work."

For more information on learning styles, go to: *http://www.collegeforadults.org/studentcenter/success.html.*

MODULE 8
Stages of Change

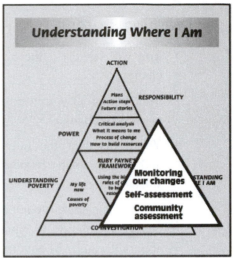

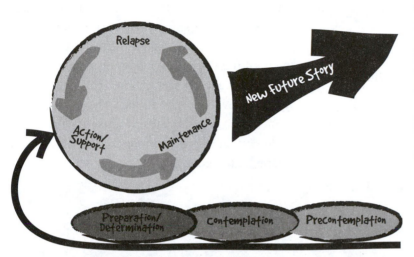

Learning Objectives

WHAT'S COVERED

You will:

Develop a definition of what it means to be motivated

Learn the stages of change

Assess your stage of change

WHY IT'S IMPORTANT

This information is important because you need to be in charge of your own changes.

All too often others are doing assessments on you and giving you plans to complete. An important part of taking charge of your life is making and monitoring your own changes. This information helps you think about where you are.

HOW IT'S CONNECTED TO YOU

Module 3 covered the process of change for this work. Module 7 named individual motivation as an important resource. The stages of change is another important concept because it is fluid—and being aware of what influences given stages of change increases your control.

Later, as you begin making your plans for building resources, you'll come back to this information. Until then, keep testing yourself and see where you are in the stages of change.

Learning Process

- You will review a theory about stages of change.

- You'll consider your journey to college as a process of change.

- You'll discover the individual variations and common patterns possible within each stage of change.

- You'll consider your experience with change in relation to what you've learned about the causes of poverty.

- You'll articulate your motivation for change.

I. The Stages of Change

A *stages of change* model was originally developed by James Prochaska and Carlo DiClemente at the University of Rhode Island where a study focused on how smokers gave up their habits (DiClemente & Velasquez, 2002). Becoming aware of the stages can help individuals identify problems, develop motivation, make plans, and develop new ways of living. The example on the next two pages relates to smokers, but it also could pertain to people trying to lose weight—or pursue higher education.

Lexicon for Module 8

Stages of change (pre-contemplation, contemplation, preparation, action, maintenance)

Stages of Change	
1. Pre-Contemplation	Ignorance is bliss. We aren't even thinking about changing. We may not know how, so we don't concern ourselves with it. We may not have suffered much (yet), so we don't see the need. We aren't willing.
Example: Take someone (let's say a woman) who has been smoking a while. She knows it's bad for her health, but she's annoyed by everyone harping about it. The more others push for her to quit, the more it feels like her rights and freedoms are being challenged. She doesn't ever expect to change and, what's more, she doesn't want to.	
2. Contemplation	Sitting on the fence. We're concerned and worried, and we begin considering a change, but we're not sold on it yet. This stage is all about thinking. We can be in this stage for a long time. Knowing this, we might be able to move through it more quickly. There are two important things that have to be dealt with in this stage: ambivalence and identity.
	Ambivalence. This is when we want to change but don't want to change. We think of the costs and benefits—what we'll gain and what we'll lose. We think about our peers, how they will or won't respect us if we make a change. We wonder what people will think or say about us.
	Identity. We worry that we won't be the same person if we change. Will the people who are in our lives now reject us if we change? Fear of failure becomes a part of this, and so does fear of success. We wonder what will happen if we do or don't change. Most of all we think, *When in doubt, put it off!*
Example: Something happens that makes the woman in our story start thinking. Someone she knows dies of cancer, a child asks her to quit, or she gets disgusted with the way her clothes smell. She stays on the fence for a long time, thinking, "I'm a smoker. Always have been, always will be." That identity is hard to change.	
3. Preparation	Testing the waters. For the first time, we begin to make the argument for change, not the others who always seem to know what's best for us. That is a sign that we're motivated. We think, "I'm going to change, and I'm figuring out what to do." We intend to change in the near future. We're in transition, so we make small behavior changes and play the "yes/but" game.
Example: Our smoker has decided to stop smoking—but only sort of. She switches to low-tar/nicotine cigarettes, tries to smoke less, might try patches, or even quits for a few days, but she doesn't tell her friends or even family (in some cases) what she's trying to do.	
4. Action	We're doing it, but it's shaky. We make a public commitment to the change, we've made a plan, and we're trying to stick to it. When we have some success we begin to think we can do it. Identity may not have changed yet, but we're thinking differently.

Example: Our smoker still thinks of herself as a smoker, and she promises never to be like others who quit and become crusading anti-smokers. Her plan develops out of the preparation phase, and she now takes a behavioral class and uses patches. She even has a plan to prevent relapse, and she tries to keep the back door of her commitment closed so she won't run out that back door the first time she gets into trouble.

5. Maintenance	"I've done it; now I'm working at keeping it going." But it's not a sure thing. Many things can trigger a relapse, so strategies have to be put into practice for some time. Efforts have to be made to prevent relapse—and to recover from relapse quickly if/when it occurs.

Example: Our non-smoker works hard to stay smoke-free and begins to gain real confidence in herself as time passes. Her sense of self slowly changes, and she increasingly becomes at ease with her new identity and lifestyle.

Note. Adapted from "Motivational Interviewing and the Stages of Change," by C. C. DiClemente and M. M. Velasquez. In *Motivational Interviewing: Preparing People for Change* (2nd ed., pp. 201–216), by W. R. Miller and S. Rollnick, 2002, New York, NY: Guilford Press. Copyright 2002 by Guilford Press.

I. A. Activity: Stages of Change for 'Going to College'

Time: 20 minutes

Materials: Flipchart paper and sticky notes

Procedure:

1. Draw lines on flipchart paper to create five sections.

2. At the top of each section, write the names of the five stages of change in order.

3. Individually write answers on the sticky notes to the following questions for each stage of change:

   - What did you say to yourself when you were in this stage?

   - What did you do?

   - How long were you in this phase?

4. Put a sticky note on each stage of change.

5. Review, compare, and contrast the results.

I. B. Discussion

1. How long did it take to move out of pre-contemplation? What created the motivation?

2. How has being a college student affected your identity—both positively and negatively?

3. Consider the stage of preparation: What was the message in your mind that prepared you to go to college? Did you "make the case for change" yourself?

4. You are here, so you took action. How secure do you feel today about this change as compared with the first day of school? Have some investigators left the group or left school? What pulled them back?

5. Think about change as it relates to research into the causes of poverty:

   ▪ What barriers to change are created by living in poverty?

   ▪ What barriers to change are created more specifically by family and friends?

   ▪ What have other people done that helped you make *progress* in the stages of change?

   ▪ What barriers to change are created by the community and political/economic structures? What assets are available in the community and college to assist?

   ▪ What barriers are created by individuals themselves? What might help overcome these obstacles?

6. What resources have been most useful in helping you move through the stages of change to come to college?

7. Consider the information from Module 7 about motivation. Describe your motivation for change.

Journal Reflections

Write or draw a picture about where you are in the stages of change in relation to a decision or life change you are experiencing.

Reading

Motivational Interviewing: Preparing People for Change (second edition) by William R. Miller and Stephen Rollnick. The authors write, "Intrinsic motivation for change arises in an accepting, empowering atmosphere that makes it safe for the person to explore the possibly painful present in relation to what is wanted and valued." From the chapter "Why do people change?" found on pages 3–12.

MODULE 9
Self-Assessment of Resources

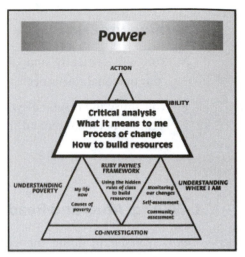

Learning Objectives

WHAT'S COVERED

You will:

Investigate the abstract, impersonal information about resources as they apply to the concrete realities of your life.

Transform your objective self-assessment back into an abstract mental model summarizing your own resource levels.

WHY IT'S IMPORTANT

The 11 resources cover all aspects of life. It's important to do your own assessment of your whole life, not just pieces of the "My Life Now" mental model.

HOW IT'S CONNECTED TO YOU

You have covered the information you need in order to form an accurate picture of your resources and the quality of your life.

You've investigated political/economic systems and learned about hidden rules, language issues, and resources.

Now it's time to use this information to make the changes you want to make.

The first step is to do an accurate assessment of your own resources.

When you're done with this, you'll do an assessment of the community, then start making your own plans.

Learning Process

- You will critically and objectively assess your personal resources.

- You'll use the results of your assessment to create a personal mental model of your resources.

I. Willing, Able, and Ready

Before you begin doing this activity, stop and think: *How am I going to approach this self-assessment? What attitude am I going to take?* This investigation takes two things: honesty and tight thinking. It's important that you make a commitment to giving this your best effort. Choose your attitude as if your future depends on it, because in a real sense it may.

I. A. Activity: Self-Assessment of Resources

Time: 45–60 minutes
Materials: Worksheets
Procedure:

1. Review all the mental models you have created for yourself as you worked through this workbook. Make any necessary revisions in order to keep them accurate and up-to-date.

2. Complete the following self-assessment on your own, each person working individually.

   - If a question doesn't make sense, ask the facilitator to explain it.

   - There are 11 sets of descriptions, one for each resource.

   - The descriptions are organized into the same five categories or levels that we used in Module 7. The descriptions provide a detailed definition of each level:

        (1) = Urgent/Crisis
        (2) = Vulnerable/High-Risk
        (3) = Stable
        (4) = Safe/Secure
        (5) = Thriving/Giving Back

3. Work your way through each resource by putting a check mark by all the descriptions that are true for you.

4. When you have completed a resource, look back over your check marks and see what was real for you. At the bottom of each resource is a place to summarize your situation; *circle the number that most closely matches the level where the majority of your check marks were.*

5. When you have done all of the resources in this way, take the scores at the bottom of each resource and transfer them to the Resources Mental Model bar chart at the end of the self-assessment. For example, if your financial resources are Vulnerable/High-Risk, or a (2), put an X in Row 2 under the "Financial" column heading. This will give you a mental model of your financial resources.

6. Do these worksheets as if your situation were just another case study, as if you were objectively looking from the outside at your life. "Detaching" yourself from any problem will help you see it more clearly.

NOTE: Sometimes doing this kind of self-assessment can be painful, especially if a number of one's resources are in crisis or vulnerable situations. It would be natural to want to reduce the pain by scoring your resources higher than they really are, but this is the time to do tough and tight thinking. However, this is also the time to identify your strongest resources because it is those resources that will help you build the urgent and vulnerable ones.

After you're finished, if you are open to sharing your thinking and scores with others, do so. Sometimes listening to others can help clarify one's thinking. At the same time, remember that this assessment is *yours,* not what someone else is saying about you. Best wishes as you do this important exercise.

Self-Assessment of Resources

Resource: Financial			
Description	**X**	**Detailed Description of Resources**	
Doesn't have enough income to purchase needed goods and services.		I'm homeless.	(1) Urgent/Crisis
		No adult in my household has a job.	
		Only one adult in my household has a job, and he or she works less than full time.	
		When an adult in my household works, the job usually pays less than $8 an hour.	
		My family income is below the Federal Poverty Line (see Module 2).	
		The worker in my household cannot afford health insurance.	
		I sometimes live in shelters.	
		I often double up in housing with people who aren't related to me.	
		Half of my household income (50%) or more goes toward housing.	
		The house I live in is unsafe.	
		My family receives government cash assistance.	
		My family uses one or more other government subsidies, such as food stamps, a medical card, and/or HEAP (Home Energy Assistance Program).	
		Someone in my household uses payday, cash-advance, and check-cashing loans.	
		Someone in my household goes to lease/purchase outlets for appliances and/or furniture.	
		My household does not have a car or other transportation.	
		The transportation that my household has isn't reliable.	
Has some, but not enough, income to purchase needed goods and services—and to save money.		No adult in my household has a full-time job.	(2) Vulnerable/High-Risk
		Only one adult in my household works and has two or more low-wage jobs.	
		The one working adult in my household is usually paid less than $10 an hour.	
		Half of my household income (50%) comes from earnings and/or child support.	
		My family income is at or just above the Federal Poverty Line (Module 2).	
		I live in subsidized housing.	
		I sometimes double up in housing with relatives or friends.	

Resource: Financial			
Description	**X**	**Detailed Description of Resources**	
(continued) Has some, but not enough, income to purchase needed goods and services—and to save money.		More than a third (33%) of my household income goes toward housing.	**(2) Vulnerable/High-Risk**
		The house I live in is unsafe.	
		My family does not receive government cash assistance.	
		My family uses one or more government subsidies, such as food stamps, a medical card, and/or HEAP.	
		We no longer borrow money from payday, cash-advance, or check-cashing lenders.	
		My family no longer uses lease/purchase outlets.	
		The working adult(s) in my household are paying off the household debts.	
		We have liability insurance for the family car(s).	
Has enough income to purchase needed goods and services—and to have money saved for a crisis.		At least one adult in the household has a full-time job—40 hours a week.	**(3) Stable**
		At least one adult has a job that pays a self-sufficient or living wage.	
		All of the household income (100%) is from earnings and/or child support.	
		Our family's annual income is 350% of the Federal Poverty Line (Module 2).	
		We have affordable health insurance.	
		Our family housing costs are 30% of the household income.	
		The adult(s) with a job made a down payment and purchased a house.	
		The house I live in is safe.	
		My family keeps money in a savings account for emergencies.	
		My family uses regular banking services: checking, savings, and loans.	
	X	Our family is reducing our debt.	
		My household has access to fair credit.	
		My household has home/renters insurance.	
		My household has liability and comprehensive insurance for our car(s).	
		My family's car(s) are reliable.	

	Resource: Financial		
Description	**X**	**Detailed Description of Resources**	
(continued) Has enough income to purchase needed goods and services, to save for emergencies, and to invest in the future.		My family income is above 400% of the Federal Poverty Line (Module 2).	**(4) Safe/Secure**
		My family has affordable health insurance.	
		The employer(s) contribute to the pension/retirement investments.	
		My family housing costs are 30% of the household income or less.	
		My family has a "rainy day" emergency fund.	
		Working adults are making investments to support retirement.	
		The household credit cards are paid off monthly.	
		My family has insurance for our home and businesses.	
		My family has dependable transportation to meet all travel needs.	
Actively seeks to increase personal financial assets over time—and to help build community assets.		My family income is well above 500% of the Federal Poverty Line (Module 2).	**(5) Thriving/Giving Back**
		The provider(s) in the family build assets: housing, businesses, investments.	
		Our family housing costs are about 10% of our household income.	
		My family uses financial services to assist in building assets.	
		My family has no debt that isn't part of a financial plan.	
		My family can access all the healthcare services it wants.	
		My family has reliable, multiple transportation options.	
		I help other community members build their financial assets.	

Summary: Circle the number that matches your resource level, according to your answers above:

    (1) = Urgent/Crisis
    (2) = Vulnerable/High-Risk
    (3) = Stable
    (4) = Safe/Secure
    (5) = Thriving/Giving Back

1	2	3	4	5

Resource: Emotional			
Description	**X**	**Detailed Description of Resources**	
Can't choose and control emotional responses. Often behaves in ways that are harmful to others or self.		I often can't name the feeling I'm having.	(1) Urgent/Crisis
		I often blame others for what I'm feeling.	
		I sometimes lose my temper and yell at others.	
		I threaten and hit others.	
		I start fights.	
		I regularly try to control the thoughts, feelings, and actions of others.	
		I have rigid rules for how others should act.	
		I often do things I'm sorry for later.	
		I often act without thinking.	
		I sometimes harm myself physically.	
		I often have a negative attitude.	
		I have trouble getting along with others at work/school.	
Can sometimes choose and control emotional responses. Sometimes behaves in ways that are harmful to others or self.		I sometimes use positive self-talk to help me deal with problems.	(2) Vulnerable/High-Risk
		I seldom lose my temper and yell at others.	
		I seldom get in fights or threaten others.	
		I try to think before I act.	
		I generally present myself in positive ways to others.	
		I alternate between a positive and negative attitude.	
		I mostly accept responsibility for my actions.	
		I get along with others at work/school more often than not.	
Can almost always choose and control emotional responses. Almost never behaves in ways that are harmful to others or self.		I identify my feelings quickly.	(3) Stable
		I use my thoughts to control my feelings.	
		I usually choose positive behaviors, even when experiencing strong feelings.	
		I usually choose positive behaviors, even in stressful situations.	
		I can solve most problems with others by talking things through.	
		I generally identify my choices before acting.	
		I usually have a positive attitude.	
		I get along well with people at work/school most of the time.	

Resource: Emotional			
Description	X	Detailed Description of Resources	
Good at choosing and controlling emotional responses. Engages in positive behaviors toward others.		I almost always manage my thoughts and feelings in positive ways.	(4) Safe/Secure
		I can set aside emotional issues so that I can focus on immediate issues.	
		I make most of my decisions based on future results rather than on feelings of the moment.	
		I almost always get along well at work/school.	
		I help create a positive climate at work/school.	
Actively seeks to improve emotional health of self and others.		I look for ways to grow emotionally.	(5) Thriving/ Giving Back
		I can teach others about feelings and emotional intelligence.	
		I help others to grow emotionally, to empower others.	
		I get along well with people who come from different backgrounds, classes, races, and political points of view.	

Summary: Circle the number that matches your resource level, according to your answers above:

(1) = Urgent/Crisis
(2) = Vulnerable/High-Risk
(3) = Stable
(4) = Safe/Secure
(5) = Thriving/Giving Back

1	2	3	4	5

Resource: Mental			
Description	**X**	**Detailed Description of Resources**	
Lacks ability, education, or skills to compete for well-paying jobs.		I dropped out of school after completing eighth grade.	**(1) Urgent/Crisis**
		I have a learning disability that I haven't had help for yet.	
		I don't usually have a plan for things I have to do.	
		I solve problems by trial and error.	
		I make decisions based on immediate needs, not the needs of the future.	
		My thinking is usually negative.	
		I am often late to work, school, and appointments.	
Has some ability, education, or skills to compete for entry-level jobs.		I dropped out of high school.	**(2) Vulnerable/High-Risk**
		I do math well enough to make change and operate a calculator.	
		I can read well enough to hold a low-wage, service-sector job.	
		I can fix things and make some home repairs.	
		I have the physical strength to do hard labor.	
		I type/keyboard well enough to do word processing.	
		I can file alphabetically and numerically.	
		I make and carry out plans for solving daily problems.	
		I'm generally on time for work, school, and appointments.	
Has enough ability, education, or skills to compete for well-paying jobs.		I graduated from high school.	**(3) Stable**
		I completed some college courses.	
		I took vocational training after high school.	
		I have mechanical and equipment-operating skills.	
		I earned a certificate in a trade or discipline.	
		I make a living through a trade: for example, carpentry, plumbing, electrical.	
		I make a living using artistic or creative skills, such as writing, playing an instrument, singing, painting, etc.	
		I make detailed plans for work and home, then carry them out.	
		I solve problems by using logical procedural steps.	
		I'm almost always on time for work, school, and appointments.	
		I meet almost all of my deadlines.	

Resource: Mental			
Description	**X**	**Detailed Description of Resources**	
Has plenty of ability, education, or skills to compete for well-paying jobs.		I have a college degree.	**(4) Safe/Secure**
		I have a master's degree.	
		I earned a license in a particular field of study or work.	
		I have the physical abilities and/or natural talent for high achievement in sports or the arts.	
		I encourage and support children to achieve educational goals.	
		I encourage and support people in the work and school settings to achieve educational goals.	
Actively seeks to improve on existing ability, education, or skills—and builds mental resources in the community.		I have a master's degree or doctorate.	**(5) Thriving/ Giving Back**
		I am a lifelong learner.	
		I enjoy taking on new learning experiences.	
		I help the community develop high-quality educational opportunities for everyone.	

Summary: Circle the number that matches your resource level, according to your answers above:

    (1) = Urgent/Crisis
    (2) = Vulnerable/High-Risk
    (3) = Stable
    (4) = Safe/Secure
    (5) = Thriving/Giving Back

1	2	3	4	5

Resource: Language			
Description	**X**	**Detailed Description of Resources**	
Lacks vocabulary, language ability, and negotiation skills needed for workplace and school settings.		I don't speak English.	(1) Urgent/Crisis
		I cannot read.	
		My vocabulary is mostly made up of concrete, specific terms.	
		I use only the casual register in my mother tongue.	
		I use only the casual register in English.	
		I have trouble using language to negotiate with people at work or school.	
Has some vocabulary, language ability, and negotiation skills needed for workplace and school settings.		I use the casual register in English.	(2) Vulnerable/High-Risk
		I use the formal register in my mother tongue.	
		I can read notices and directions at school.	
		I understand most of the instructions I get from instructors.	
		I can explain myself well enough to solve most problems at school.	
		I can hold a job that doesn't require much language knowledge.	
Has enough vocabulary, language ability, and negotiation skills needed for workplace and school settings.		My vocabulary includes some abstract terms, particularly those needed in school or in the workplace.	(3) Stable
		I can write in the formal register.	
		I can speak in the consultative register, with generally proper syntax and grammar.	
		I can translate from the formal to the casual and vice versa.	
		I can use casual register appropriately.	
		I'm able to use language to explore the point of view of others and to negotiate solutions.	
		I can present ideas in a linear, sequential manner.	
		I can use the "voices" appropriately.	
		I sometimes use "mediation" with co-workers.	
Has plenty of vocabulary, language ability, and negotiation skills need for workplace and school settings.		I have the vocabulary to be comfortable in a variety of work and school settings.	(4) Safe/Secure
		I use language to express complex ideas.	
		I use language to develop and maintain a profession.	
		I can be bilingual; that is, I can function easily in both casual and formal register.	

Resource: Language			
Description	**X**	**Detailed Description of Resources**	
(continued) Has plenty of vocabulary, language ability, and negotiation skills need for workplace and school settings.		I provide children with a varied and rich language experience.	**(4) Safe/Secure**
		I use language to understand the point of view of others.	
		I use language to negotiate at work and school, as well as in personal settings.	
Actively seeks to improve upon already strong vocabulary and language ability foundation— and works to develop language resources in the community.		I'm reasonably fluent in at least one language besides my mother tongue.	**(5) Thriving/ Giving Back**
		I use language to debate and persuade.	
		I use language to resolve conflicts.	
		I'm bilingual in that I can use both the casual and formal registers appropriately.	
		I work in the community to develop language resources for everyone.	

Summary: Circle the number that matches your resource level, according to your answers above:

  (1) = Urgent/Crisis
  (2) = Vulnerable/High-Risk
  (3) = Stable
  (4) = Safe/Secure
  (5) = Thriving/Giving Back

1	2	3	4	5

Resource: Support Systems			
Description	**X**	**Detailed Description of Resources**	
Lacks positive friends, family, and connections that can be accessed to improve resources.		Some people in my home and/or neighborhood are dangerous to me and others.	**(1) Urgent/Crisis**
		Most family members and friends don't support my efforts to make positive changes in my life.	
		Situations with my family often interfere with work and/or my education—such as truancy, drug use, or violence.	
		My neighborhood is unsafe.	
		I have very little positive contact with people from the community: social services, police, healthcare, etc.	
		I have no influence or voice on important community issues.	
Has some positive friends, family, and connections that can be accessed to improve resources.		One or two people in my neighborhood are dangerous to me and others.	**(2) Vulnerable/High-Risk**
		Many but not all of my family members and friends support my efforts to make positive changes.	
		Situations with my family—such as truancy, drug use, or violence—rarely interfere with my work and/or my education.	
		I have some positive contact with people from the community: social services, police, healthcare, etc.	
		Sometimes my neighborhood is safer than at other times.	
		I have very little influence or voice on important community issues.	
Has enough positive friends, family, and connections that can be accessed to improve resources.		I have plenty of positive friends, family, and connections that can be accessed to improve resources.	**(3) Stable**
		Nearly all of my family members and friends support my efforts to make positive changes.	
		Serious, problematic behaviors by my sibling(s) are now basically under control.	
		I have positive relationships with some people in community organizations and agencies.	
		My neighborhood is safe.	
		I have relationships of mutual respect with several people outside of my usual circle of family and friends.	
		I have influence or a voice on important community issues that matter to me.	

Resource: Support Systems			
Description	**X**	**Detailed Description of Resources**	
Has plenty of positive friends, family, and connections that can be accessed to improve resources.		I live in a neighborhood that is safe—in part because of the close relationships I have with my neighbors.	**(4) Safe/Secure**
		My family and friends encourage and support my efforts to make positive changes.	
		My siblings and I are usually engaged in positive social activities with peers and adults.	
		I belong to groups or organizations that improve community life.	
		I help people at work or school gain influence and voice on important work- and school-related community activities.	
Actively develops networks and social resources that can be accessed to improve personal and community resources.		I have a large circle of friends and family who support me and help my parent(s) or guardian(s) raise me.	**(5) Thriving/ Giving Back**
		I have a substantial network of positive professional colleagues.	
		I have extensive social and financial connections.	
		I help people from other backgrounds and economic classes gain influence and power with regard to important community issues.	

Summary: Circle the number that matches your resource level, according to your answers above:

 (1) = Urgent/Crisis
 (2) = Vulnerable/High-Risk
 (3) = Stable
 (4) = Safe/Secure
 (5) = Thriving/Giving Back

1	2	3	4	5

Resource: Physical			
Description	**X**	**Detailed Description of Resources**	
Lacks physical health and mobility for workplace or school settings.		I need help to care for my own body.	**(1) Urgent/Crisis**
		I regularly do things that are bad for my health.	
		I have a drinking/drug problem and/or a mental illness.	
		I have a stress-related disease.	
		I have a chronic illness or illnesses.	
		I have problems with my teeth that aren't being addressed.	
		I am very overweight.	
		I take care of someone who is chronically ill or elderly.	
		I have trouble getting healthcare for myself or others.	
		I cannot ride a bike.	
		I spend a great deal of time on health issues and getting healthcare, which often affects my ability to work or attend school during regular hours.	
		I use free clinics.	
Has some physical health and mobility problems that could limit effectiveness in the workplace or school.		I'm getting treatment for an addiction and/or a mental illness.	**(2) Vulnerable/High-Risk**
		I'm receiving medical care for stress-related diseases.	
		I'm developing a way to manage a chronic illness or illnesses.	
		I'm receiving dental care.	
		I'm helping to care for someone who is chronically ill or elderly.	
		My siblings and I have minimal healthcare coverage.	
		My parent(s) or guardian(s) don't have healthcare coverage for themselves.	
		I can ride a bike.	
		I can do light physical work.	
		Health problems sometime interfere with my work or school schedule.	
Has the physical health and mobility needed for workplace and school settings.		I do preventive healthcare.	**(3) Stable**
		I do preventive dental care.	
		More often than not I eat healthful foods and balanced meals.	
		I exercise or play sports fairly often.	
		I can do hard physical work.	

Resource: Physical			
Description	**X**	**Detailed Description of Resources**	
(continued) Has the physical health and mobility needed for workplace and school settings.		My parent(s) or guardian(s) have good care arrangements for the children and adults in my household.	(3) Stable
		I'm considered to be physically attractive.	
		I have above-average athletic ability.	
		My parents' or guardians' employer pays for our family's health coverage.	
		Health problems seldom interfere with work or school.	
Consistently maintains physical health and mobility needed for self and others in the workplace and/or school.		I have no ongoing physical health concerns; except for the occasional cold, I'm in excellent health.	(4) Safe/Secure
		I have no addiction issues or mental health problems.	
		I use prevention and early-detection strategies.	
		I exercise at least three times a week.	
		I'm exceptionally attractive.	
		Health concerns almost never interfere with work or school.	
		I support healthy lifestyle programs in the workplace and school.	
Actively develops physical resources for self, workplace, school, and community.		My family has access to private healthcare providers of choice.	(5) Thriving/ Giving Back
		I have outstanding athletic ability.	
		I exercise daily.	
		I have actively worked toward the development of high-quality and affordable community facilities and healthcare systems for all members of the community.	

Summary: Circle the number that matches your resource level, according to your answers above:

   (1) = Urgent/Crisis
   (2) = Vulnerable/High-Risk
   (3) = Stable
   (4) = Safe/Secure
   (5) = Thriving/Giving Back

1	2	3	4	5

Resource: Spiritual			
Description	**X**	**Detailed Description of Resources**	
Lacks cultural connections or a sense of spiritual purpose that offers support and guidance.		I believe in fate—that my choices really don't make any difference.	**(1) Urgent/Crisis**
		I hope my luck will change.	
		I go to church or other religious institutions when I need clothes, food, housing, or other emergency assistance.	
		I don't feel a sense of belonging to any particular group.	
		I feel mostly isolated from other people.	
		I'm part of a hate group.	
Has some cultural connections and a sense of spiritual purpose that offers personal support and guidance.		I believe that choices can sometimes make a difference but that there's little point in trying to make changes.	**(2) Vulnerable/ High-Risk**
		I go to church or other religious institutions for help with emergency needs and spiritual needs.	
		I identify with a cultural group, but I'm not very active in its activities.	
Has sufficient cultural connections and a sense of spiritual purpose that offers personal support and guidance.		I believe in a higher power that is larger than myself.	**(3) Stable**
		I read spiritual texts for guidance.	
		I attend services at a church, temple, synagogue, or mosque.	
		I have some social relationships with people from my religious group.	
		I have some cultural relationships with people from my cultural, ethnic, or racial group.	
Has plenty of cultural connections and a sense of spiritual purpose that offers personal support and guidance.		I engage in a daily spiritual practice based on a particular religious faith.	**(4) Safe/Secure**
		I regularly participate in services at a church, temple, synagogue, or mosque.	
		I have many social relationships with people from my religious group.	
		I regularly participate in the cultural, ethnic, or racial events of my group.	
		I engage in regular spiritual activities outside of organized religion.	
		I believe that the choices I make today will affect my future.	

Resource: Spiritual			
Description	**X**	**Detailed Description of Resources**	
Actively seeks cultural connections and encourages spiritual growth in self and others.		My spiritual practice is a very important part of my life.	**(5) Thriving/ Giving Back**
		I'm tolerant of people of other beliefs and faiths.	
		I devote considerable time and energy to helping others.	
		I actively work to develop understanding and compassion between and among groups in the community.	

Summary: Circle the number that matches your resource level, according to your answers above:

    (1) = Urgent/Crisis
    (2) = Vulnerable/High-Risk
    (3) = Stable
    (4) = Safe/Secure
    (5) = Thriving/Giving Back

1	2	3	4	5

Resource: Integrity/Trust			
Description	**X**	**Detailed Description of Resources**	
Cannot be trusted to keep one's word, to accomplish tasks, and to obey laws even when under supervision.		I often lie and deceive others.	**(1) Urgent/Crisis**
		I steal from others and/or from work or school.	
		I cheat on tests.	
		I don't give my employer or teachers my full effort.	
		I fix my scores.	
		I obey the laws but only when they're being enforced.	
		I just about always take care of my own needs and interests first.	
		I often don't do what I say I'll do.	
		I'm not accountable to anyone.	
		I often blame others when things go wrong.	
Can sometimes be trusted to keep one's word, to accomplish tasks, and to obey laws when under supervision.		I sometimes lie and deceive others.	**(2) Vulnerable/High-Risk**
		I rarely steal from others or from work or school.	
		I obey laws most of the time.	
		I cheat on my tests in small ways.	
		I trust a few people.	
		I give my employer or instructor a full day's effort most of the time.	
		I'm accountable to those who have power.	
Can usually be trusted to keep one's word, to accomplish tasks, and to obey laws without supervision.		I'm truthful.	**(3) Stable**
		I try to do what is fair and right for all concerned.	
		I always obey laws, unless it's a law with which I have a philosophical or moral disagreement.	
		I trust many people.	
		I almost always give my employer or instructor a full day's work.	
		I generally accept responsibility for myself and don't blame others.	
		I usually do what I say I'll do.	
Can invariably be trusted to keep one's word, to accomplish tasks, to obey laws, and to inspire others to do the same.		I hold positions of trust at work or school.	**(4) Safe/Secure**
		I take on difficult problems and accept responsibility for myself.	
		I live by high ethical standards.	
		I feel comfortable talking about moral and ethical standards with people who work and/or go to school with me.	

185

Resource: Integrity/Trust			
Description	**X**	**Detailed Description of Resources**	
Actively seeks to build integrity and trust—and sets high ethical standards at work, at school, and in the community.		I'm accountable to myself.	**(5) Thriving/ Giving Back**
		I make myself accountable to others.	
		I work with others to set high ethical standards at work or school and in community life.	
		I lead by example.	
		I actively work with others to change laws and policies that I consider immoral or unjust.	

Summary: Circle the number that matches your resource level, according to your answers above:

    (1) = Urgent/Crisis
    (2) = Vulnerable/High-Risk
    (3) = Stable
    (4) = Safe/Secure
    (5) = Thriving/Giving Back

1	2	3	4	5

		Resource: Motivation/Persistence	
Description	**X**	**Detailed Description of Resources**	
Lacks energy or drive to prepare for, plan, and complete projects, jobs, and personal change.		I avoid work or school when possible.	**(1) Urgent/Crisis**
		I have low energy most of the time.	
		I watch way too much TV.	
		I would rather not be promoted at work, and I hate training events.	
		I don't like the hassle of learning new things.	
		I work hard sometimes but often goof off while at work or school.	
		I give up easily.	
		I work only for money.	
		I usually wait until things get really bad before I make changes.	
Has some energy or drive to prepare for, plan, and complete projects, jobs, and personal change.		I have low energy some of the time.	**(2) Vulnerable/High-Risk**
		I'm cautious about taking on new duties at work or school.	
		I don't enjoy training events, but I usually attend because it's expected.	
		I work just hard enough to keep supervisors and instructors off my back.	
		I work hard if I like the people I'm working for.	
		I'll work at making changes in my life if things will get better right away.	
Has enough energy or drive to prepare for, plan, and complete projects, jobs, and personal change.		I work hard most of the time.	**(3) Stable**
		I set short-term goals.	
		I usually stick with the goals I set until I finish them.	
		I have fairly steady energy.	
		I seek promotion for the power or recognition.	
		I attend and value most training opportunities.	
Has plenty of energy or drive to prepare for, plan, and complete projects, jobs, and personal change.		I have high energy almost all of the time.	**(4) Safe/Secure**
		I try to do the right thing for the business or school or organization.	
		I sometimes seek out training on my own.	
		I see opportunities coming and prepare myself for them.	
		I seek promotions because they reflect excellence.	
		I have planning strategies that usually work very well for me.	
		I'm self-motivated.	

Resource: Motivation/Persistence			
Description	**X**	**Detailed Description of Resources**	
Actively seeks to maintain motivation and persistence—and to assist others in finding theirs.		I see the big picture and can make plans for the organization or school.	**(5) Thriving/Giving Back**
		I see opportunities for the organization and other individuals and prepare the organization and others for such opportunities.	
		I work with others to set goals and enjoy achieving positive results in an atmosphere that emphasizes teamwork.	
		I promote motivation and persistence by creating quality and improvement structures at the organizational and community level.	

Summary: Circle the number that matches your resource level, according to your answers above:

    (1) = Urgent/Crisis
    (2) = Vulnerable/High-Risk
    (3) = Stable
    (4) = Safe/Secure
    (5) = Thriving/Giving Back

1	2	3	4	5

Resource: Relationships/Role Models			
Description	**X**	**Detailed Description of Resources**	
Lacks access to others who are safe, supportive, and nurturing.		Many people I know personally are negative and unsuccessful people.	(1) Urgent/Crisis
		Many people I know say negative things about themselves and others.	
		Many people I know think that life happens to them—that they really don't have much control over things.	
		Many people I know have heard that they're "no good" a large number of times.	
		Many people I know let fear and obstacles stop them from trying to succeed.	
		Many people I know don't like to learn new things.	
		Many people close to me will undercut just about any efforts I make to improve my life.	
Has limited access to others who are safe, supportive, and nurturing.		Some people I know are negative and unsuccessful people.	(2) Vulnerable/High-Risk
		Some people I know say negative things about themselves and others.	
		Some people I know think that life happens to them.	
		Some people I know have heard that they're "no good" many times.	
		Some people I know let fear and obstacles stop them.	
		Some people I know don't like to learn.	
		Some people close to me will undercut just about any efforts I make to improve my life.	
Has enough access to others who are safe, supportive, and nurturing.		Some people I know often think, "By my choices I can create my life."	(3) Stable
		Some people I know are eager to change and to succeed.	
		Some people I know like to learn.	
		There are some people in my life who give steady support to me.	
		Some people in my life will support the changes I want to make to improve my life.	
		I have several relationships of mutual respect with people at work or school.	
		I have someone I can model myself after in one or more areas of my life.	

Resource: Relationships/Role Models			
Description	**X**	**Detailed Description of Resources**	
Has plenty of access to others who are safe, supportive, and nurturing.		Most people I know usually think, "By my choices I can create my life."	(4) Safe/Secure
		Most people I know are eager to change and succeed.	
		Most people I know like to learn.	
		Most of my family and friends give me steady support.	
		Most of the people in my life support the changes I want to make to improve my life.	
		I have many relationships of mutual respect with people at work or school.	
		I have someone who is a strong role model, mentor, or sponsor for me.	
Actively seeks out others who are safe, supportive, and nurturing—and is safe, supportive, and nurturing of others.		Most people I know focus on opportunities.	(5) Thriving/Giving Back
		Most people I know are positive, successful people.	
		Most people I know are continually learning and growing.	
		Most of the people in my life are positive, supportive, and nurturing to me.	
		I have mentors or sponsors with whom I meet regularly.	
		I'm a mentor or sponsor to others in the community.	
		I assist the community in building relationships that are supportive of people from all economic classes and backgrounds.	

Summary: Circle the number that matches your resource level, according to your answers above:

 (1) = Urgent/Crisis
 (2) = Vulnerable/High-Risk
 (3) = Stable
 (4) = Safe/Secure
 (5) = Thriving/Giving Back

1	2	3	4	5

		Resource: Knowledge of Hidden Rules	
Description	**X**	**Detailed Description of Resources**	
Lacks knowledge of hidden rules of other economic classes.		I know the hidden rules only of the class in which I was raised.	(1) Urgent/Crisis
		As a person in poverty, I don't know the environment or the hidden rules of school and work—that is, the middle class.	
		As a person in poverty, I don't know the environment or the hidden rules of people in positions of power and influence—that is, wealth.	
		As a person in middle class, I don't know the environment or hidden rules of people in poverty.	
		As a person in middle class, I don't know the environment or hidden rules of people in wealth.	
		As a person in wealth, I don't know the environment or hidden rules of people in poverty.	
		As a person in wealth, I don't know the environment or hidden rules of people in middle class.	
Has some awareness of hidden rules of other economic classes but cannot use them.		As a person in poverty, I know some of the rules of middle class, but I don't know how to use them.	(2) Vulnerable/High-Risk
		As a person in poverty, I know some of the rules of wealth, but I don't know how to use them.	
		As a person in middle class, I know some of the rules of poverty, but I don't know how to use them.	
		As a person in middle class, I know some of the rules of wealth, but I don't know how to use them.	
		As a person in wealth, I know some of the rules of poverty, but I don't know how to use them.	
		As a person in wealth, I know some of the rules of middle class, but I don't know how to use them.	
Knows the hidden rules of other economic classes and can use some of them in personal ways.		As a person in poverty, I know some of the rules of middle class and can use some of them to be more skillful at work, school, and in other middle-class settings.	(3) Stable
		As a person in poverty, I know some of the rules of wealth, but I almost never have the opportunity to use them.	
		As a person in middle class, I know some of the rules of poverty and can use some of them to be more skillful in my relationships.	
		As a person in middle class, I know some of the rules of wealth, but I seldom know how to use them.	

Resource: Knowledge of Hidden Rules			
Description	**X**	**Detailed Description of Resources**	
(continued) Knows the hidden rules of other economic classes and can use some of them in personal ways.		As a person in wealth, I know some of the rules of poverty and can use them to improve policies and programming for people in the community.	**(3) Stable**
		As a person in wealth, I know some of the rules of middle class and can use them to improve policies and programming for people in the community.	
Knows the hidden rules of all three economic classes and can use most of them effectively in limited settings.		As a person in poverty, I know most of the rules of middle class and can use most of them to be more skillful at work, school, and in other middle-class settings—and have some influence on policy and programming for community well-being.	**(4) Safe/Secure**
		As a person in poverty, I know most of the rules of wealth and know how to have some influence on policy and programming for community well-being.	
		As a person in middle class, I know most of the rules of poverty and can use them in my relationships, as well as in the design of policy and programming for community well-being.	
		As a person in middle class, I know most of the rules of wealth and have some influence on policy and programming for community well-being.	
		As a person in wealth, I know most of the rules of poverty and can use them to improve personal relationships and develop policies and programming for community well-being.	
		As a person in wealth, I know most of the rules of middle class and can use them to improve personal relationships, as well as policies and programming for community well-being.	
Actively seeks to understand the hidden rules of all three economic classes—and to use them effectively in a variety of settings.		As a person in poverty, I have relationships of mutual respect with people in middle class and work with them on community sustainability issues.	**(5) Thriving/ Giving Back**
		As a person in poverty, I have relationships of mutual respect with people in wealth and sit at the decision-making table with them and work with them on community sustainability issues.	
		As a person in middle class, I have relationships of mutual respect with people in poverty and work with them on community sustainability issues.	

Resource: Knowledge of Hidden Rules			
Description	**X**	**Detailed Description of Resources**	
(continued) Actively seeks to understand the hidden rules of all three economic classes—and to use them effectively in a variety of settings.		As a person in middle class, I have relationships of mutual respect with people in wealth and sit at the decision-making table with them and work with them on community sustainability issues.	**(5) Thriving/Giving Back**
		As person in wealth, I have relationships of mutual respect with people in poverty and sit at the decision-making table with them to work on community sustainability issues.	
		As person in wealth, I have relationships of mutual respect with people in middle class and sit at the decision-making table with them to work on community sustainability issues.	

Summary: Circle the number that matches your resource level, according to your answers above:

    (1) = Urgent/Crisis
    (2) = Vulnerable/High-Risk
    (3) = Stable
    (4) = Safe/Secure
    (5) = Thriving/Giving Back

1	2	3	4	5

Resources Mental Model

	Financial	Emotional	Mental	Language	Support Systems	Physical	Spiritual	Integrity/Trust	Motivation/ Persistence	Relationships/ Role Models	Knowledge of Hidden Rules
5											
4											
3											
2											
1											

I. B. Discussion

1. Looking at the mental model, which are your highest or strongest resources?

2. Where did each of your resources come from? To what extent were they from family or friends or both?

3. How did your community help your family build resources?

4. To what extent does your community provide fair opportunities for good jobs, good healthcare, a good education, and fair credit?

5. Did you build your resources yourself? Was it something inside you, a decision you made, a way of thinking, a talent, or a gift?

6. What did you learn about your situation and your life by doing this exercise?

7. How are certain resources linked to each other in relation to your situation?

8. Which resources are your lowest?

9. How might you use your higher resources to build your lower resources?

10. Thinking back over everything that we have investigated so far, how does this piece fit into it?

11. Where are you with regard to the stages of change?

Journal Reflections

Write or draw your ideas, thoughts, and feelings about your identified resources.

MODULE 10
Community Assessment

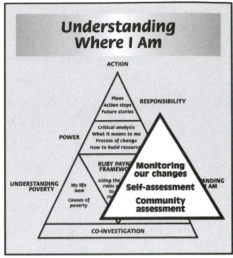

Understanding Where I Am

ACTION

Plans
Action steps
Future stories

RESPONSIBILITY

POWER

Critical analysis
What it means to me
Process of change
How to build resources

RUBY PAYNE FRAMEWORK

UNDERSTANDING POVERTY

My life now

Using the rules to...

Causes of poverty

Monitoring our changes
Self-assessment
Community assessment

...ANDING I AM

CO-INVESTIGATION

Learning Objectives

WHAT'S COVERED

You will:

Investigate the capacity of the community to provide a high quality of life for its members from the point of view of people in poverty

Complete the community assessment

Identify community assets (individuals, associations, and institutions) that can help investigators build resources

Identify campus services that can help students build resources

WHY IT'S IMPORTANT

Resource development can only happen locally—at the community level.

The community contributes to the quality of life by helping people build resources. An accurate assessment is needed that includes information from people in poverty.

It's important because we'll need to identify people, associations, and organizations that can help build resources.

It's important to hold the community accountable for a community's quality of life and for the steps needed to become a sustainable community.

It's important that members of this group participate in solving community problems, not just their own.

HOW IT'S CONNECTED TO YOU

There are two themes in *Investigations:* the individual and the community.

This goes back to the Research Continuum we studied in Module 4. Our communities must have strategies from all four areas of research for fighting poverty. When we make our final plans, we'll need to include what needs to be done in the community—alongside what needs to happen in our personal lives.

Learning Process

- You will investigate community assets for key quality-of-life indicators.

- You'll seek out individuals, associations, and institutions that can help you build resources.

- You'll identify campus services and programs that can help you stay in school, build resources, and graduate.

- You'll consider roles you might have or take on as a member of the community.

Lexicon for Module 10

Capacity
Community assets
Community Reinvestment Act
Concentrated poverty
Digital divide
Employee stock ownership
Persistent poverty
Profit sharing
Social health index
Stock-ownership plans
Workers' compensation violations

I. Assessing Your Community

Where you live has a great deal to do with the quality of life and how easy it will be for someone to get out of poverty. It's going to be harder to establish a stable and prosperous life if you live in a region of the United States where poverty is concentrated and persistent than if you live in a community that is a center of economic pros-

perity and cultural vitality. According to Amy K. Glasmeier (2006) in *An Atlas of Poverty in America,* poverty is concentrated in Appalachia, the Mississippi Delta, the border region with Mexico, Native American lands, rural America, and segregated areas within cities (pp. 51–80).

Many community leaders and residents are concerned with their community's ability to provide a good life and whether they will be able to pass that good life on to the next generation. These quality-of-life issues cannot be described by economic indicators and market reports alone. The measure needed to provide a clear picture of life is called a social health index. This index takes into account not only economic issues like wages, unemployment, and poverty rates, but health and safety information, environmental conditions, educational opportunities, along with recreation and civic opportunities. Every developed nation has a social health index except the U.S. (Miringoff & Miringoff, 1999, p. 27). There are a few states (Ohio, Connecticut, Montana, and Wyoming) that have a social health index. These typically provide data by city and county. There are a few cities (such as Portland, Oregon) and counties (Montgomery County, Ohio) that have their own social health index. Ideally, these should be web-based and interactive, capable of providing up-to-date information that provides a context for trends and tells, at a deep level, the stories about our communities.

If your state or community has a social health index, it will make the following investigation easier. The survey you'll conduct, like a social health index, can be used in many ways. The focus here is to hold the leaders and ourselves accountable for the quality of life and to help you find the positive aspects of your community that can help you build your resources.

This is important information because nearly all quality-of-life solutions will have to be found locally. Regardless of international and national trends, well-paying jobs, healthcare, education, and flourishing social capital are local matters. In terms of the lexicon developed in *Investigations,* the question is: To what extent does your community encourage individuals to build resources?

For example, it's easier to lose weight and be fit in a community that is safe, where there are walking trails and bike paths, where there are many sporting and outdoor activities available, and where there is healthful food available than it is in a community that generally has the opposite characteristics. Denver and Boulder, Colorado, consistently rank high among the fittest U.S. cities. But, if you live in a neighborhood where parents don't want their kids to play outdoors be-

cause of safety issues, where there are no walking trails and bike paths, and where healthful food is a long bus ride away, it will be harder to work and be successful with a fitness program.

The fact that solutions usually must be found at the local level is a good thing because it's at the local level that individuals can make connections and have influence.

In the following Community Assets Assessment the task is to determine how adequate your community response is to poverty issues. You will be examining a number of key measures that describe what is available for those trying to achieve economic stability and build resources. This is designed as an informal survey from the perspective of people who understand and are familiar with life in poverty neighborhoods.

I. A. Activity: Community Assets Assessment

Time: 1 hour

Materials: Assessment forms (following pages)

Procedure:

1. Read and discuss the following nine tables that make up the survey of communities' responses to poverty issues.
2. The first table is about economic conditions in your community. Review the results of the investigation and write a brief summary in the space provided.
3. Working in teams, answer the questions in each of the next eight tables. Investigation techniques can include use of the Internet, libraries, local reports and documents, and interviews with people in poverty neighborhoods, as well as with informed community members.
4. Compile your findings and data, share the results with the whole group, and determine the ranking on the five-point scale in the space provided. Then write a brief summary of your findings in the space below each of the eight tables.
5. Transfer the evaluation scores to the bar chart.

Community Assets Assessment

Economic Conditions in the Community
1. What percentage of the people in your community have an income below the official poverty guideline?
2. What percentage of children in your community are living in poverty? What percentage are on food stamps?
3. What is the average free and reduced lunch rate in the community schools?
4. Are there some schools where the free and reduced lunch rate is very high? If so, which ones?
5. To what extent are there pockets of poverty in the community?
6. What are the trends in the poverty rate?
7. In terms of poverty, where does your community rank in the state?
8. Is the community losing population? If so, how much?
9. Are middle-class and upper-class families moving out of the city or county? If so, in what kinds of numbers?
10. What are the utilization trends of homeless shelters in your city and county?
11. What is the unemployment rate? What are the trends in unemployment?
12. What entry-level jobs are available? What do the pay? What kinds of pay-advancement opportunities are there?
13. How does the community rank in health, wellness, and fitness studies?
14. To what degree do students coming out of your community's schools have the knowledge, skills, and attitudes to compete successfully with students from across the globe?
15. How much do leaders in all sectors of the community have the intention to address poverty in a comprehensive way?
16. To what extent do the leaders have the knowledge, tools, and strategies to do so?
Given the economic conditions for people in your community, how adequate is the community response?   5 = excellent, 4 = very good, 3 = good, 2 = fair, 1 = poor

Summary statement about economic conditions in the community:

Housing
1. What is the quality of housing in poor neighborhoods in your community?
2. What is the trend in the number of vacant and abandoned buildings (is the number increasing or decreasing)?
3. What is the typical monthly rental fee for a two-bedroom apartment?
4. What is the trend in "doubling up," of people moving in together?
5. What is the trend in homeownership for low-wage workers?
6. To what extent is "third sector" housing ownership (such as community land trust, housing cooperatives, and mutual housing) available in the community?
Given the housing situation for people in poverty, how adequate is the community response?   5 = excellent, 4 = very good, 3 = good, 2 = fair, 1 = poor

Summary statement about housing conditions in the community:

Banking
1. To what extent are banks offering typical banking services to low-income workers without charging excessive fees?
2. Are banks offering low-interest loans for microeconomic opportunities and business startups? If so, which ones?
3. What are the Community Reinvestment Act (CRA) scores for each bank?
4. To what extent do community groups participate in the development of the CRA plans?
5. Do the CRA plans adequately address the issues of people in all classes and races? If not, why not?
Given the banking situation, how adequate is the community response for those who are in poverty?   5 = excellent, 4 = very good, 3 = good, 2 = fair, 1 = poor

Summary statement about banking conditions in the community:

Jobs, Wages, and Wealth Creation
1. What is the mix of jobs in the knowledge, manufacturing, service, and construction sectors?
2. To what degree are new manufacturing jobs and/or green manufacturing jobs coming into the community?
3. What are the wages for entry-level workers at the last five big employers that came into the community?
4. Does your community have a living-wage ordinance?
5. What is the self-sufficient wage for your community?
6. Is there downward pressure on wages? Are employees being asked to take cuts in wages and/or benefits?
7. Does your community have reasonable CEO-to-front-line-staff salary ratios in the private sector? In the public sector?
8. To what extent are employers using more temporary and part-time employees?
9. To what extent are union jobs available? If so, is the starting pay a living wage, or has the union been forced to greatly lower its standards?
10. To what extent are apprenticeships and certificate programs that lead to well-paying jobs available to high school graduates?
11. Is employee ownership widely available? Employee stock-ownership plans? Profit-sharing and stock-option plans?
12. To what extent is affordable, high-quality childcare available during working hours?
13. Are new companies moving into the community? What is the trend in recent years?
Given the employment/jobs situation, how adequate is the community response?   5 = excellent, 4 = very good, 3 = good, 2 = fair, 1 = poor

Summary statement about jobs, wages, and wealth creation in the community:

Protection from Predators
1. Are payday lenders, cash-advance shops, and check-cashing outlets charging fees and interest rates above 30%? If so, what efforts been made to stop unfair practices?
2. How sufficient and effective are your community's lending services for low-income families that could be used to replace lease/purchase stores?
3. Does your community have lending services that could be used to replace buy-here, pay-here, used-car dealers? If so, how sufficient and effective are they?
4. What, if any, is your community's strategy for dealing with slum landlords?
5. How much are employers asking employees to work "off the clock" (during meal times and breaks, after shifts) without pay? Are there minimum-wage violations? Pay-stub violations? Violations of workers' compensation?
6. What is your community's strategy for dealing with illegal drugs? How effective is it?
Given the current predatory practices, how adequate is the community response?   5 = excellent, 4 = very good, 3 = good, 2 = fair, 1 = poor

Summary statement about protection from predators in the community:

Health and Safety
1. What is the healthcare situation in your community for people in poverty? To what extent is healthcare affordable?
2. What percentage of people in your community do not have health insurance?
3. Can people get to doctor's offices, clinics, and hospitals using public transportation?
4. To what extent is high-quality food available locally at a reasonable cost?
5. From an environmental standpoint, how safe are poor neighborhoods?
6. To what degree do parents feel that their children are safe playing outside and in local parks?
7. To what degree are the streets and neighborhoods safe from violence and crime?
8. How available and affordable are mental health and addiction services?
9. How effective are prenatal-to-age-6 services for people in poverty?
10. To what extent are people in poverty accessing preventive healthcare programs?
Given the health and safety status, how adequate is the community response for people in poverty? 5 = excellent, 4 = very good, 3 = good, 2 = fair, 1 = poor

Summary statement about health and safety conditions in the community:

Education
1. To what extent are high-quality preschool opportunities available to families in poverty?
2. Is Early Head Start available? What percentage of eligible children are enrolled in Early Head Start?
3. What is the graduation rate for high schools, community colleges, and universities?
4. To what extent are students prepared with the skills needed in this economy?
5. To what extent are financial literacy classes available for all stages of life?
6. What is being done about your community's "digital divide"—computer access and computer skills for low-income areas of the community and low-income families?
7. How effective are strategies to improve retention and graduation rates of first-generation, low-income students in the institutions of higher education in your community?
8. To what extent do technical schools provide certifications and apprenticeship programs that lead to well-paying jobs for high school graduates?
Given the status of education, how adequate is the community response for people in poverty? 5 = excellent, 4 = very good, 3 = good, 2 = fair, 1 = poor

Summary statement about educational conditions in the community:

Public Services
1. How sufficient is your community's tax base for maintaining high-quality services?
2. How efficient is your community's public transportation in moving people to the workplace, school, groceries, healthcare facilities, and agencies?
3. How affordable is public transportation?
4. How safe is the public transportation?
5. To what degree do all neighborhoods have high-quality water, sewer, garbage pickup, electricity, public safety, and street cleaning services?
6. To what degree do all neighborhoods have high-quality police and fire services?
Given the investigation into public services, how adequate is the community response for people in poverty?   5 = excellent, 4 = very good, 3 = good, 2 = fair, 1 = poor

Summary statement about public services in the community:

Leadership (governmental, civic, business, education, social services, law enforcement, judicial, healthcare, and faith community)
1. Is your city on the list of "meanest cities in the U.S." for how it treats people in poverty?
2. To what extent does the leadership in each sector (above) ensure that people from of all classes are engaged in planning, program design, implementation, and evaluation of major initiatives?
3. How intentional is the leadership in each sector about helping people in poverty move toward prosperity?
4. How extensively does the leadership in each sector have the knowledge, tools, and strategies that will help people in poverty move toward prosperity?
5. How effectively does the leadership create a culture of mutual respect for people of all classes and races?
Given the status of leadership, how adequate is the community response for people in poverty? 5 = excellent, 4 = very good, 3 = good, 2 = fair, 1 = poor

Summary statement about leadership in the community:

Mental Model: Community Assets Assessment

Housing	Banking	Jobs and Wages	Predators	Health and Safety	Education	Public Services	Leadership
5	5	5	5	5	5	5	5
4	4	4	4	4	4	4	4
3	3	3	3	3	3	3	3
2	2	2	2	2	2	2	2
1	1	1	1	1	1	1	1

Overall summary of community response to poverty:

I. B. Discussion

1. What are the strengths and weaknesses of your community?

2. What does this investigation suggest about the quality of life (social health index) in the community?

3. What opportunities might your community have in the near future?

4. List individuals, associations, and organizations that stand out as potential partners for building resources.

5. List local leaders who are committed to a wide range of strategies to eliminate poverty.

Journal Reflections

Write or draw your thoughts about the conditions in your community.

Community Assets Map

```
┌─────────────────────────────────────────────────────────────┐
│                      ┌─────────────────┐                      │
│   Businesses         │Local Institutions│         Schools     │
│                      └─────────────────┘                      │
│              ┌────────────────────────────────┐               │
│              │      ┌──────────────────┐       │               │
│   Churches   │      │Citizens' Associations│   Block clubs     │
│              │      └──────────────────┘       │               │
│              │  ┌──────────────────────────┐   │               │
│   Parks      │  │  Income │Gifts of Individuals│ Artists │  Libraries │
│              │  │         └────────────────┘   │               │
│              │  │  Youths │ Elderly │ Labeled  │               │
│              │  │         │         │ people   │               │
│              │  └──────────────────────────┘   │               │
│              │         Cultural Groups          │               │
│              └────────────────────────────────┘               │
│   Hospitals                    Community colleges              │
└─────────────────────────────────────────────────────────────┘
```

Note. Adapted from *Building Communities from the Inside Out: A Path Toward Finding and Mobilizing a Community's Assets* (p. 7), by J. P. Kretzmann and J. L. McKnight, 1993, Chicago, IL: ACTA. Copyright 1993 by ACTA.

II. Asset-Based Community Development

In Module 9 you completed a self-assessment of resources that defined and named the current realities of your life. You can use that assessment to hold yourself accountable for your resources and for whatever happens next in your life. If you hold yourself accountable, it's only reasonable that the communities should be held accountable too. The Community Assets Assess-

ment that we just completed was in part about holding the community accountable.

The next investigation is to find the individuals, associations, and institutions that have the vision, knowledge, and connections to help solve community problems in innovative, exciting ways.

Investigations is based on the premise that people who live in poverty are problem solvers who have unique skills, talents, and knowledge that can help them in any setting. John Kretzmann and John McKnight, authors of *Building Communities from the Inside Out: A Path Toward Finding and Mobilizing a Community's Assets,* share that philosophy. They take a "capacity" approach that "… leads toward the development of policies and activities based on the capacities, skills and assets of lower income people and their neighborhoods" (Kretzmann & McKnight, 1993, p. 5).

They have documented that poverty neighborhoods are full of unrecognized assets. They say, "The key to neighborhood regeneration, then, is to locate all the available local assets, *to begin connecting them with one another in ways that multiply their power and effectiveness,* and to begin harnessing those of local institutions that are not yet available for local development purposes" [emphasis added] (Kretzmann & McKnight, 1993, p. 5).

Kretzmann and McKnight begin by "releasing" individual capacities, then expand to include the capacities of citizens associations, and finally identify the capacities of local institutions as seen in the preceding "Community Assets Map."

The Community Assets Map is a way to begin to organize an inventory that unlocks the gifts available from individuals, associations, and institutions.

What *Investigations* has brought to the task of making connections is the lens of economic class. Having already identified our strongest resources, investigated our social capital, and

named the hidden rules that have helped us navigate our world, we know the value of one-on-one relationships. Combining the relationship-based approach of poverty with the achievement-based approach of the middle class—and knowing the hidden rules of class—allow us to visualize a community of expanding relationships of mutual respect and expanding opportunities for everyone.

In the chart on the next page, Kretzmann and McKnight represent how to develop one-on-one relationships. This example is for "local youths"; in their book there are similar charts for senior citizens, disabled individuals, welfare recipients, and artists. The point is that each "group" interacts with a variety of community associations and institutions. And within each of those groups are people who might share an affinity for the particular concerns of the associations and institutions. Each of the interactions represented in the chart illustrates a matching of the gifts and capabilities of "local youths" with those in various organizations and institutions.

The purpose of this activity is to develop one-on-one relationships that have the potential to turn into partnerships that will help you (1) complete the plan you'll make in Module 12, (2) stabilize your environment, (3) build resources, (4) earn your degree or credential, and (5) benefit future students.

One-on-One Relationships

Note. Adapted from *Building Communities from the Inside Out: A Path Toward Finding and Mobilizing a Community's Assets* (p. 44), by J. P. Kretzmann and J. L. McKnight, 1993, Chicago, IL: ACTA. Copyright 1993 by ACTA.

Analyze the chart to expand your thinking of how you can build relationships with associations and institutions in your community. It is in those relationships that you might find the key to new solutions.

II. A. Activity: Creating a One-on-One Relationships Mental Model

Time: 45 minutes

Materials: Paper, pencils, community directories, campus directories

Procedure:

1. Working as a group, use flipchart paper and draw a circle in the center of the paper, labeling the circle COLLEGE STUDENTS.

2. Brainstorm the local associations, institutions, and organizations with which college students might partner. Consider both the college campus and the community.

3. Review the following Sample Community Map for additional ideas of the associations, institutions, individuals, physical spaces, and activities in the local economy that might be considered. Again, think both "on campus" and "off campus."

4. List the local individuals and organizations that came up in Steps 1–3. If possible, find and document the contact information for each.

5. Create a One-on-One Relationships mental model by drawing lines between a center circle (COLLEGE STUDENTS) and the various on- and off-campus community assets. Write brief descriptions of the possible connections. Where might there be matches of gifts and capabilities?

6. Develop another One-on-One Relationships mental model for your individual use, one that is specific to your interests, gifts, capabilities, and connections. Re-create a list of the people with whom you have a relationship—or need to have one; include contact information for them.

Sample Community Map

Physical Spaces

Gardens
Parks
Playgrounds
Parking Lots
Bike Paths
Walking Paths
Forests/Forest Preserves
Picnic Areas
Campsites
Fishing Spots
Duck Ponds
Zoos
Wildlife Centers
Natural Habitats—coastal,
marine, amphibious
Bird Watching Sites
Stargazing Sites
Housing
Vacant Land and Buildings
Transit Stops and Facilities
Streets

Associations

Animal Care Groups
Anti-Crime Groups
Business Organizations
Charitable Groups
Civic Events Groups
Cultural Groups
Disabilities/Special Needs Groups
Education Groups
Elderly Groups
Environmental Groups
Family Support Groups
Health Advocacy/Fitness
Heritage Groups
Hobby and Collectors Groups
Men's Groups
Mutual Support Groups
Neighborhood Groups
Political Organizations
Recreation Groups
Religious Groups
Service Clubs
Social Groups
Union Groups
Veterans' Groups
Women's Groups
Youth Groups

Individuals

Gifts, Skills, Capacities,
Knowledge, and Traits of:

Youths
Older Adults
Artists
Welfare Recipients
People with Disabilities
Students
Parents
Entrepreneurs
Activists
Veterans
Ex-Offenders

Local Economy

For-Profit Businesses
Consumer Expenditures
Merchants
Chamber of Commerce
Business Associations
Banks
Credit Unions
Institutional—purchasing power
and personnel
Barter and Exchange
Community Development
Corporations (CDCs)
Corporations and Branches

Institutions

Schools
Universities
Community Colleges
Police Departments
Hospitals
Libraries
Social Service Agencies
Non-Profits
Museums
Fire Departments
Media
Foundations

Note. Adapted from "Discovering Community Power: A Guide to Mobilizing Local Assets and Your Organization's Capacity" (p. 15), by J. P. Kretzmann and J. L. McKnight, with S. Dobrowolski and D. Puntenney, 2005, Evanston, IL: Asset-Based Community Development Institute. Copyright 2005 by Asset-Based Community Development Institute.

II. B. Discussion

1. This is information that can be used by the entire group. How might it be used by other groups in the community?

2. What community assets did this investigation uncover that surprised you?

3. Who are some of the individuals identified by the group who can address policy issues on campus?

4. Who are the individuals in a position to help students complete a degree and build resources?

5. What associations and institutions can help students complete a degree and build resources?

Readings

An Atlas of Poverty in America: One Nation, Pulling Apart, 1960–2003 by Amy K. Glasmeier. From the back cover: "The atlas serves as a standard reference volume for students and researchers trying to understand one of the most pressing and longstanding social problems in America."

The Careless Society: Community and Its Counterfeits by John McKnight. "The discussions point out that our problem is not ineffective service-producing institutions. In fact, our institutions are too powerful, authoritative, and strong. Our problem is weak communities, made ever more impotent by our strong service systems" (p. ix).

Class Matters: Cross-Class Alliance Building for Middle-Class Activists by Betsy Leondar-Wright. "I see such a difference between privileged communities and low-income communities. Parents with power feel worthy of calling decision makers and saying, 'I need an appointment'" (p. 96). From the chapter "Obstacles to Alliances?" found on pages 88–130. Provides a look at classism.

Just and Lasting Change: When Communities Own Their Futures by Daniel Taylor-Ide and Carl E. Taylor. "The only meaningful counterbalance to corporate globalization is communities. The momentum of globalized trade cannot be stopped, but it can be redirected. Communities are small enough to be able to understand their own self-interest, yet large enough to be able to access resources and generate efficiencies of scale. When communities are weak, they are inevitably exploited" (p. 19).

The Measure of America: American Human Development Report 2008–2009 by Sarah Burd-Sharps, Kristen Lewis, and Eduardo Borges Martins. This report introduces the American Human Development Index, a single measure of well-being for all Americans. Reports are available by state, congressional district, gender, race, and ethnicity. It reveals huge disparities in health, education, and living standards among different groups.

The Social Health of the Nation: How America Is Really Doing by Marc Miringoff and Marque-Luisa Miringoff. Discusses how the social health index provides an interesting way to measure and monitor a community's health in Chapter 7, "Judging the Nation's Social Performance," found on pages 149–156.

Toward Sustainable Communities: Resources for Citizens and Their Governments by Mark Roseland. Using the concept of "community capital," this book describes how to naturally build social and economic capital. Look up "poverty" in the book's index and learn how sustainability and poverty are linked.

Who Are the Question-Makers? A Participatory Evaluation Handbook edited by Janet Donnelly. See in particular "Part Four: How to Do a Participatory Evaluation" found on pages 25–32.

MODULE 11
Building Resources

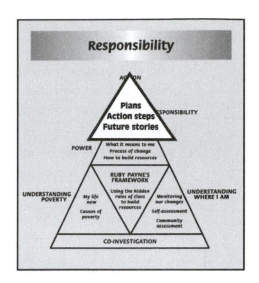

Responsibility

Learning Objectives

WHAT'S COVERED

You will:

Create a list of ways to develop each resource

Explore how hidden rules can be used to build resources

WHY IT'S IMPORTANT

People build a high quality of life by building resources.

Brainstorming ways to build resources prepares you for the planning phase.

HOW IT'S CONNECTED TO YOU

The learning and analysis phases of *Investigations* are leading to the action phase.

Soon you are going to apply to your plan everything you have learned during *Investigations.*

You also can use the ideas developed by the group to build resources.

Learning Process

- You will explore two different types of resource development activities, both of which ask you to brainstorm any number of possible options.

- You'll listen to other investigators' ideas, which might spark even more ideas to share.

Lexicon for Module 11

Interlocking resources
Mere-measurement effect

I. Key Points About Building Resources

Building resources is easier said than done. Now that you have developed a deeper understanding of the impact of poverty on individuals and communities, you can appreciate how difficult it is to build resources. In this module, we'll investigate ways to build resources *theoretically*. In other words, think of *all* possibilities, and don't restrict your thinking because it isn't a resource that you personally intend to build. In the next module, you'll do the *practical* thinking as you decide more specifically what you wish to work on. This module helps you explore the possibilities. While you're doing this, keep these points in mind:

1. Building resources can lead to a more balanced life. Have you ever known of someone who had high financial resources but very low emotional or spiritual resources? Or someone who was intelligent but just couldn't get along with others? That person might have high mental resources and low emotional resources; raising emotional resources will lead to a more balanced life.

2. Be aware of the natural inclination to focus on building resources that are already high. For example, a woman who is physically fit already has high physical resources; she doesn't need to build that particular resource any more. But it wouldn't be surprising if she still focused on fitness. This tendency is understandable because she's familiar with going to the gym and confident that she'll feel comfortable there. Therefore, when doing this activity, you'll be able to tell which of your resources are already high, because it will be easy to list many ways to build them.

3. Earlier we discussed the interlocking nature of resources. When a teacher was involved in a serious accident, he suffered brain and pelvic damage that over a period of five years led to the loss of his job, his physical strength to hike and camp, and the loss of his circle of friends with whom he had hiked. Resources are linked as we lose them, but they're linked as we grow them too. For example, building mental resources by earning a degree can lead to higher financial, emotional, and social resources.

4. Building resources begins with forming the intention to build them. Researchers are learning more about the "mere-measurement effect," which suggests that simply by forming (and measuring) an intention we increase the likelihood that we'll engage in one or more new behaviors. If we articulate the in-

tention, we're more likely to act on it (Chapman, 2001). In Module 8 (in the five-part Stages of Change chart) we investigated a way to measure our motivation for change. If you are motivated to build resources and to change—and you monitor that intention—you will be more likely to be successful. Some investigators report that they redo the self-assessment from Module 9 once or twice a year. In some colleges students continue to meet with other investigators to discuss their self-assessments, resources, and plans, as well as to support one another in other ways.

5. The last activity in Module 10 identified individuals, associations, and organizations that are potential partners. In the following activities, you'll be able to name the individuals and organizations that can help you stabilize your environment and build resources.

6. We are now well aware that poverty isn't just about individual choices. As our investigations revealed, there are systemic issues that contribute to poverty too. Right now, though, the task is to work as a group to prepare for creating individual plans. In the following activities you will break into teams of two or three and work together to capture ideas on how to build resources. The whole group will then get back together and expand on the small groups' ideas. By the time each individual begins to work on his or her plans, we will have tapped the experience, knowledge, and wisdom of the entire group.

I. A. Activity: Building Resources
Time: 30–45 minutes
Materials: Chart paper, markers
Procedure:

1. Choose one of the two following strategies to brainstorm ideas for resource development.

2. Break into small groups

3. Assign as many resources to each group as necessary so that all 11 resources are covered.

Option 1: Tic-Tac-Toe Technique

1. On chart paper re-create the following Tic-Tac-Toe diagram (without the examples) for each resource assigned to your small group. In the center circle of the center square, name the resource that the group will be working on. When naming each resource, add a more specific goal to help focus thinking. For example, if your group is working on physical resources, the specific goal may be to "lose weight and exercise." In the following example, the group is working on mental resources; specifically group members are thinking about earning a college degree.

2. Then brainstorm eight issues that will have to be addressed when building that resource. In one or two words, label the eight circles surrounding the resource named in the center. In the following diagram, three issues are identified: managing time, making good grades, and managing relationships.

3. Now take the first issue (in the circle marked A in the center square) and rewrite it in the center circle marked A of the upper-left square. Do the same with each issue from the center square.

4. Then continue the brainstorming to identify strategies for each issue in circles A through H. In the example below for A (time) members of the small group decided they would need to spend less (<) time at parties and more (>) time studying.

5. When the small groups are done brainstorming for each resource assigned to them, they will share their results with the entire class.

6. The whole class will add more ideas to the charts developed by the small group, thus capturing the best thinking of everyone.

7. Individuals will be able to access these charts when they develop their own plans in Module 12.

Resource Tic-Tac-Toe

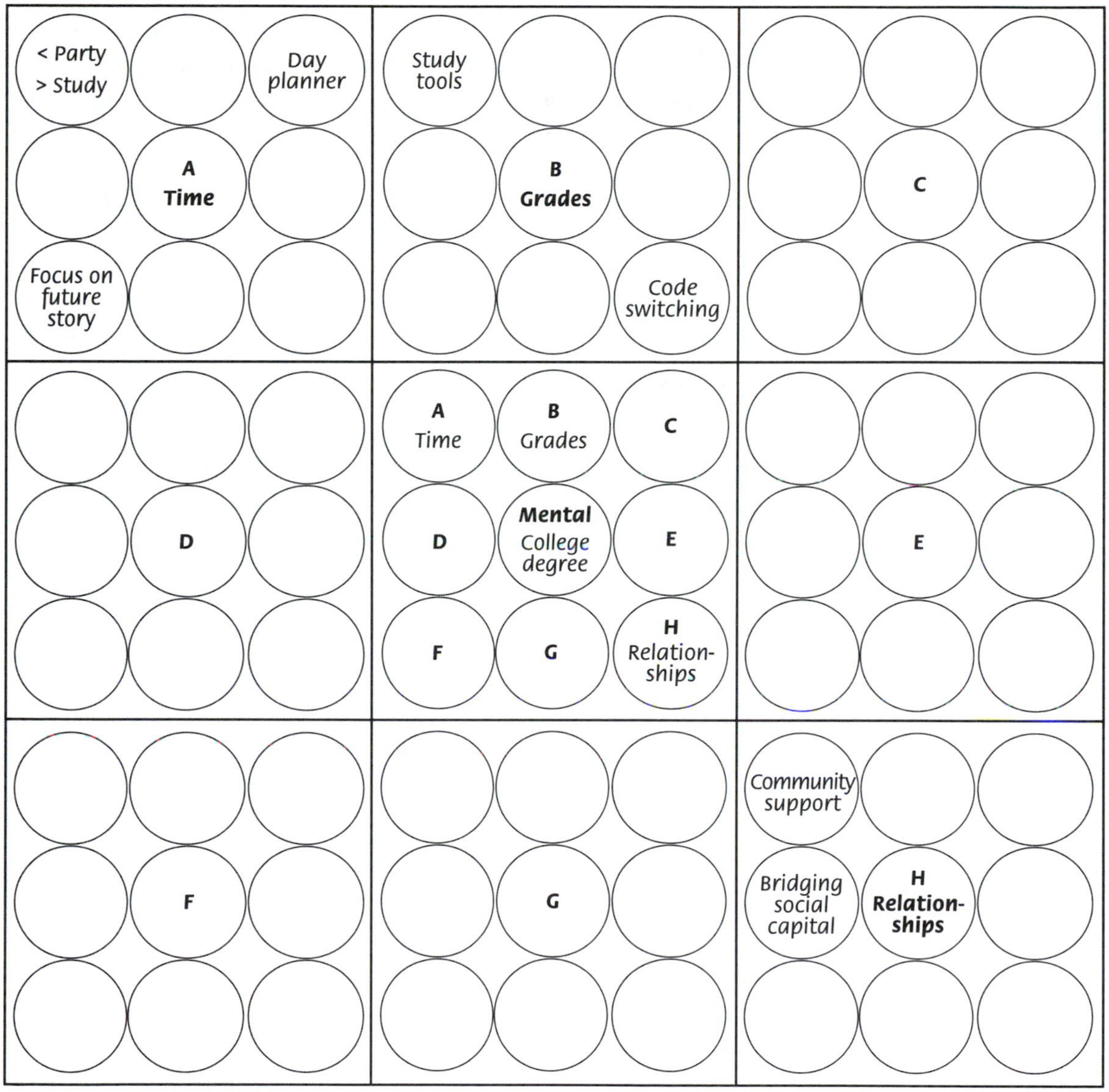
< Party
> Study
Day planner
A
Time
Focus on future story
Study tools
B
Grades
Code switching
C
D
A
Time
B
Grades
C
Mental
College degree
D
E
F
G
H
Relation-ships
E
F
G
Community support
Bridging social capital
H
Relation-ships

Option 2: Brainstorming

1. Working in small groups at tables, with each table taking one or two resources, brainstorm ideas on how to build resources. When brainstorming, remember that you don't stop to criticize ideas; you want to let them flow so that different ideas spark new thinking. Using chart paper, draw a line down the middle of the page from top to bottom. Then label the left side, "Building _____ Resources." List the ideas under that heading. Use one page for each of the 11 resources.

Resource Brainstorming

Building _____ Resources	Hidden Rules

2. Label the right-hand column "Hidden Rules." Now under that heading list the hidden rules that are needed to build that particular resource. Indicate which class's hidden rules would be needed—poverty, middle, or wealth. It's

possible that one, two, or all three might be needed. For example, if you're working on building social support and decide that volunteering at a service agency will increase your bridging capital, what hidden rules would you need to use? Speaking in formal register would make things easier for the people you meet, so that's one option. You might think it would be OK to use casual register too in certain circumstances, so in that case you would be using language rules from two classes. It also might help if you used the middle-class rules regarding driving forces (work and achievement) because, even though it's volunteer work you'll be doing, it will still be about achieving the goals of the organization. The middle-class rule on punctuality is another that you might want to use.

3. Share ideas from all the tables and expand the brainstorming by letting the whole group suggest ideas.

4. Have a volunteer type up the list for all the resources so that everyone has a copy to look at when it's time to make individual plans.

I. B. Discussion

1. What ideas did you get from this exercise?

2. How might someone still be able to build resources even when his or her environment is very unstable?

3. How might someone build resources when community assets are low?

4. Which resources were the most difficult to build? Why?

5. Which resources were the easiest to build? Why?

6. Which hidden rules of poverty, middle class, and wealth were listed most often?

7. Where are you now with regard to the stages of change?

"I finally understood that, in the end, I may not be responsible for what I was, but I am responsible for what I am, what I hope to become, and what I hope my children will become. I'm the role model now. I cannot possibly demand moral behaviors from others, demand integrity and forthrightness, if my own life does not exemplify it."

—Carl Upchurch, *Convicted in the Womb*

I. C. Activity: Read a Good Book

Read a book from the list on p. 228. These are autobiographies and stories about people in different economic classes, mostly poverty. Analyze the book using the lens of economic class that was introduced in *Investigations*—and in resource development in particular.

I. D. Discussion

1. When did the main character become motivated for change?

2. What was the person's highest resource? What other resources for the individual also were high?

3. Which resource did he or she build first?

4. How did the characters manage their relationships during periods of change?

5. Who supported the development of and access to the resources?

6. What, if any, community assets did he or she use?

Journal Reflections

Write or draw your thoughts and ideas about building your own resources.

Readings

The Absolutely True Diary of a Part-Time Indian by Sherman Alexie. Can be read as a case study of how to build resources.

All Over but the Shoutin' by Rick Bragg. Can be read as a case study of how to build resources.

Angela's Ashes: A Memoir by Frank McCourt. Can be read as a case study of how to build resources.

Class Matters: Cross-Class Alliance Building for Middle-Class Activists by Betsy Leondar-Wright. How to bring people together across class lines to improve lives.

Convicted in the Womb by Carl Upchurch. Can be read as a case study of how to build resources.

Makes Me Wanna Holler by Nathan McCall. Can be read as a case study of how to build resources.

"Measuring Intent: There's Nothing 'Mere' about Mere Measurement Effects" by Kenneth J. Chapman. Highlights the importance of measuring progress and the value of regularly doing a self-assessment of resources.

Welfare Brat: A Memoir by Mary Childers. The author's life story illustrates many concepts of class and poverty that are covered in *Investigations*. From the back cover: "With poetic prose that sings and moans, Mary Childers strips away the mythology, the pity, the phony notions of heroism that usually mask the realities of being poor. It's also a page-turner that makes you think and think, even after you put it down," writes David K. Shipler, author of *The Working Poor: Invisible in America*.

MODULE 12
Personal Plan for Building Resources

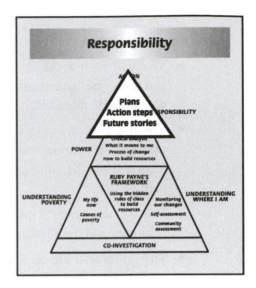

ACTION

Plans
Action steps RESPONSIBILITY
Future stories

POWER

Critical analysis
What it means to me
Process of change
How to build resources

RUBY PAYNE'S
FRAMEWORK

UNDERSTANDING
POVERTY

My life
now

Using the hidden
rules of class
to build
resources

Monitoring
our changes

UNDERSTANDING
WHERE I AM

Causes of
poverty

Self-assessment

Community
assessment

CO-INVESTIGATION

Learning Objectives

WHAT'S COVERED

You will:

Review the work completed to date: mental models, notes, assessments, and stages of change

List your strongest and weakest resources

Rank the resources you need to work on first

Create SMART goals—specific, measurable, attainable, realistic, and time-specific

Develop your plans for building the first three resources that need the most attention

Create immediate action steps

Complete the Support for Change mental model

Create a mental model of your plan

As a group, create a mental model for Community Prosperity or a mental model for How the Campus Can Support Transition

Revise your plans based on your vision or on mental models

WHY IT'S IMPORTANT

It's important that you make your own plans—plans that fit your overall situation and are based on your priorities.

HOW IT'S CONNECTED TO YOU

The investigations are done, and it's now time to move to the action phase.

Everything you've done in this course up to this point is part of the foundation for this module. Now you can create a plan that works for you. Then you and your co-investigators can create plans to help find solutions for the community or the campus.

Learning Process

- You will review the investigative process and what you have learned, then develop a plan to build resources.

- You'll use the Support for Change mental model to determine who will be on your team during the time you work on your plan.

- You'll create a mental model that represents your plan and future story.

- The group will create a mental model for how the community or the campus can support students and build a prosperous community.

Lexicon for Module 12

Back door
Future story
Support for Change mental
    model

I. Building Resources

Your plans will focus on building your personal resources—and also considering your role in the community. Consider this quote from Carl Upchurch:

> In reality, no single group has created the conditions of our inner cities. No single race can be charged with committing the whole array of economic, political and social crimes perpetrated against the poor and their children. We are all at fault, we who preach peace and justice yet enjoy the bounty of exploitation and oppression; we who don't give our national crises the same priority we give international ones; we who barter away human rights for a slice of the power pie; and we, the poor, who intentionally or not, help perpetuate our own condition by refusing to hold society accountable for what it does to us—and for refusing to hold ourselves accountable for what we *allow* it to do. (Upchurch, 1996, p. 198)

I. A. Activity: Personal Plan for Building Resources

Time: 2 hours

Materials: Worksheets, mental models

Procedure:

1. First consider what you want to work on and why it's important to you.

2. Work through the following seven steps thoroughly, using the blank worksheets at the end of the module. Talk things over with other group members and the facilitator as you see fit.

3. If you're comfortable disclosing your work, share it with other investigators so they can use your ideas to help build their own plans.

Prepare to Work

Review all seven mental models and notes that you've made in your workbook. They are:

- "My Life Now"
- Process of Change
- Social Capital
- Resources Self-Assessment (bar chart)
- Community Assessment (bar chart)
- One-on-One Relationships
- Tic-Tac-Toe and/or Brainstorming Worksheet

Decide *What* to Work On

Reviewing the Self-Assessment of Resources mental model (Module 9), identify and list your three strongest resources.

Three Strongest Resources	Three Weakest Resources

Define *Why* You Want to Work on These Resources

Now choose the three weakest resources you want to work on and rank them, the most important one first. For example, you may have just been offered a job and so you want to start with building your financial resources. On reflection, however, if the job offer is for minimal pay or has few hours, you might decide that it's more important to pursue your degree (building your mental resources) than to work another low-wage job right now. This step might take considerable thought because sometimes what seems obvious at first is not in your best interests longer term.

Rank your three most important resources to work on	How important is it to you that you change? 1–10 scale: 1= not important at all, 10 = extremely important	Explain in your own words why change is important to you
1	Circle your score: 1 2 3 4 5 6 7 8 9 10	
2	Circle your score: 1 2 3 4 5 6 7 8 9 10	
3	Circle your score: 1 2 3 4 5 6 7 8 9 10	

Step 1

Establish a SMART goal for each of the three resources on your list. Before listing your goals, refer back to the work the group did in Module 11 about how to build your particular three resources. It is *very important* that you set goals well. SMART goals are specific, measurable, attainable, realistic, and time-specific. Use a worksheet to work on these goals first. When you have the first one exactly the way you want it, write it on the worksheet at the end of the module. What follows is an example.

NOTE: As stated, blank worksheets are available at the end of this module and also at *www.gettingaheadnetwork.com/college.*

Example: Setting a SMART Goal

Resource: Support Systems
Goal: One year from now I will have more bridging social capital. I'll join two groups or organizations where I will have regular (at least monthly) contact with positive and diverse people.
Monitor for SMART standards: Check each box that meets the standards of a SMART goal. Get feedback from at least one other person that it is a SMART goal.
☐ Specific   ☐ Measurable   ☐ Attainable   ☐ Realistic   ☐ Time-specific

Analysis: Let's check to see if this example meets the SMART standard: *Is it specific?* Yes, it's about building bridging capital. *Is it measurable?* Yes, this person will join *two* groups and will have *monthly* contact. *Is it attainable or doable?* The answer to this is not so obvious. We would have to know more about the person setting the goal, but let's say that most people could find the time to join two groups if it was important to them. *Is it realistic?* The answer to this is similar to the "attainable" question. *Is it time-specific?* Yes, it must be done within a year.

Step 2

Create procedural steps for each goal. Write the goal in the appropriate space, then put the procedural steps in a logical order, first things first. What do you need to do to accomplish your goal? Identify the hidden rules that you may use. Finally, think through how long it will take to do each step, then pick the starting date for each. Below is the example we looked at in Step 4.

Example: Procedural Steps

Goal: One year from now I will have more bridging social capital. I'll join two groups or organizations where I will have regular (at least monthly) contact with positive and diverse people.		
Steps	**Hidden Rules**	**Starting Date**
1. Make a list of things that interest you personally and/or a list of college or community issues that you want to do something about.	*Driving force:* middle class = work and achievement *Language:* casual and formal registers, language to negotiate	Today
2. Find organizations that deal with those issues and interests. Choose five organizations that interest you the most.	*Time:* middle class = keep the future in mind; be on time, reliable	Today
3. Make contact—face to face or by phone, mail, or e-mail—with the five organizations. Ask for information about when and where the next meeting is and if it's OK for you to attend.	*Personality:* poverty = entertainment and humor; middle class = stability and achievement	Tomorrow
4. Attend meetings and meet people from five organizations.		Two weeks from today
5. Sign up with or join two of them.		
6. Attend meetings and get involved in a regular way. Keep a journal to record your thoughts and feelings—and how you use information from *Investigations* within these organizations.		Eight weeks from today for one, 12 weeks from today for the other

Step 3

Make a list of where you will get help. When we begin to make changes, we almost always need the help of other individuals, groups, organizations, and agencies. Review the ideas this group created on how to build resources. Make a list for each goal.

Example: Where to Go to Get Help

Goal 1:	One year from now I will have more bridging social capital. I'll join two groups or organizations where I will have regular (at least monthly) contact with positive and diverse people.
1. Support systems	1. For ideas on interests: friends, family, college handbook, campus newspaper, people who are well-connected, newspapers, library, Internet.
	2. For ideas on organizations and groups: Office of Student Organizations on campus, Office of Equal Opportunity and Diversity, academic departments for subject areas I'm interested in (like English, art, technology, etc.), campus and community newspaper, library, Internet, agency lists, Chamber of Commerce lists, phone book. Also talk to people outside of my bonding circle.
	3. For first meeting: Find someone who is already connected or a member of the group and go with him or her. Invite one of the people from the *Investigations* group to go along as well.
	4. If I don't know anyone in the organization, I can ask a contact person to meet ahead of time with one group member in order to find out what to expect.

Step 4

Develop a monthly and weekly plan. Put the action steps you need to take into a monthly and weekly plan. The first week of the month is laid out in an example below.

Example: Weekly Plan

Goal 1: One year from now I will have more bridging social capital. I'll join two groups or organizations where I will have regular (at least monthly) contact with positive and diverse people.						
Sun	*Mon*	*Tue*	*Wed*	*Thu*	*Fri*	*Sat*
Read news-paper; talk to family and friends; check phone book.	Chamber of Commerce; agency lists; library; make lists of interests and organiza-tions.	Contact two of five organi-zations.	Contact other three organi-zations.	Research interests and organiza-tions to find out what's expected.	Talk with positive friends—people who support my changes.	Talk with positive friends—people who support my changes; prepare plans for next week.

Step 5

Keep a daily plan or "To Do" list. On a 3x5 card, write down everything you're going to do today. Carry it with you and cross off the items as you get them done. You could have one card for each goal, or keep all your to-do's on the same card.

Step 6

Create backup plans for when things go wrong. It's very easy to slip back into old ways of functioning. Sometimes we make wonderful plans for change but keep a "back door" open to escape if the going gets tough. The following strategy comes from the American Lung Association, and it's used to help people stop smoking. There are hundreds of reasons to stop smoking, but people often relapse by leaving the back doors open, using a phrase like, "If I start gaining weight … then I'll smoke again." The last half of that sentence often isn't spoken, but it's there. Well, many people who stop smoking gain some weight, at least at first, so there's the escape hatch. You have to close the back doors so that you can stick with your plans.

Example: Closing 'Back Doors'

Back Doors	How to Close Them
1. "If things don't go well, I'll throw in the towel." (It's always easier to give up than keep trying.)	1. Recognize that you are about to fly out the back door. 2. Tell yourself that you can do this. Wait a few minutes, and the negative feeling will pass. 3. Talk to someone who supports what you're doing. Have his or her phone number handy and tell this person ahead of time that it's his or her "job" to encourage you when things get rough. Have a sense of humor about this "job description," but still be firm in your expectations of your friend.
2. "I'll do it tomorrow. Too much is going on today. Gotta let it slide for now."	1. Recognize the negative thinking you're engaging in. 2. Make the phone call to your friend. 3. Tell yourself that nothing short of death or the house burning down is going to keep you from doing the one or two things on your daily list.
3. "If the people around me don't support me, I won't be able to do it."	1. Recognize the inclination to do back-door thinking. 2. Make a list of people who do support your changes—and stay in touch with them. 3. Have more than one plan for getting things done. If Person A won't help, have Person B ready to go. If Plan A falls apart, be ready with Plan B.

Step 7

It's time to put together the team that will support you for as long as it takes to build your resources. The following Support for Change mental model will help you pick your team. Building different resources may require different people, so make a model for each of the three resources.

1. At the top of the paper, fill in the name of the resource that you're planning to build.

2. Put your name in the center circle.

3. Think of the people who will be affected by the changes you make: children, family, friends, employers, and so on. These are people who have influence on your life and people you influence. To refresh your thinking, go back to the earlier mental models you made. Draw a circle for all persons and put their names in those circles.

4. Using a pen or pencil, draw a line between each person and yourself—the more support they are likely to give you the thicker the line. For example, if the person will give you total support and actively help you make the change, draw a thick line. If his or her support is halfhearted or weak, use a thin or dotted line. If the person will oppose the idea of your change and will work against you, leave it blank or draw an arrow going away from you.

5. Now begin to select the members of your support team.

    a. Look at the mental model and select people who are already supporting your efforts to change. List them as "current team members."

    b. Then think of fellow investigators from this class whom you want on your team. List them as "current team members" also.

    c. Think back to the Social Capital mental model created in Module 7 and the people you listed in the section on bridging social capital. Select and list the people from that mental model whom you need to "recruit."

    d. Review the investigation into campus and community assets and the One-on-One Relationships mental model you created in Module 10. Add the names of the people and organizations to the "recruit" list that will support you as you build your resources; write down their names.

6. Share your plan with the people and organizations you have selected and ask for their commitment.

Example: Personal Support for Change Mental Model

"I'm going to build my _____ resource."

SUPPORT TEAM

**Current Team Members
You Want to Keep**

People to Recruit

_____   _____

_____   _____

_____   _____

_____   _____

_____   _____

Complete Steps 1–7 for each of the three resources you chose to develop.

Your facilitator may provide you with blank planning pages, or you can find them on the *www.gettingaheadnetwork.com/college* website.

Journal Reflections

Write or draw your thoughts, ideas, and feelings about your personal plan for prosperity.

I. B. Activity: Personal Mental Model of Future Story

Time: 1 hour
Materials: Worksheets, mental models
Procedure:

1. Look back over the mental models that you've created and think about how far you've come. Also reflect on the story you were living when you started and the future story you are now making. This is the narrative of your life.

2. Look at the plans you just made, the goals and action steps, the people who will support you, and the work that lies ahead.

3. Using these thoughts, think of a way to draw a mental model or write a brief story of the changes you are already making and are going to keep making. This is a picture or vision of your coming journey and your goals. You can hold this mental model in your mind more easily than all the words that went into the SMART plan. This mental model will help you remember your plan. The vision will help you persist and avoid back-door escapes.

4. Share your mental model with others. How many times have we found that building on each other's ideas helps to improve our thinking? Consider their ideas, and perhaps use them in your mental model.

5. Your latest vision might help you see missing pieces in your plan—people who could support you, things to do, organizations to work with, or even specifics about your goals. Revise anything that needs to be revised

 I. C. Discussion

1. When you think back over the investigations, what things stand out as the most important for you?

2. When you think about what it took for you to create your own path, what did you learn about yourself?

3. Where are you now in relation to the stages of change?

4. When was it that you became most motivated to change?

5. What changes have you already made in the way you think and act?

6. Who is going on the journey with you?

Journal Reflections

Write or draw your thoughts and ideas about completing your plans for building your resources.

I. D. Activity: Mental Model for Community Prosperity and the College Campus

Time: 45 minutes

Materials: Chart paper, markers

Procedure:

1. Have a group discussion about the difference between taking responsibility for solving personal problems—such as taking action to build your own resources—and taking responsibility for community solutions (e.g., to fight poverty) or campus solutions (e.g., to help students from poverty succeed). We've often said that poverty is about more than the choices of the individual. If we hold the community responsible for creating a wide range of strategies to fight poverty, then we can help the community create those strategies. If we hold the college accountable for educating under-resourced college students, then we also can help the college meet that challenge. Now that we are taking responsibility for our own choices, it's time to consider how we also can be problem solvers in the community and/or on campus.

2. Decide as a group if you will work on the community model or the campus model.

3. If you choose to work on a mental model for the community, discuss what it means to have prosperity and economic security for all people. What would it take to have that happen? Think back over the information on the wealth gap and the research on poverty. What strategies are needed? How can we get the community to work on those strategies?

4. If you choose to work on a mental model for the campus, think about what it would take for the campus to support under-resourced students so that they could live in a stable environment, achieve academically, and earn a degree.

5. Make a list of the ideas generated by the group.

6. Work on a mental model together.

7. Decide how to share this mental model and your ideas with the community or campus.

I. E. Discussion

1. Did the mental model for Community Prosperity include strategies from all four areas of research on the causes of poverty? Or did the mental model for College Success include strategies from all four areas of research?

2. Has your attitude toward the college and the community changed since beginning this workbook? If so, in what ways?

3. Has your perspective of the middle class changed? Toward the wealthy? If so, how?

4. How might you build more and stronger partnerships with people from other economic classes?

5. In what ways do you think of yourself differently now that you have contributed ideas for the betterment of the college and the community?

Journal Reflections

Write or draw your thoughts, ideas, and dreams about community prosperity.

Personal Plan for Building Resources

Step 1: SMART Goals

Resource:
Goal:
Monitor for SMART standards: Check each box that meets the standards of a SMART goal. Get feedback from at least one other person that it is a SMART goal.
☐ Specific   ☐ Measurable   ☐ Attainable   ☐ Realistic   ☐ Time-specific

Step 2: Procedural Steps

Goal (from Step 1):		
Steps	**Hidden Rules**	**Starting Date**
1.		
2.		
3.		
4.		
5.		
6.		
7.		
8.		
9.		
10.		

Step 3: Where to Go to Get Help

Step	Where to Go to Get Help
1. Support systems	1. 2. 3. 4.

Step 4: Weekly and Monthly Plan

Plan for first week

Sun	Mon	Tue	Wed	Thu	Fri	Sat

Step 4: Weekly and Monthly Plan *(continued)*

Plan for next month

Sun	Mon	Tue	Wed	Thu	Fri	Sat
Sun	Mon	Tue	Wed	Thu	Fri	Sat
Sun	Mon	Tue	Wed	Thu	Fri	Sat
Sun	Mon	Tue	Wed	Thu	Fri	Sat

Step 5: Daily 'To Do' List

Keep a daily plan or "To Do" list—on a 3x5 card.

Step 6: Back-Up Plans for Closing Back Doors

Back Doors	How to Close Them
1.	1. 2. 3.
2.	1. 2. 3.
3.	1. 2. 3.

Step 7: Establish Support Team

Sample Diagram: Personal Support for Change Mental Model

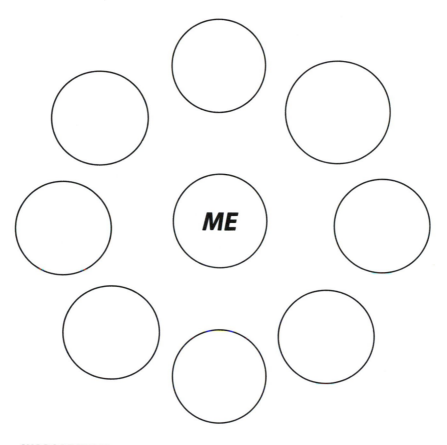

SUPPORT TEAM

**Current Team Members
You Want to Keep**

People to Recruit

_____   _____
_____   _____
_____   _____
_____   _____
_____   _____

That's a plan!

Appendix

Movies, Literature, and Poetry on Economic Class

Films

Allen, W. (Director). (1969). *Take the money and run* [Motion picture]. USA: American Broadcasting Company. Cast: Woody Allen, Janet Margolin, Marcel Hillaire. Uses documentary style to tell the story of a compulsive thief.

Apted, M. (Director). (1980). *Coal miner's daughter* [Motion picture]. USA: Universal Pictures. Cast: Sissy Spacek, Tommy Lee Jones, Beverly D'Angelo, Levon Helm. Life story of country singer Loretta Lynn, chronicling her rise from poverty to fame and her struggles with identity.

Avildsen, J. G. (Director). (1976). *Rocky* [Motion picture]. USA: Chartoff-Winkler Productions. Cast: Sylvester Stallone, Burgess Meredith, Talia Shire, Burt Young. Story of a prizefighter who makes it back to the top through spirit and hard work. Won an Academy Award for best picture, director, and editing. Followed by four sequels.

Bauman, S., & Heller, R. (Directors). (1986). *The women of summer* [Motion picture]. USA: The National Endowment for the Humanities. Documentary of 1920s Bryn Mawr Summer School for Women Workers in Industry. Present-day interviews are used to reflect back on this period of labor schools in America.

Benedek, L. (Director). (1951). *Death of a salesman* [Motion picture]. USA: Stanley Kramer Productions. Cast: Fredric March, Cameron Mitchell, Mildred Dunnock. Arthur Miller's Pulitzer Prize-winning drama of a middle-aged salesman facing age and business decline.

Biberman, H. (Director). (1954). *The salt of the earth* [Motion picture]. USA: Independent Production Company. Cast: Will Geer, David Wolfe, Rosaura Revueltas. New Mexico mineworkers are abused for going on strike. Strong women characters help them survive. Docudrama tone. Film resulted in blacklisting of Geer, Biberman, producer Paul Jarrico, and screenwriter Michael Wilson.

Bird, S., & Shaffer, D. (Directors). (1979). *The Wobblies* [Motion picture]. USA: Joint Federation for Support. Documentary of Industrial Workers of the World. History intermixing archival footage and present-day interviews with old Wobblies.

Borden, L. (Director). (1986). *Working girls* [Motion picture]. USA: Alternate Current. Cast: Louise Smith, Ellen McElduff, Amanda Goodwin. Depicts a New York City brothel in docudrama style.

Brown, P., & Jason, W. (Directors). (1951). *The Harlem Globetrotters* [Motion picture]. USA: Columbia Pictures Corporation. Cast: Thomas Gomez, Dorothy Dandridge, Bill Walker, Angela Clarke. Documentary-style tale of exhibition black basketball team as it struggles for recognition in racist 1950s America.

Burnett, C. (Director). (1990). *To sleep with anger* [Motion picture]. USA: SVS Films. Cast: Paul Butler, Danny Glover, Carl Lumbly, Mary Alice. African American working-class family struggles with a wicked visitor in their Los Angeles home.

Cassavetes, N. (Director). (2002). *John Q* [Motion picture]. USA: New Line Cinema. Parents are financially ruined by their child's illness.

Cattaneo, P. (Director). (1997). *The full monty* [Motion picture]. United Kingdom: Redwave Films. Cast: Robert Carlyle, Tom Wilkinson, Mark Addy, Paul Barber, Steve Huison. An unlikely bunch of out-of-work steel laborers decide to reverse their fortunes by performing as male strippers in a local club.

Chapman, M. (Director). (1983). *All the right moves* [Motion picture]. USA: Lucille Ball Productions. Cast: Tom Cruise, Craig T. Nelson, Lea Thompson. A high school football player struggles to leave his future in the local steel mills for a future at college.

Cimino, M. (Director). (1978). *The deer hunter* [Motion picture]. USA: EMI Films. Cast: Christopher Walken, Robert DeNiro, Meryl Streep, John Savage. Examines the hellish worlds of the Vietnam War and an Ohio Valley steel town with some depth. Won the Academy Award for best picture.

Coen, J. (Director). (1996). *Fargo* [Motion picture]. USA: Polygram Filmed Entertainment. Cast: Frances McDormand, William H. Macy, Steve Buscemi. A car salesman's kidnapping plot goes awry and leads to murder. A female police detective investigates. Set in Fargo, North Dakota. Script by Joel and Ethan Coen.

Coles, J. D. (Director). (1990). *Rising son* [Motion picture]. USA: Sarabande Productions. Cast: Brian Dennehy, Piper Laurie, Matt Damon. A working class family struggles to survive the collapse of their Georgia factory town.

Dash, J. (Director). (2002). *The Rosa Parks story* [Motion picture]. USA: Chotzen/Jenner Productions. Angela Bassett plays Rosa Parks, who helped spark the civil rights movement in the United States.

Eastwood, C. (Director). (2004). *Million dollar baby* [Motion picture]. USA: Warner Brothers Pictures. Cast: Clint Eastwood, Hilary Swank, Morgan Freeman. A female prizefighter earns money and tries to help her family out of poverty.

Fincher, D. (Director). (1999). *Fight club* [Motion picture]. USA: Fox 2000 Pictures. Cast: Edward Norton, Brad Pitt, Helena Bonham Carter. A young office employee and a soap salesman build a global organization to help vent male aggression.

Fleischer, R. (Director). (1972). *The new centurions* [Motion picture]. USA: Chartoff-Winkler Productions. Cast: George C. Scott, Stacy Keach, Jane Alexander, Scott Wilson. A sensitive portrayal of rookie cops on the Los Angeles police force as they struggle with work and family life. Stirling Silliphant's script is based on Joseph Wambaugh's novel.

Ford, J. (Director). (1940). *The grapes of wrath* [Motion picture]. USA: Twentieth Century Fox. Cast: Henry Fonda, Jane Darwell, John Carradine. Adaptation of John Steinbeck's 1939 novel of Dust Bowl Okies headed west to the promised land of California where they find the American dream gone sour.

Forman, M. (Director). (1975). *One flew over the cuckoo's nest* [Motion picture]. USA: Fantasy Films. Cast: Jack Nicholson, Louise Fletcher, William Redfield, Brad Dourif, Danny DeVito. Film adaptation of Ken Kesey's novel of a social misfit committed to an insane asylum where he turns inmates into an organized rebellion against the system.

Freedman, J. (Director). (1986). *Native son* [Motion picture]. USA: American Playhouse. Cast: Carroll Baker, Matt Dillon, Victor Love, Elizabeth McGovern, Oprah Winfrey. A young black man struggles in racist 1930s Chicago. Richard Wright's novel is co-produced with PBS's American Playhouse series.

Gilbert, L. (Director). (1983). *Educating Rita* [Motion picture]. United Kingdom: Acorn Pictures. Cast: Michael Caine, Julie Walters. Adaptation of Willy Russell's play about a young working-class wife going to the university where she becomes entangled in the life of a boozing professor of literature.

Herek, S. (Director). (1995). *Mr. Holland's opus* [Motion picture]. USA: Hollywood Pictures. Cast: Richard Dreyfuss, Glenne Headly, Jay Thomas, Olympia Dukakis. Musician-composer resorts to teaching high school music and finds he loves it.

Higgins, C. (Director). (1980). *9 to 5* [Motion picture]. USA: IPC Films. Cast: Jane Fonda, Lily Tomlin, Dolly Parton, Dabney Coleman. Secretarial revolt against a harassing boss. This comedy is based on a story by screenwriter Patricia Resnick.

Hughes, J. (Director). (1985). *The breakfast club* [Motion picture]. USA: A&M Films. Teens from poor and middle-class backgrounds have conflicts with teachers and each other during Saturday detention.

James, S. (Director). (1994). *Hoop dreams* [Motion picture]. USA: KTCA Minneapolis. Documentary of two African American high school students who face the manipulative world of a career in basketball.

Kopple, B. (Director). (1977). *Harlan County, U.S.A.* [Motion picture]. USA: Cabin Creek. Academy Award-winning documentary of Kentucky mineworkers' strike against the Eastover Mining Company.

LaGravenese, R. (Director). (2007). *Freedom writers* [Motion picture]. USA: Paramount Pictures. A white teacher in an inner-city high school learns the rules and how to build relationships of mutual respect with students.

Lyne, A. (Director). (1983). *Flashdance* [Motion picture]. USA: Paramount Pictures. Cast: Jennifer Beals, Michael Nouri, Lilia Skala. A woman welder/stripper seeks romance and a career as a dancer.

Malle, L. (Director). (1985). *Alamo Bay* [Motion picture]. USA: Delphi IV. Cast: Ed Harris, Amy Madigan. Texas Gulf Coast fishing meets migration of Vietnamese immigrants.

Mandel, R. (Director). (1992). *School ties* [Motion picture]. USA: Paramount Pictures. Cast: Brendan Fraser, Chris O'Donnell, Matt Damon. A working-class Jewish student wins a football scholarship to a preparatory school, where he encounters anti-Semitism. Set in the 1950s.

Menéndez, R. (Director). (1988). *Stand and deliver* [Motion picture]. USA: American Playhouse. A teacher works with under-resourced students.

Nava, G. (Director). (1983). El Norte [Motion picture]. USA: American Playhouse. Cast: Trinidad Silva, Zaide Silvia Gutiérrez, Rodrigo Puebla. Saga of a brother and sister who come north from violence-torn Guatemala. Their struggle to migrate is followed by their struggle to survive in "El Norte"—the United States. Written and produced by Anna Thomas for the PBS American Playhouse series.

Nava, G. (Director). (1995). *My family, mi familia* [Motion picture]. USA: American Playhouse. Cast: Jimmy Smits, Esai Morales, Edward James Olmos. A Mexican American family's saga of coming to and surviving in Los Angeles.

Nichols, M. (Director). (1988). *Working girl* [Motion picture]. USA: Twentieth Century Fox. Cast: Harrison Ford, Melanie Griffith, Sigourney Weaver, Joan Cusack. Romantic comedy about a secretary with ambition and the struggle to rise up the corporate ladder.

Pearce, R. (Director). (1990). *The long walk home* [Motion picture]. USA: Dave Bell Associates. Cast: Sissy Spacek, Whoopi Goldberg, Dwight Schultz; narrated by Mary Steenburgen. Mid-1950s racial tensions in the segregated U.S. South as they affect a middle-class woman and her hardworking black housekeeper.

Peerce, L. (Director). (1969). *Goodbye, Columbus* [Motion picture]. USA: Willow Tree. Cast: Richard Benjamin, Ali MacGraw, Jack Klugman. Adaptation of Philip Roth's novel portraying urban and suburban Jewish families.

Petersen, W. (Director). (2000). *The perfect storm* [Motion picture]. USA: Baltimore Spring Creek Productions. Cast: George Clooney, Mark Wahlberg, Diane Lane, Mary Elizabeth Mastrantonio, John C. Reilly. A fishing crew and captain off Gloucester, Massachusetts, fight the threat of losing their ship and their lives in a storm.

Petrie, D. (Director). (1961). *A raisin in the sun* [Motion picture]. USA: Columbia Picture Corporation. Cast: Sidney Poitier, Claudia McNeil, Ruby Dee, Diana Sands. Adaptation of Lorraine Hansberry's play depicting a black Chicago family as it struggles to survive; Hansberry also wrote the screenplay.

Pollack, S. (Director). (1969). *They shoot horses, don't they?* [Motion picture]. USA: American Broadcasting Company. Cast: Jane Fonda, Michael Sarrazin, Gig Young. Based on the 1935 novel by Horace McCoy. Desperate attempts to win a marathon dance contest.

Rash, S. (Director). (1978). *The Buddy Holly story* [Motion picture]. USA: ECA. Cast: Gary Busey, Charles Martin Smith, Don Stroud, Maria Richwine. Biographical story of the teen rocker's rise from Lubbock, Texas, to national stardom, then early death.

Redford, R. (Director). (1988). *The Milagro beanfield war* [Motion picture]. USA: Esparza. Cast: Ruben Blades, Richard Bradford, Sonia Braga, Melanie Griffith, John Heard. Adaptation of John Nichols' novel of New Mexico struggle between landowners and rugged workers.

Reitman, J. (Director). (2007). *Juno* [Motion picture]. USA: Mandate Pictures. A teenage girl from a working-class background becomes pregnant and elects to allow a middle-class family to adopt the child.

Ritt, M. (Director). (1979). *Norma Rae* [Motion picture]. USA: Twentieth Century Fox. Cast: Sally Field, Beau Bridges, Ron Leibman, Pat Hingle, Barbara Baxley. Field plays a real-life southern textile worker who is won over to unionization by a northern labor organizer, then becomes a local champion. Field won an Academy Award for this role.

Roemer, M. (Director). (1964). *Nothing but a man* [Motion picture]. USA: DuArt. Cast: Ivan Dixon, Julius Harris, Abbey Lincoln. A young black man, with the help of a woman, struggles to survive in the repressive U.S. South of the 1960s.

Rydell, M. (Director). (1984). *The river* [Motion picture]. USA: Universal Pictures. Cast: Sissy Spacek, Mel Gibson, Scott Glenn. A family struggles to work and keep its farm despite threats from the bank and from a flooding river. Screenplay by Robert Dillon.

Schlesinger, J. (Director). (1969). *Midnight cowboy* [Motion picture]. USA: Florin Productions. Cast: Dustin Hoffman, Jon Voight, Sylvia Miles. A dishwashing cowboy comes to New York City to become a sexual stud, yet meets the cold reality of prostitution and homelessness shared with a city friend. Received Academy Awards for best picture, director, and screenplay. Based on a novel by James Leo Herlihy; the film was given an early X rating.

Schlöndorff, V. (Director). (1985). *Death of a salesman* [Motion picture]. USA: Bioskop film. Cast: Dustin Hoffman, John Malkovich, Charles Durning, Kate Reid. More recent version of Arthur Miller's Pulitzer Prize-winning drama of a middle-aged salesman facing age and business decline.

Scorsese, M. (Director). (1974). *Alice doesn't live here anymore* [Motion picture]. USA: Warner Brothers Pictures. Cast: Ellen Burstyn, Kris Kristofferson, Diane Ladd. A single mom's quest to find herself lands her in a western diner.

Scorsese, M. (Director). (2002). *Gangs of New York* [Motion picture]. USA: Miramax Films. Cast: Leonardo DiCaprio, Daniel Day-Lewis, Cameron Diaz. Set in early New York City where youth gangs battle.

Shankman, A. (Director). (2003). *Bringing down the house* [Motion picture]. USA: Touchstone Pictures. Depicts clashes based on the hidden rules of wealth and other classes at home and in the office.

Smith, J. N. (Director). (1995). *Dangerous minds* [Motion picture]. USA: Hollywood Pictures. Cast: Michelle Pfeiffer, George Dzundza, Courtney B. Vance. An inexperienced teacher (and ex-Marine) takes on a class of "unteachable" students in an inner-city school.

Spielberg, S. (Director). (1985). *The color purple* [Motion picture]. USA: Amblin Entertainment. Cast: Whoopi Goldberg, Danny Glover, Margaret Avery, Oprah Winfrey. Adaptation of Alice Walker's acclaimed novel of a poor black girl who gains self-esteem and control of her life.

Stack, J. (Director). (1995). *Harlem diary* [Motion picture]. USA: Discovery Channel Pictures. Documentary of nine Harlem youths who chronicle their life stories of trying to survive in the projects. Produced for the Discovery Channel but shown in theaters as well.

Stone, O. (Director). (1989). *Born on the fourth of July* [Motion picture]. USA: Ixtlan. Cast: Tom Cruise, Willem Dafoe, Caroline Kava. A wounded Vietnam veteran's questioning of the United States of America, based on the real-life saga of author Ron Kovic.

Stuart, M. (Director). (1979). *The Triangle factory fire scandal* [Motion picture]. USA: Alan Landsburg Productions. Cast: Tom Bosley, David Dukes, Tovah Feldshuh, Lauren Frost. A retelling of the Triangle Shirtwaist Factory abuse and fire of March 25, 1911.

Valdez, L. (Director). (1987). *La bamba* [Motion picture]. USA: Columbia Pictures. Cast: Lou Diamond Phillips, Esai Morales, Rosana De Soto. Story of Mexican American rock singer Ritchie Valens and his tragic death in a plane crash.

Van Sant, G. (Director). (1997). *Good will hunting* [Motion picture]. USA: Be Gentlemen Limited Partnership. Cast: Robin Williams, Matt Damon, Ben Affleck, Minnie Driver. A rough Boston youth with a genius for math shows up MIT academics, wins girl, and gains confidence with counselor. Written by Damon and Affleck, who received an Academy Award for the screenplay.

Van Sant, G. (Director). (2000). *Finding Forrester* [Motion picture]. USA: Columbia Pictures Corporation. An African American student struggles with hidden rules and social capital as he attends private school.

Wang, W. (Director). (2002). *Maid in Manhattan* [Motion picture]. USA: Revolution Studios. Cast: Jennifer Lopez, Ralph Fiennes, Natasha Richardson, Stanley Tucci. A single mom works as a maid uptown and meets a politician.

Wyler, W. (Director). (1946). *The best years of our lives.* [Motion picture]. USA: Samuel Goldwyn Company. Cast: Dana Andrews, Harold Russell, Myrna Loy, Fredric March. Returning veterans from World War II reintegrate with hometown lives, yet struggle with war wounds; won seven Academy Awards.

Yates, P. (Director). (1979). *Breaking away* [Motion picture]. USA: Twentieth Century Fox. Cast: Dennis Christopher, Dennis Quaid, Daniel Stern. Reveals rivalry and class distinctions between college students and working class "cutters" (stonecutters) in Bloomington, Indiana.

Literature

Alexie, S. (1993). *The Lone Ranger and Tonto fistfight in heaven.* New York, NY: Atlantic Monthly Press.

Alexie, S. (2007). *The absolutely true diary of a part-time Indian.* New York, NY: Little, Brown.

Allison, D. (1988). *Trash: Stories.* Ann Arbor, MI: Firebrand Books.

Allison, D. (1993). *Bastard out of Carolina.* New York, NY: Plume.

Anderson, S. (1919). *Winesburg, Ohio.* New York, NY: B. W. Huebsch.

Arnow, H. (1954). *The dollmaker.* New York, NY: Macmillan.

Bell, T. (1941). *Out of this furnace.* New York, NY: Little, Brown.

Bellow, S. (1953). *The adventures of Augie Marsh.* New York, NY: Viking Press.

Berry, W. (1960). *Nathan Coulter.* Boston, MA: Houghton-Mifflin.

Berry, W. (1967). *A place on Earth.* San Francisco, CA: Harcourt, Brace.

Berry, W. (1974). *The memory of Old Jack.* Bellmawr, NJ: Harcourt, Brace, Jovanovich.

Bragg, R. (1998). *All over but the shoutin'.* New York, NY: Vintage Books.

Brooks, G. (1953). *Maud Martha.* New York, NY: AMS Press.

Cahan, A. (1917). *The rise of David Levinsky.* New York, NY: Harper.

Caldwell, E. (1932). *Tobacco road.* New York, NY: Charles Scribner's Sons.

Caldwell, E. (1933). *God's little acre.* New York, NY: Viking Press.

Carver, R. (1981). *What we talk about when we talk about love: Stories.* New York, NY: Vintage Books.

Carver, R. (1983). *Cathedral.* New York, NY: Vintage Books.

Chute, C. (1985). *The beans of Egypt, Maine.* New York, NY: Ticknor and Fields.

Chute, C. (1994). *Merry men.* Bellmawr, NJ: Houghton Mifflin Harcourt.

Cisneros, S. (1991). *Woman Hollering Creek: And other stories.* New York, NY: Random House.

Coles, N., & Oresick, P. (Eds.). (1995). *For a living: The poetry of work.* Urbana, IL: University of Illinois Press.

Coles, N., & Zandy, J. (Eds.). (2006). *American working class literature*. New York, NY: Oxford University Press.

Crane, S. (1984). *Maggie: A girl of the streets*. New York, NY: Random House.

Davis, R. H. (1993). *Life in the iron mills and other stories* (2nd ed.). New York, NY: The Feminist Press at CUNY.

DeMott, B. (Ed.). (1996). *Created equal: Reading and writing about class in America*. New York, NY: HarperCollins.

Doctorow, E. L. (1975). *Ragtime*. New York, NY: Random House.

Dybek, S. (1990). *The coast of Chicago: Stories*. New York, NY: Alfred A. Knopf.

Ehrlich, G. (1988). *Heart Mountain*. New York, NY: Viking Adult.

Ellison, R. (1952). *Invisible man*. New York, NY: Random House.

Erdrich, L. (1984). *Love medicine*. New York, NY: Holt, Rinehart, and Winston.

Evans, W. (1941). *Let us now praise famous men*. Boston, MA: Houghton-Mifflin.

Faulkner, W. (1926). *Soldier's pay*. New York, NY: Boni and Liveright.

Faulkner, W. (1932). *Light in August*. New York, NY: Smith and Haas.

Faulkner, W. (1940). *The hamlet*. New York, NY: Random House.

Faulkner, W. (1962). *The reivers*. New York, NY: Random House.

Ford, R. (1987). *Rock Springs: Stories*. Boston, MA: The Atlantic Monthly Press.

Henson, M. (1980). *Ransack*. New York, NY: West End Press.

Henson, M. (1983). *A small room with trouble on my mind*. New York, NY: West End Press.

Gold, H. (1966). *Fathers: A novel in the form of a memoir*. New York, NY: Random House.

Grey, Z. (1919). *Desert of wheat*. New York, NY: Grosset and Dunlap.

Hijuelos, O. (1993). *The fourteen sisters of Emilio Montez O'Brien*. London, England: Farrar Straus Giroux.

Kennedy, W. (1983). *Ironweed*. New York, NY: Viking Press.

Kerouac, J. (1950). *The town and the city*. New York, NY: Harcourt Brace.

Kerouac, J. (1957). *On the road.* New York, NY: Viking Press.

Kerouac, J. (1958). *The subterraneans.* New York, NY: Grove Press.

Kesey, K. (1962). *One flew over the cuckoo's nest.* New York, NY: Viking Press.

Kesey, K. (1964). *Sometimes a great notion.* New York, NY: Viking Press.

Kingsolver, B. (1993). *Pigs in heaven.* New York, NY: HarperCollins.

Kingsolver, B. (2000). *Prodigal summer.* New York, NY: Perennial.

Kingston, M. H. (1975). *The woman warrior: Memories of a girlhood among ghosts.* New York, NY: Vintage Books.

Le Sueur, M. (1990). *Harvest song: Collected essays and stories.* New York, NY: West End Press.

Lewis, S. (1920). *Main street.* New York, NY: Harcourt Brace.

Lewis, S. (1922). *Babbitt.* New York, NY: Harcourt Brace.

Linkon, S. L., & Russo, J. (2003). *Steeltown, USA: Work and memory in Youngstown.* Lawrence, KS: University Press of Kansas.

London, J. (1903). *The call of the wild.* New York, NY: Macmillan.

London, J. (1904). *The sea-wolf.* New York, NY: Macmillan.

Lopez, L. M. (Ed.). (2009). *An angle of vision: Women writers on their poor and working-class roots.* Ann Arbor, MI: University of Michigan Press.

Mann, H. (1904). *Adam Clarke: A story of the toilers.* New York, NY: Popular Book Company.

Martz, S. (Ed.). (1990). *If I had a hammer: Women's work in poetry, fiction, and photographs.* Watsonville, CA: Papier-Mache Press.

Mason, B. A. (1982). *Shiloh and other stories.* New York, NY: Harper & Row.

Mason, B. A. (1985). *In country: A novel.* New York, NY: Harper & Row.

Mason, B. A. (1988). *Spence and Lila.* New York, NY: Harper & Row.

McCall, N. (1995). *Makes me wanna holler.* New York, NY: Vintage Books.

McCourt, F. (1996). *Angela's ashes: A memoir.* New York, NY: Scribner.

McCrumb, S. (2001). *The songcatcher.* New York, NY: Dutton.

McCrumb, S. (2003). *Ghost riders*. New York, NY: Dutton.

Morrison, T. (1970). *The bluest eye*. New York, NY: Holt, Rinehart, and Winston.

Morrison, T. (1987). *Beloved*. New York, NY: Alfred A. Knopf.

Nekola, C., & Rabinowitz, P. (Eds.). (1987). *Writing red: An anthology of American women writers, 1930–1940*. New York, NY: The Feminist Press.

Nichols, J. (1974). *The Milagro beanfield war*. New York, NY: Holt, Rinehart, and Winston.

O'Brien, T. (1973). *If I die in a combat zone, box me up and ship me home*. New York, NY: Delacorte Press.

O'Brien, T. (1990). *The things they carried*. Boston, MA: Houghton-Mifflin Harcourt.

Olsen, T. (1961). *Tell me a riddle: Stories*. New York, NY: Lippincott.

Oresick, P., & Coles, N. (Eds.). (1990). *Working classics: Poems on industrial life*. Urbana, IL: University of Illinois Press.

Pancake, B. D. (1983). *The stories of Breece D'J Pancake*. New York, NY: Little, Brown.

Phillips, J. A. (1984). *Machine dreams*. New York, NY: Dutton.

Phillips, J. A. (2000). *Motherkind*. New York, NY: Alfred A. Knopf.

Pransky, J. (1998). *Modello: A story of hope for the inner city and beyond*. Cabot, VT: Northeast Health Realization Institute.

Sanders, D. (1993). *Her own place*. Chapel Hill, NC: Algonquin Books.

Sayles, J. (1991). *Los gusanos*. New York, NY: HarperCollins.

Shevin, D., & Smith, L. (Eds.). (1996). *Getting by: Stories of working lives*. Huron, OH: Bottom Dog Press.

Shevin, D., Smith, L., & Zandy, J.(Eds.). (1999). *Writing work: Writers on working-class writing*. Huron, OH: Bottom Dog Press.

Sinclair, U. (1906). *The jungle*. New York, NY: Doubleday.

Sinclair, U. (1917). *King coal*. New York, NY: Macmillan.

Steinbeck, J. (1932). *The pastures of heaven: Stories*. New York, NY: Covici-Friede.

Steinbeck, J. (1935). *Tortilla Flat*. New York, NY: Covici-Friede.

Steinbeck, J. (1936). *In dubious battle.* New York, NY: Covici-Friede.

Steinbeck, J. (1937). *Of mice and men.* New York, NY: Covici-Friede.

Steinbeck, J. (1938). *The long valley.* London, England: Penguin.

Steinbeck, J. (1939). *The grapes of wrath.* New York, NY: Viking Press.

Steinbeck, J. (1945). *Cannery Row.* New York, NY: Viking Press.

Steinbeck, J. (1952). *East of Eden.* New York, NY: Viking Press.

Stockett, K. (2009). *The help.* New York, NY: Penguin.

Twain, M. (1882). *The prince and the pauper.* Boston, MA: J. R. Osgood.

Twain, M. (1894). *Pudd'nhead Wilson.* New York, NY: Charles L. Webster.

Upchurch, C. (1996). *Convicted in the womb.* New York, NY: Bantam Books.

Vonnegut, K., Jr. (1979). *Jailbird.* New York, NY: Delacorte Press.

Walker, A. (1970). *The third life of Grange Copeland.* New York, NY: Harcourt Brace Jovanovich.

Walker, A. (1982). *The color purple.* New York, NY: Harcourt Brace Jovanovich.

Zandy, J. (Ed.). (1990). *Calling home: Working class women's writings.* New Brunswick, NJ: Rutgers University Press.

Poetry

Anderson, M. (2000). *Windfall: New and selected poems*. Pittsburgh, PA: University of Pittsburgh Press.

Angelou, M. (1994). *The complete collected poems of Maya Angelou*. New York, NY: Random House.

Antler. (1986). *Last words*. New York, NY: Ballantine Books.

Baraka, A. (1999). *The LeRoi Jones/Amiri Baraka reader* (2nd ed.). New York, NY: Basic Books.

Beatty, J. (1995). *Mad river*. Pittsburgh, PA: University of Pittsburgh Press.

Blair, P. (1999). *Last heat*. Washington, DC: Word Works.

Bryner, J. (1999). *Blind horse*. Huron, OH: Bottom Dog Press.

Coffman, L. (1996). *Likely*. Kent, OH: Kent State University Press.

Daniels, J. (1985). *Places/everyone*. Madison, WI: University of Wisconsin Press.

Daniels, J. (2003). *Show and tell: New and selected poems*. Madison, WI: University of Wisconsin Press.

Dobler, P. (2005). *Collected poems*. Pittsburgh, PA: Autumn House Press.

Knight, E. (1986). *The essential Etheridge Knight*. Pittsburgh, PA: University of Pittsburgh Press.

Kooser, T. (1980). *Sure signs: New and selected poems*. Pittsburgh, PA: University of Pittsburgh Press.

Laux, D. (1994). *What we carry*. Rochester, NY: BOA Editions.

Levine, P. (1991). *What work is: Poems*. New York, NY: Alfred A. Knopf.

Llewellyn, C. (1987). *Fragments from the fire*. New York, NY: Penguin.

McKinney, I. (1989). *Six o'clock mine report*. Pittsburgh, PA: University of Pittsburgh Press.

Paulenich, C. (2009). *Blood will tell*. Buffalo, NY: BlazeVOX Books.

Sandburg, C. (1920). *Smoke and steel*. New York, NY: Harcourt, Brace, and Howe.

Vollmer, J. (1998). *The door open to the fire*. Cleveland, OH: Cleveland State University Press.

Bibliography

Albelda, R., Folbre, N., & Center for Popular Economics. (1996). *The war on the poor: A defense manual.* New York, NY: The New Press.

Alexie, S. (1993). *The Lone Ranger and Tonto fistfight in heaven.* New York, NY: Atlantic Monthly Press.

Alexie, S. (2007). *The absolutely true diary of a part-time Indian.* New York, NY: Little, Brown.

Alvarez, L., & Kolker, A. (Directors). (2001). *People like us: Social class in America* [Motion picture]. United States of America: WETA and Center for New American Media.

American Psychological Association. (2000). Resolution on Poverty and SES. Retrieved from http://www.apa.org/about/government/council/policy/poverty-resolution.aspx

America's fortunes [Editorial]. (2004). *The Atlantic Monthly, 293*(1). Retrieved from http://www.theatlantic.com/doc/200401/editors

Andreas, S., & Faulkner, C. (Eds.). (1994). *NLP: The new technology of achievement.* New York, NY: Quill.

Andrews, E. L. (2009). *Busted: Life inside the great mortgage meltdown.* New York, NY: Norton.

Barkai, J. (1996). Teaching negotiation and ADR: The savvy samurai meets the devil. *Nebraska Law Review, 75,* 704–751.

Becker, K. A., Krodel, K. M., & Tucker, B. H. (2009). *Understanding and engaging under-resourced college students: A fresh look at the influence of economic class on teaching and learning in higher education.* Highlands, TX: aha! Process.

Berne, E. (1996). *Games people play: The basic handbook of transactional analysis.* New York, NY: Ballantine Books.

Bragg, R. (1998). *All over but the shoutin'.* New York, NY: Vintage Books.

Brooks, D. (2000). *Bobos in paradise: The new upper class and how they got there.* New York, NY: Touchstone.

Burd-Sharps, S., Lewis, K., & Martins, E. B. (2008). *The measure of America: American human development report 2008–2009.* New York, NY: Columbia University Press.

Chapman, K. J. (2001). Measuring intent: There's nothing 'mere' about mere measurement effects. *Psychology and Marketing, 18*(8), 811–841.

Childers, M. (2005). *Welfare brat: A memoir.* New York, NY: Bloomsbury.

Covey, S. R. (1989). *The 7 habits of highly effective people: Powerful lessons in personal change.* New York, NY: Simon & Schuster.

Daniels, C. (2007). *Ghettonation: A journey into the land of bling and the home of the shameless.* New York, NY: Doubleday.

DeParle, J. (2004). *American dream: Three women, ten kids, and a nation's drive to end welfare.* New York, NY: Viking Penguin.

de Soto, H. (2000). *The mystery of capital: Why capitalism triumphs in the West and fails everywhere else.* New York, NY: Basic Books.

DiClemente, C. C., & Velasquez, M. M. (2002). Motivational interviewing and the stages of change. In W. R. Miller & S. Rollnick (Eds.), *Motivational interviewing: Preparing people for change* (2nd ed., pp. 201–216). New York, NY: Guilford Press.

Donnelly, J. (Ed.). (1997). *Who are the question-makers? A participatory evaluation handbook.* New York, NY: Office of Evaluation and Strategic Planning, United Nations Development Program.

Doran, G. T. (1981). There's a S.M.A.R.T. way to write management's goals and objectives. *Management Review, 70*(11), 35–36.

Estimated state median income, by family size and by state for FY 2009. (2008, October 8). Retrieved from http://www.acf.hhs.gov/programs/ocs/liheap/guidance/SMI75FY09.pdf

Fairbanks, M. (2000). Changing the mind of a nation: Elements in a process for creating prosperity. In L. E. Harrison & S. P. Huntington (Eds.), *Culture matters: How values shape human progress* (pp. 268–281). New York, NY: Basic Books.

Farson, R. (1997). *Management of the absurd: Paradoxes in leadership.* New York, NY: Touchstone.

Fisher, R., & Ury, W. (1983). *Getting to YES: Negotiating agreement without giving in.* New York, NY: Penguin.

Florida, R. (2002). *The rise of the creative class: And how it's transforming work, leisure, community, and everyday life.* New York, NY: Basic Books.

Freedman, J., & Combs, G. (1996). *Narrative therapy: The social construction of preferred realities.* New York, NY: Norton.

Freire, P. (1999). *Pedagogy of the oppressed.* New York, NY: Continuum.

Fussell, P. (1983). *Class: A guide through the American status system.* New York, NY: Touchstone.

Galeano, E. (1998). *Upside down: A primer for the looking-glass world.* New York, NY: Metropolitan Books.

Gladwell, M. (2008). *Outliers: The story of success.* New York, NY: Little, Brown.

Glasmeier, A. K. (2006). *An atlas of poverty in America: One nation, pulling apart, 1960–2003.* New York, NY: Routledge.

Goleman, D. (1995). *Emotional intelligence.* New York, NY: Bantam Books.

The growing divide: Inequality and the roots of economic insecurity [Trainer's manual]. (2009). Boston, MA: United for a Fair Economy.

Harrison, L. E., & Huntington, S. P. (Eds.). (2000). *Culture matters: How values shape human progress.* New York, NY: Basic Books.

Hart, B., & Risley, T. R. (1995). *Meaningful differences in the everyday experience of young American children.* Baltimore, MD: Paul H. Brookes.

hooks, bell. (2000). *Where we stand: Class matters.* New York, NY: Routledge.

Istook, E. (2009, December 9). Taxes are more certain than death? Retrieved from http://blog.heritage.org/2009/12/09/taxes-are-more-certain-than-death/

Jaworski, J. (1996). *Synchronicity: The inner path of leadership.* San Francisco, CA: Berrett-Koehler.

Joos, M. (1967). The styles of the five clocks. In R. D. Abraham & R. C. Troike (Eds.), *Language and cultural diversity in American education* (pp. 145–149). Englewood Cliffs, NJ: Prentice Hall.

Kadi, J. (1966). *Thinking class: Sketches from a cultural worker.* Boston, MA: South End Press.

Kelly, M. (2001). *The divine right of capital: Dethroning the corporate aristocracy.* San Francisco, CA: Berrett-Koehler.

Kiyosaki, R. T., & Lechter, S. L. (1998). *Rich dad, poor dad.* Paradise Valley, AZ: TechPress.

Klein, N. (2007). *The shock doctrine: The rise of disaster capitalism.* New York, NY: Metropolitan Books.

Kling, A., & Schulz, N. (2009). *From poverty to prosperity: Intangible assets, hidden liabilities and the lasting triumph over scarcity.* New York, NY: Encounter Books.

Kretzmann, J. P., & McKnight, J. L. (1993). *Building communities from the inside out: A path toward finding and mobilizing a community's assets.* Chicago, IL: ACTA.

Kretzmann, J. P., & McKnight, J. L. (with Dobrowolski, S., & Puntenney, D.). (2005). Discovering community power: A guide to mobilizing local assets and your organization's capacity. Evanston, IL: Asset-Based Community Development Institute. Retrieved from http://www.abcdinstitute.org/docs/kelloggabcd.pdf

Lareau, A. (2003). *Unequal childhoods: Class, race, and family life.* Berkley, CA: University of California Press.

Leondar-Wright, B. (2005). *Class matters: Cross-class alliance building for middle-class activists.* Gabriola Island, Canada: New Society Publishers.

Lind, M. (2004). Are we still a middle-class nation? *The Atlantic, 293*(1), 120–128.

Lopez, L. M. (Ed.). (2009). *An angle of vision: Women writers on their poor and working-class roots.* Ann Arbor, MI: University of Michigan Press.

Lui, M., Robles, B., Leondar-Wright, B., Brewer, R., & Adamson, R. (2006). *The color of wealth: The story behind the U.S. racial wealth divide.* New York, NY: The New Press.

McCall, N. (1995). *Makes me wanna holler.* New York, NY: Vintage Books.

McCarthy, N., Poole, K. T., & Rosenthal, H. (2006). *Polarized America: The dance of ideology and unequal riches.* Cambridge, MA: MIT Press.

McCourt, F. (1996). *Angela's ashes: A memoir.* New York, NY: Touchstone.

McKnight, J. (1995). *The careless society: Community and its counterfeits.* New York, NY: Basic Books.

Mehrabian, A. (1981). *Silent messages: Implicit communications of emotions and attitudes.* Belmont, CA: Wadsworth.

Michaels, W. B. (2006). *The trouble with diversity: How we learned to love identity and ignore inequality.* New York, NY: Metropolitan Books.

Miller, A. F., & Cunningham, J. A. (1981). How to avoid costly job mismatches. *Management Review, 70*(11), 29–31.

Miller, M. (2006). Make 150,000% today! *Fortune, 153*(2), 36.

Miller, M. (2009). *The tyranny of dead ideas: Letting go of the old ways of thinking to unleash a new prosperity.* New York, NY: Times Books.

Miller, W. R., & Rollnick, S. (2002). *Motivational interviewing: Preparing people for change* (2nd ed.). New York, NY: Guilford Press.

Miringoff, M., & Miringoff, M-L. (1999). *The social health of the nation: How America is really doing.* New York, NY: Oxford University Press.

National College Transition Network. (2009). College for adults. Retrieved from http://www.collegeforadults.org

O'Connor, A. (2001). *Poverty knowledge: Social science, social policy, and the poor in twentieth century U.S. history.* Princeton, NJ: Princeton University Press.

Payne, R. K. (2005). *A framework for understanding poverty* (4th rev. ed.). Highlands, TX: aha! Process.

Payne, R. K. (2008). *Under-resourced learners: 8 strategies to boost student achievement.* Highlands, TX: aha! Process.

Payne, R. K., DeVol, P. E., & Smith, T. D. (2006). *Bridges out of poverty: Strategies for professionals and communities* (3rd rev. ed.). Highlands, TX: aha! Process.

People like us: Resources. (n.d.). Retrieved from http://www.pbs.org/peoplelikeus/resources/index.html

Peterson, C., Maier, S. F., & Seligman, M. E. P. (1993). *Learned helplessness: A theory for the age of personal control.* New York, NY: Oxford University Press.

Pfarr, J. R. (2009). *Tactical communication: Law enforcement tools for successful encounters with people from poverty, middle class, and wealth.* Highlands, TX: aha! Process.

Pransky, J. (1998). *Modello: A story of hope for the inner city and beyond.* Cabot, VT: Northeast Health Realization Institute.

Prante, G. (2009). Summary of latest federal individual income tax data. Retrieved from http://www.taxfoundation.org/research/show/250.html

Putnam, R. D. (2000). *Bowling alone: The collapse and revival of American community.* New York, NY: Simon & Schuster.

Roseland, M. (2005). *Toward sustainable communities: Resources for citizens and their governments.* Gabriola Island, Canada: New Society Publishers.

Seligman, M. E. P. (2002). *Authentic happiness: Using the new positive psychology to realize your potential for lasting fulfillment.* New York, NY: Free Press.

Senge, P. M. (1990). *The fifth discipline: The art and practice of the learning organization.* New York, NY: Currency Doubleday.

Senge, P. M., Ross, R., Smith, B., Roberts, C., & Kleiner, A. (1994). T*he fifth discipline fieldbook: Strategies and tools for building a learning organization.* New York: Currency Doubleday.

Shipler, D. K. (2004). *The working poor: Invisible in America.* New York, NY: Alfred A. Knopf.

Smith, A. (1994). *An inquiry into the nature and causes of the wealth of nations.* New York, NY: The Modern Library.

Smith, H. (1994). *The illustrated world's religions: A guide to our wisdom traditions.* New York, NY: HarperCollins.

Sowell, T. (1997). *Migrations and cultures: A world view.* New York, NY: HarperCollins.

Sowell, T. (1998, October 5). Race, culture, and equality. *Forbes,* 144–149.

Taylor-Ide, D., & Taylor, C. E. (2002). *Just and lasting change: When communities own their futures.* Baltimore, MD: Johns Hopkins University Press.

Twin Cities RISE! (2009). *Empowerment: A course in personal empowerment.* Minneapolis; MN: Author.

Upchurch, C. (1996). *Convicted in the womb.* New York, NY: Bantam Books.

Washburne, C. (1958). Conflicts between educational theory and structure. *Educational Theory, 8*(2), 87–94.

WETA. (2010). Home. Retrieved from http://www.ldonline.org/index.php

Wheeler, R. S. (2008). Becoming adept at code-switching. *Educational Leadership, 65*(7), 54–58.

Wheeler, R. S., & Swords, R. (2006). *Code-switching: Teaching Standard English in urban classrooms.* Urbana, IL: National Council of Teachers of English.

Wheeler, R. S., & Swords, R. (2010). *Code-switching lessons: Grammar strategies for linguistically diverse writers.* Portsmouth, NH: Heinemann.

Wilkinson, R. G. (2007). *The impact of inequality: How to make sick societies healthier.* Oxfordshire, England: Routledge.

Wilkinson, R. G., & Pickett, K. (2009). *The spirit level: Why more equal societies almost always do better.* London, England: Penguin.

World Bank. (2005). *World development report 2006: Equity and development.* New York, NY: Oxford University Press.

Index

NOTE: Page numbers in *italics* refer to display material.

A

Abstract, 45
Accountability
    of community, 211
    to learning group, 3, 9
    to self, 3
Action
    change process, *163*
    Triangle mental model, 9
Active listening, 129
Adult voice, 118
Affordable Housing Payment Threshold Calculator, 18–19
Alexie, Sherman, 16
American Psychological Association, 159
Andreas, Steve, 145, 146
Andrews, Edmund L., 27
Assessment
    individual resources, case studies, 149–156
    See also Community resources assessment;
        Self-assessment of resources
Auditory learning style, 140

B

Backwards planning, 86–87
Balanced life, 220
Barkai, John, 128
Becker, K. A., 122
Berne, Eric, 116
Body language, 117, 118
Bonding capital, 140–141, 143, 144
Bridging capital, 141, 143, 144
Briggs, Xavier de Souza, 141
Building resources
    assessment and planning for, 10
    for balanced life, 220
    brainstorm technique, 224–225
    discussion questions, 225, 226
    group activities, 221
    intentionality, 220–221
    journal reflections, 227
    learning objectives, 219
    learning process, 220
    lexicon, 220
    partners for, 221
    stories about, 226
    theoretical approach, 220
    tic-tac-toe technique, 221–222, *223*
    See also Community resources assessment;
        Personal plan for building resources;
        Resources; Self-assessment of resources

C

Carey, Sandra, 144
Change process
    agency investigation, 38, 39–40, 41
    being able to change, 145–146
    college experience and, 41–43, 164
    difficult changes, 145
    discussion questions, 40, 148, 165
    goals, 10
    Investigations model, 45–46
    journal reflections, 43, 47, 166
    learning objectives, 37, 161
    learning process, 38, 162
    lexicon, 38, 162
    mental model, 44–45
    models of, 41
    motivation for, 145–147
    persistence for, 145
    readiness, 146
    resistance to, 40–41
    righting reflex, 40
    self-assessment, 44
    significance of, 44
    stages of, 161–166
    Support for Change mental model, 238, 239, *249*
    willingness in, 145
    wisdom for, 145
Child voice, 117–118
Circles™ Campaign, 143
Circular story pattern, 113, 120
Clarian Health Partners, 46
Clark County, Ohio, 84–85
Code switching, 114–116

Co-investigation, 6

College
- Circles™ Campaign, 143
- effects on relationships, 95
- financial aid, 105
- hidden rules, 101–106
- lexicon, 103
- mediation learning technique, 123–124
- mental model for College Success, 243, 244
- process of change in, 41–43
- relationships, 102
- resource identification, 157, 216
- resources for adults, 160
- social life, 106

Community Assets Map, *211,* 212, *215*

Community involvement
- access to credit, 78
- coalition building for, 84
- community accountability, 211
- goal of *Investigations,* 11
- social capital resources, 140–141
- sustainability goals, 83

Community Reinvestment Act, 78

Community resources assessment, 198–199
- for asset-based approach to community development, 211–213
- banking services, *202*
- discussion questions, 210, 216
- economic conditions, *200*
- educational access and quality, *206*
- health and safety, *205*
- housing, *201*
- importance of, 197, 199
- jobs and wages, *203*
- journal reflections, 210
- leadership, *208*
- learning activity, 199, 214
- learning objectives, 197
- learning process, 198
- lexicon, 198
- map, *211,* 212, *215*
- mental model, *209*
- mental model for Community Prosperity, 243, 244
- one-on-one relationships, 212–*213,* 214
- protection from predators, *204*
- public services, *207*
- social health index, 198

Community Sustainability Grid, 84–85

Concrete, 45

Contemplation stage of change, *163*

Contrastive analysis, 114

Covey, Stephen, 47–48, 86

D

Debt-to-income ratio, 27–29

DiClemente, C., 162

Disciplining children, 125, 127

Distribution of wealth, 71

E

Economic class
- consideration in negotiations, 127–128
- effect on relationships of change in, 94–95
- generational, 93
- language development and, 120–121
- poverty viewed through lens of, 93
- relative perception, 93
- self-examination, 2
- situational, 93–94
- study objectives, 1–2
- *See also* Hidden rules of economic class

Economic conditions
- community resources assessment, *200*

Economic stability
- building individual plans for, 9
- goals, 2–3
- resource assessment, 8
- savings for, 26–27

Educational system
- community resources assessment, *206*
- hidden rules, 94, 100

Emotional functioning
- emotional intelligence, 139–140
- mental–emotional balance, 220
- regulation, 139
- resource evaluation, *152, 173–174*
- resources, *137,* 139
- self-defeating patterns, 139

Employment opportunities
- community resources assessment, *203*

Exploitation and predation
- community resources for protection from, assessment of, *204*
- discussion questions, 65
- learning activity, 64–65
- of people in poverty, 60

F

Facilitator, group, 3–4
Fairbanks, Michael, 14
Families
    culture of talk, 119
    disciplining children, 125, 127
    income growth, 65–67
    racial differences in income, 68
    racial differences in net worth, 73, 74
Farson, Richard, 41
Faulkner, Charles, 145, 146
Federal Poverty Guidelines, 23, 136
Feuerstein, Reuven, 122
Financial management
    debt-to-income ratio, 27–29
    hidden rules of college financial aid, 105
    housing costs, 18–21, 24
    knowledge needs, 27, 138
    savings cushion calculation, 26–27
Financial resources, *137, 138*
    community resources assessment, *202*
    scoring table for individual evaluation, *152*
    self-assessment, *170–172*
Future stories
    goals, 2, 3, 9
    personal mental model, 241

G

Geographical distribution of poverty, 198
Getting Ahead in a Just-Gettin'-By World, 1
Glasmeier, Amy K., 198
Globalization, 77
Goleman, Daniel, 139
Group activities
    facilitator role, 3–4
    ground rules, 9
    individual accountability, 3, 9
    Mental Model of Poverty, 15–16
    personal discomfort in, 10
    support for investigators, 4
    working vocabulary for, 10

H

Hart, Betty, 63, 120
Healthcare resources, community assessment, *205*
Hidden rules of economic class
    approach to investigating, 95–97
    breaking, 96
    college rules, 101–106

conceptual basis, 93–94
conflicts over, 96
definition and scope, 92
discussion questions, 93, 94, 104, 106
examples, 97–99
institutional rules, 100
journal reflections, 107
knowledge of, as resource, 138, *154*
language as, 7
learning objectives, 91
learning process, 92
lexicon, 92
as patterns of differences, 94
in personal plan for building resources, 234
power and, 100–101
self-assessment and self-knowledge, 94, 95, 96,
    191–193
source of, 92–93
transmission in families and cultures, 92
use of, 7
workplace rules, 100
Housing
    affordable housing payment calculator, 18–19
    community resources assessment, *201*
    income related to cost of, 24
    mental model of Floor Plan, 21
    Mental Model of Poverty, 18–21

I

Income. *See* Wages and income
Integrity and trust
    resource evaluation, *153, 185–186*
    safety and, *138*
Investigations into Economic Class in America
    approach to hidden rules, 95–97
    ground rules, 9
    group activities, 3
    journal writing, 9–10
    mental model for, 5–9
    mental model of change, 45–46
    objectives, 1–3
    self-knowledge and, 1, 2, 3

J

Joos, Martin, 110
Journal reflections
    community assessment, 210
    community prosperity, 244
    discrimination, 74

hidden rules, 107
language, 133
Mental Model of Poverty, 14, 17, 20, 30
personal plan for prosperity, 240
process of change, 43, 47
resource building, 227, 242
resources, 156, 196
social capital, 144
stages of change, 166
use of, 9–10

K

Keller, Fred, 96
Kinesthetic learning style, 140
Kretzmann, John, 212
Krodel, K. M., 122

L

Language
  casual/informal register, 111, 113, 114
  circular story pattern, 113
  code switching, 114–116
  discourse patterns, 112–113
  discussion questions, 111–112, 113, 118–119,
    120, 121, 124
  economic class and learning of, 120–121
  formal register, 7, 111, *137, 153*
  hidden rules of economic class, 7
  journal reflections, 133
  learning objectives, 109
  learning process, 110
  lexicon, 110
  mediation learning technique, 122–124
  of negotiation, 127–132
  registers, 110–112
  to resolve differences, 125–127
  resource evaluation, *153, 177–178*
  resources, *137*
  skills self-assessment, 132
  story structure, 119–120
  vocabulary size, 111, 121
  voices, 116–119
  working vocabulary for group learning, 10
Learned helplessness, 139
Learning
  disabilities, 160
  facilitator role, 3–4
  group process, 3
  objectives, 4

as process, 1, 5
setting for, 9
structure of workbook, 5
styles, 3, 140
Lexicon
  building resources, 220
  of college, 103
  community resources assessment, 198
  hidden rules of economic class, 92
  language rules and resources, 110
  personal plan for building resources, 230
  processes of change, 38
  purpose, 10
  resources, 136
  rich/poor gap, 56
  stages of change, 162
Lind, Michael, 61
Living wage, 23
Lockheed Martin, 77

M

McKnight, John, 212
Mediation
  language learning technique, 122–124
  to resolve differences, 125
Mehrabian, Albert, 131
Mental/cognitive resources
  definition and scope, *137,* 140
  learning styles, 140
  mental–emotional balance, *220*
  scoring table for individual evaluation, *152*
  self-assessment, 140, *175–176*
  staying focused, 147
  thinking strategies for motivation, 146–147
Mental Model of Poverty
  agency linkages, 39
  group mental model, 15–16
  housing investigation, 18–21
  income investigation, 22–25
  ournal and notebook entries, 14, 17, 20, 30
  learning objectives, 13, 15
  learning process, 14
  savings investigation, 26–27
Mental models
  of change, 44–45
  community prosperity/college success, 243, 244
  community resources assessment, *209*
  definition, 14
  eleven resources, *194*

middle class and wealth, 79
one-on-one relationships, 214
personal support for change, 238, *239, 249*
principles for, 14
purpose, 14, 15
self-awareness, 78, 168
social capital, 142
Triangle framework, 5, 6
use of, 78–79
See also Mental Model of Poverty
Metacognition, 45
Middle class
    characteristics, 80, 136
    current trends, 63
    registers of language, 111
    systemic factors in creation of, 61–63
    See also Hidden rules of economic class
Miller, W. R., 40, 145
Minimum wage, 22–23
Motivation and persistence
    for building resources, 220–221
    change and, 145
    components, 145–146
    definition, *138*
    discussion questions, 148
    journal reflections, 148
    scoring table for individual resource evaluation, *154*
    self-assessment, *187–188*
    staying focused, 147
    thinking strategies, 146–147
    values and, 145
    willingness as part of, 145
    wisdom in, 145
"My Life Now" mental model, 29, 44, 137

N

National Community Reinvestment Coalition, 78
Negotiations
    asking questions in, 130
    communication in, 131
    discussion questions, 129, 130, 132
    distinctive qualities, 127
    economic class considerations, 127–128
    emotional aspects, 128–129
    importance of, 127
    information needs for, 130
    learning activity, 127
    listening in, 129
    perspective, 128
    skills self-assessment, 131–132
Niebuhr, Reinhold, 147

O

O'Connor, Alice, 57
One-on-one relationships, 212, *213,* 214
Organisation for Economic Cooperation and Development, 136

P

Parent voice, 117
Payne, Ruby K., 7, 91, 92, 109, 136
Penance/forgiveness cycle in relationships, 125–126, 127
Persistence. *See* Motivation and persistence
Personal plan for building resources
    backup plans, 237
    community context, 230
    daily to-do list, 236, *248*
    discussion questions, 241
    forms, *245–249*
    group activities for, 221
    hidden rules in, 234
    journal reflections, 240, 242
    learning objectives, 229
    learning process, 230
    lexicon, 230
    mental model of Community Prosperity/College Success, 243, 244
    mental model of Future Story, 241
    monthly and weekly plans, 236, *246–247*
    procedural steps and starting dates, 234, 245
    process, 231–239
    resource selection, 231–232
    SMART goals, 233, 245
    Support for Change mental model, 238, 239, 249
    support systems for, 235, 246
    team recruitment, 238, 249
Pfarr, J. R., 93, 94, 100
Physical resources, 137, 153
    self-assessment, 181–182
Political functioning
    campaign contributions, 77
    coalition building, 84
    community leadership resources, 208
    distribution of wealth and political power, 76–77
    hidden rules, 100

Poverty
absence of resources in, 136, 137
asset-based approach to community development, 212
causal models, 57–60
community factors, 59–60, 198
community resource assessment, 198, 199
definition, 136
discussion questions, 16, 19, 21, 25, 29, 77, 82
exploitation risk, 60, 64–65
federal guidelines, 23, 136
generational, 93
geographical distribution, 198
goals of *Investigations,* 2, 7
individual behaviors and circumstances contributing to, 59
language development and, 121
living wage, 23
multicausal conceptualization, 58–59
penance/forgiveness cycle in relationships, 125–126
planning tool for addressing causes of, 84–85
political perspectives, 58
registers of language, 111
Research Continuum, 57–58
situational, 93–94
sustainability and, 83
systemic factors, 58, 59, 60
through lens of economic class, 93
See also Hidden rules of economic class; Mental Model of Poverty; Rich/poor gap
Power
hidden rules of, 100–101
rich/poor gap and, 76–77
Triangle mental model, 8
Private sector
corporate tax burden, 75
executive pay as multiple of worker pay, 69–70
hidden rules of economic class, 94
return on political investments, 77
revolving door between government and, 77
Proactive planning strategies, 45
Procedural steps, 45
Prochaska, James, 162
Public services access and quality assessment, 207
Putnam, Robert, 140, 141

Q
Quality of life, community assessment, 198

R
Race/ethnicity
median family income, 68
median family net worth, 73, 74
systemic factors in development of racial wealth gap, 62–63
Reactive problem solving, 45
Registers of language, 110–111
resource evaluation, 153
resources, 137
Relationships
Community Assets Map, 212
one-on-one, 212–213, 214
as resources, 138
resource self-assessment, 154, 189–190
See also Community involvement; Support systems
Research Continuum, 56, 57, 59, 197
Resources
asset-based approach to community development, 212–213
case study evaluations, 149–152, 155–156
characteristics of poverty, 136, 137
college services, 157
discussion questions, 154, 156
eleven resources, 137–138
emotional resources, 137, 139–140
financial resources, 137, 138
goals of *Investigations,* 138
importance of, 135
interlocking nature of, 220
journal reflections, 156
learning activity, 149–152, 157
learning objectives, 135
learning process, 136
levels of vulnerability and safety, 149, 152–154
lexicon, 136
mental/cognitive, 137, 140
motivation and persistence, 138, 145–148
personal strategy for, 138
scoring table for individual evaluation, 152–154
support systems and social capital, 137, 140–144
See also Building resources; Community resources assessment; Self-assessment of resources

Responsibility, Triangle mental model, 8–9
Rich/poor gap
    concept of wealth, 72
    discussion questions, 69, 70, 72, 77, 82
    distribution of wealth, 71
    executive pay as multiple of worker pay, 69–70
    family net worth, 73
    globalization and, 77
    hidden rules of economic class and, 92–93
    journal reflections, 74, 82
    learning objectives, 55
    learning process, 56
    lexicon, 56
    non-monetary assets, 72
    patterns and trends, 60–61, 65–68
    political power and, 76–77
    racial differences, 68, 73, 74
    systemic factors in development of, 61–63
    tax payment and, 75–76
Righting reflex, 40–41
Risley, Todd R., 63, 120
Role model resources, 138
    self-assessment, 189–190
Rollnick, S., 40, 145

S
Savings Cushion Calculation, 26–27
Self-assessment of resources
    commitment for, 168
    difficulty in, 169
    discussion questions, 195
    emotional, 173–174
    financial, 170–172
    importance of, 8
    integrity/trust, 185–186
    journal reflections, 196
    knowledge of hidden rules, 191–193
    language, 177–178
    learning activity, 168–169
    learning objectives, 167
    learning process, 168
    mental/cognitive, 175–176
    mental model, 194
    motivation and persistence, 187–188
    physical, 181–182
    relationships and role models, 189–190
    spiritual, 183–184
    support systems, 179–180

Self-knowledge
    emotional functioning, 139–140
    hidden rules of economic class, 94, 95, 96
    housing affordability, 18–19
    Investigations into Economic Class in America,
        and, 1, 2, 3
    language skills, 132
    of learning style, 3, 140
    mental models, 78, 168
    negotiating skills, 131–132
    personal mental model, 29–30
    process of change, 44
    societal experience, 2
    time management, 31–34, 49, 51
    See also Self-assessment of resources
Seligman, M. E. P., 139
Senge, Peter, 14, 78
Serenity Prayer, 147
Shipler, David, 57
SMART goals, 86, 229, 233, 245
Social capital. See Support systems
Social health index, 198, 210, 217
Sowell, Thomas, 83
Spiritual resources, 138, 153
    self-assessment, 183–184
St. Joseph County, Indiana, 84
Stages of change, 161–166
Standard American English (SAE), 109, 111, 114
Standard of living, international comparison, 60–61
Support systems, 140–141
    bonding and bridging resources, 140–141
    for building personal resources, 235
    community as, 140
    definition, 137
    discussion questions, 143
    journal reflections, 144
    mental model of Social Capital, 142
    resource self-assessment, 179–180
    scoring table for individual evaluation, 153
    as social capital, 140
Sustainability
    Community Sustainability Grid, 84–85
    definition, 83
    implications of disenfranchisement and poverty
        for, 83
    importance of, 83
Swords, R., 114

Systemic factors
    causes of poverty, 58, 59, 60
    creation of middle class, 61–63

T
Tacit knowledge, 78
Taxes
    capital gains, 75
    corporate share, 75
    discussion questions, 76
    distribution of tax burden, 75
    estate taxes, 75
    individual income tax, 75, 76
    payroll tax, 75
    urban revenue, 76
Time management and planning
    backwards planning, 86–87
    discussion questions, 32, 46, 51, 87
    hidden rules of college, 102, 103
    matrix, 47–50
    self-assessment, 31–34, 49, 51
Triangle (mental model)
    purpose, 5
    structure, 6–9
Tucker, B. H., 122
Twin Cities RISE!, 139
Tyranny of the moment, 37, 38, 45, 46, 47, 60, 91,
    128, 138

U
Upchurch, Carl, 42, 75, 225, 230
Urban areas, tax revenues, 76

V
Values, 145
Visual learning style, 140

W
Wages and income
    community resources assessment, 203
    debt-to-income ratio, 27–29
    distribution of wealth, 71
    executive pay as multiple of worker pay, 69–70
    family income growth, 65–67
    Mental Model of Poverty, 22–23
    See also Poverty
Washburne, Chandler, 38
Wealth
    characteristics, 81
    community resources assessment, 203
    Mental Models of Middle Class and Wealth, 79
    relative perception, 93
    worries of, 137
    See also Hidden rules of economic class;
        Rich/poor gap
Wheeler, Rebecca, 114
Wisdom, 145
Workplace, hidden rules, 100
Writing, code switching, 116